Race Talk in the Age of the Trigger Warning

Praise for *Race Talk in the Age of the Trigger Warning: Recognizing and Challenging Classroom Cultures of Silence*

"Grayson offers a vital resource for college and secondary English and writing teachers who wish to deepen their social justice practices and discussions in the classroom with students. Her careful nuancing of trigger warnings, how one might use them in the classroom and the problems with using them are nicely explained. This book also details pedagogical ways to work with trauma among students in classes that may inadvertently add to that trauma or trigger it. Those discussions nicely weave important related topics about White fragility, academic freedom, and antiracist pedagogies, all of which make for more conscientious thinking about how to be a socially just teacher. Furthermore, Grayson contextualizes her own white, female subjectivity, as well as her own past trauma, into the discussion in ways that many teachers might learn from."

—**Asao B. Inoue**, associate dean for academic affairs, equity, and inclusion, College of Integrative Sciences and Arts, Arizona State University, and 2019 Conference on College Composition and Communication Chair

"How can educators honor the cultural, linguistic, and social history of their students while challenging them to reflect and consider the experiences of others knowing, that some topics may evoke painful memories or imaginations? Teaching in culturally diverse classrooms, being sensitive to the unsettling nature of the homophobic, White male supremacy narrative in the United States, some educators use trigger statements in hopes of avoiding emotional or psychological trauma during class discussion. We welcome Dr. Mara Lee Grayson's book that exposes, composes, explains, explores, and expands our thinking about social, political, racial, cultural, and gender issues that influence what and how we teach. Avowing that valuable learning occurs in conversations that disrupt and disturb one's thinking, Dr. Grayson urges us to weigh the cost, then persist and design lessons that cultivate thoughtful, nurturing learning communities and explore equitable curricula with the students in our classrooms."

—**Anna J. Small Roseboro**, National Board Certified teacher, author, mentor, and coach

"Mara Lee Grayson is one of an emerging generation of composition and rhetoric scholars who are not only writing at the leading edge of research in our field, but whose activism is transforming our profession. If this generation is standing on the shoulders of giants to see what may be seen from there, they are also calling us to account for that which too many of us have refused to see. Fiercely and tenderly, in turns, this new generation is leading scholars, teachers, and students in the field to an understanding of equity richly conceived and insisting that we make it and keep it real."

"In *Race Talk in the Age of the Trigger Warning: Recognizing and Challenging Classroom Cultures of Silence*, Mara Lee Grayson has accomplished the remarkable feat of producing a book in the field of composition studies that is exceptionally well researched, well theorized, and supremely readable. While Grayson has written most directly to teachers, this is a book for students—undergraduate and graduate—as well as for 'seasoned' professionals who might be inclined to believe they no longer need such books. They do. We do. *Race Talk in the Age of the Trigger Warning* fills a space in the literature of composition studies that has been empty for too long.

"In prose that is both elegant and accessible, Grayson argues for equitable, trauma-informed pedagogical practice built upon the framework of racial literacy. Drawing on feminist and intersectional theory, critical race theory, Whiteness studies, and trauma studies, as well as critical discourse analysis and her own empirical study of composition teachers, she offers readers a thorough historical context, clearly defined terms, and astute critique of direct and oblique manifestations of racism and White supremacy that manifest in everyday teaching practices that too often function as 'common sense' in the writing classroom.

"In particular, Grayson notes the ways and degrees to which the 'trigger warning' often serves the interests of more privileged students while doubling down on the silencing and marginalization of students of color and Indigenous students. Further, she argues, debates about the efficacy of 'trigger warnings' frame students from historically marginalized and excluded groups who have been traumatized by racism, White supremacy, and their most common manifestation in quotidian microaggressions as members of a 'victim culture.'

"But Grayson accomplishes more in this text than telling us what we ought not do. Using the very pedagogical strategies for which she advocates, Grayson shuttles between narrative, analysis, critique, and counternarrative to weave a racially literate, critical pedagogical praxis. Theoretically grounded and eminently pragmatic, Grayson offers her readers a way to move that we can learn, use, and build upon as we work to create and sustain equitable writing classrooms.

"I am delighted to endorse and recommend this book and am looking forward to including it as required reading for both undergraduate and graduate courses I will soon be teaching."

—**Frankie Condon**, associate professor, Department of English Language and Literature, University of Waterloo

Race Talk in the Age of the Trigger Warning

Recognizing and Challenging Classroom Cultures of Silence

Mara Lee Grayson

ROWMAN & LITTLEFIELD
Lanham • Boulder • New York • London

Published by Rowman & Littlefield
An imprint of The Rowman & Littlefield Publishing Group, Inc.
4501 Forbes Boulevard, Suite 200, Lanham, Maryland 20706
www.rowman.com

6 Tinworth Street, London SE11 5AL

Copyright © 2020 by Mara Lee Grayson

All rights reserved. No part of this book may be reproduced in any form or by any electronic or mechanical means, including information storage and retrieval systems, without written permission from the publisher, except by a reviewer who may quote passages in a review.

British Library Cataloguing in Publication Information Available

Library of Congress Cataloging-in-Publication Data

Names: Grayson, Mara Lee, 1985- author.
Title: Race talk in the age of the trigger warning : recognizing and challenging classroom cultures of silence / Mara Lee Grayson.
Description: Lanham : Rowman & Littlefield, [2020] | Includes bibliographical references and index. | Summary: "This book tracks the rise of the trigger warning within historical and contemporary educational contexts"—Provided by publisher.
Identifiers: LCCN 2019045970 (print) | LCCN 2019045971 (ebook) | ISBN 9781475851601 (cloth) | ISBN 9781475851618 (paperback) | ISBN 9781475851625 (epub)
Subjects: LCSH: Trigger warnings—United States. | Culturally relevant pedagogy—United States. | School psychology—United States. | Multicultural education—United States. | Anti-racism—Study and teaching—United States. | Racism in education—United States.
Classification: LCC LB1091.5 .G73 2020 (print) | LCC LB1091.5 (ebook) | DDC 370.89—dc23
LC record available at https://lccn.loc.gov/2019045970
LC ebook record available at https://lccn.loc.gov/2019045971

Contents

Acknowledgments	ix
Introduction: Trigger Warning as Apologia	xi
1 Racism, Antiracism, and Education: Classroom Spaces as Microcosms	1
2 The Rise of the Trigger Warning	19
3 Speaking Truth to Trauma: Schooling and Suffering in the United States	43
4 Academic Discourse and the Inequity of the Politeness Protocol	63
5 Coping in the Classroom: Emotions and Education	89
6 Reading Lives, Writing Lives: Languaging and Counternarrating Trauma	115
7 Career Considerations: Managing Challenges to Emotional Health and Academic Freedom	141
Bibliography	167
Index	175
About the Author	181

Contents

Acknowledgments	ix
Introduction: Trigger Warning as Apologia	xi
1 Racism, Antiracism, and Education: Classroom Spaces as Microcosms	1
2 The Rise of the Trigger Warning	19
3 Speaking Truth to Trauma: Schooling and Suffering in the United States	43
4 Academic Discourse and the Inequity of the Politeness Protocol	63
5 Coping in the Classroom: Emotions and Education	89
6 Reading Lives, Writing Lives: Languaging and Counternarrating Trauma	115
7 Career Considerations: Managing Challenges to Emotional Health and Academic Freedom	141
Bibliography	167
Index	175
About the Author	181

Acknowledgments

I want to thank foremost the following teachers and scholars, who shared their stories, offered feedback on the work in progress, or bounced ideas around with me: Cristine Busser, Frankie Condon, Rachel Golland, Irene Lietz, Ruth Osario, Matthew Rosenbloom, Seth Rosenbloom, Iris D. Ruiz, Cheryl Hogue Smith, Ryan Witt, and Adam Wolfsdorf. This work exists because of the teachers and students whose voices and experiences populate these chapters.

I am grateful to the Conference on College Composition and Communication for supporting the larger research project which I draw upon in the following pages with a 2019 Emergent Researcher Award, and to my editorial team at Rowman & Littlefield, especially acquisitions editor Sarah Jubar, assistant editors Emily Tuttle and Kira Hall, and production editor Megan DeLancey, without whom this book would not be in your hands today.

Finally, my heartfelt thanks to my friends across the country, who text to see how I'm doing even when they know that "busy" is my default response, and to the family that taught me to question everything and to keep working toward a better world. Last but not least, love and gratitude to my spouse, Alex Doyban, for loving, challenging, and encouraging me.

Introduction

Trigger Warning as Apologia

Not long after I began working on this book, I had dinner with my spouse at a local pub known for their homebrews, barbecue, and (at least to me and perhaps a few random vegetarians in accompaniment of their more carnivorous spouses) their pimiento cheese sandwich. We sat at the bar on stools that spun and as I rotated to face Alex, I noticed a framed t-shirt hanging by the door. I read the words on the shirt: "If a cow is in a coma, does that make it a vegetable?"

I was horrified.

I pointed to the wall. Alex did a double take.

"That's pretty tasteless," he said. "Do you want to leave?"

Alex's question wasn't a commentary on the crudeness or political incorrectness of the words. Tasteless joke aside, he was alluding to a part of my history that he didn't share, but which he knows lingers in my mind and my emotional memory even now, more than a decade later.

On a random Saturday night less than a month before my college graduation, the man with whom for three years I'd had the sort of tumultuous on-again-off-again relationship characteristic of postadolescent, long-distance affairs, was violently attacked outside a popular bar. He was beaten unconscious and kicked into the concrete; to minimize the swelling in his brain, doctors placed him in a medically induced coma.

We were at an off point in our relationship so I found out about the incident and his treatment, indirectly, a week later. I moved through the last few weeks of college in a sort of trance. I went to classes and took finals, but I remember none of that now. I told only two friends and my parents about the attack and, except for a few short conversations with my ex-boyfriend's best friend, I spoke to no one.

Doctors had attempted to bring my ex-boyfriend out of the coma but had not been able to do so, and he was now in a comatose state somewhere in the middle of the Glasgow scale; no one could say for sure how much of his brain function remained, how long he would be in that state, or what he might be like if he were to awaken. He was transferred to a trauma center only a few miles from the cheap apartment I shared with two roommates. I wanted to see him, but our relationship had not ended on good terms that time around; doctors warned his family, who passed the message along to his best friend, who passed it on to me, that, if he could sense his surroundings, my presence might be too emotionally disruptive.

The therapist I spoke to told me that, in order to function in the absence of closure, I had to compartmentalize. I had to, for lack of a better phrase, pretend my ex-boyfriend was dead. I had to move on, a difficult feat that became impossible when the man who attacked him jumped bail and fled the country. Overnight, the personal tragedy I'd until then had to pretend wasn't mine turned into an international incident that commanded the attention of the news media and two United States senators. My ex-boyfriend's picture was in the paper; his name was on the evening news. The family members and acquaintances from whom I had kept the story were asking how he was, how I was.

With a few previous traumatic experiences already under my belt, I did not handle any of it well. My until-then occasional social cigarette turned into chain-smoking; I took Valium to get through four hours each day at the real estate office where I worked part-time; I drank from happy hour until the wee hours with friends who, like me, were trying to avoid the harder parts of our new adult realities; and I stopped eating. Years later, looking back, I wondered if I had been trying, unconsciously, to whittle myself away.

When, at the end of the summer, my ex-boyfriend arose from a three-month coma and agreed to see me, I was as petrified as I was relieved. I broke down in tears at work, chain-smoked on the way to the hospital, and had to physically steady myself when I first saw him in his hospital bed, body wasted to little more than bent bones and flesh. He smiled at me. Later we watched television and laughed. We spent two years together after that and, like many couples who repeatedly split apart and come back together, we eventually broke up for reasons remarkably similar to the ones that had broken us up the first time around.

During those two years, while his family wanted revenge on the man who attacked him, he wanted nothing but to move on. He grew stronger, relearned how to walk, then run. He started working as an accountant then resigned to start a nonprofit for victims of traumatic brain injury and go back to school. I hear now he became a social worker and runs marathons. I wasn't focused on revenge, but I couldn't move on either. I saw danger everywhere: In the faces of strangers, I saw the potential for cruelty; in every staircase, I saw a fall. I turned off the news whenever an act of violence was reported. I cried during crime movies. Now, writing this, I am shaking; I have had to pause to compose myself many times.

I was finally diagnosed with Post-Traumatic Stress Disorder (PTSD) a few years later, initially for reasons unrelated to the secondary traumatization I suffered living with and often caring for my ex-boyfriend. But the trauma was cumulative, my psychotherapist told me: some of it had begun long before I'd met him and some of it happened long after our relationship ended.

Alex and I didn't leave the bar that night after seeing the t-shirt on the wall. I did, however, mention to the bartender (who I'm sure had no part in the design of the thoughtless t-shirt) that I found the joke insensitive. He nodded, said he had always disliked the display, and, at the end of the night, took a round of drinks off of our bill.

Why didn't we leave? Alex was willing, but he left the decision to me. I vacillated for a while, debating the merits of making a statement against the appeal of the grilled cheese and trying to figure out if the discomfort I felt jumping beneath my skin would soon abate. It did, eventually, and we enjoyed our dinner. I didn't leave, I suppose, because I wanted to enjoy my evening, because I've been told to choose my battles, and because I didn't want to let the pain of my past win.

But as we paid the bill, the uncomfortable knot I'd managed to untangle during dinner reappeared in my stomach. How could I contribute money I'd earned teaching and writing about rhetoric and equity to a business that showed so little regard for either?

And late that night, trying to sleep beside the person I'd married, I could not shake the intrusive images flashing across my mind of my ex-boyfriend's emaciated body, or his smiling face on the cover of the *Daily News*, or the face of his attacker.

I woke the next morning knowing I had to write this book.

All this, you might wonder, because of two lines printed on a t-shirt? Trauma triggers, as many who have experienced PTSD know, are neither logical nor predictable. For me, jokes about the comatose are not merely distasteful—they invite in painful memories, like a door left open during a flood.

WHY I DON'T USE TRIGGER WARNINGS: A NOTE ON POSITIONALITY

Based solely on my history, one might assume I'd be a strong proponent of the trigger warning, a brief statement that informs students of distressing or potentially retraumatizing content, and, perhaps, an ideal example of the type of student for whom it is intended. I do not use trigger warnings, though I have written about the broad policies and content notes I include on my own course syllabi.[1]

I don't remember teachers using trigger warnings when I was in school—but this is not because trigger warnings, as some Baby Boomers and Gen-Xers suggest, are a modern creation intended to protect so-called Millennial snowflakes[2] from experiencing discomfort. Rather, the topics that today are most often prefaced with trigger warnings, such as racism and sexual assault, were not a part of the curricula throughout most of my secondary and undergraduate education.

Though I was educated primarily in diverse public schools in New York City, my education was steeped in whiteness and patriarchy. I am White identified and was born to middle-class, educated parents, so perhaps this is not very surprising. At the same time, however, I was raised by labor and antiracist activists in a family that is more racially and ethnically diverse than one would guess just by looking at me. As my cousin says, "we learned sociology around the dinner table."

In the first high school I attended, classroom talk was regulated to the point that my parents were advised to arrange a transfer to another school: "This is a conservative school," my English teacher told my parents at our first parent-teacher conference of the year, "and your daughter marches to the beat of her own drummer."

Earlier that week, after his lecture on *Julius Caesar* had somehow turned into a discussion of what we were doing for Christmas, I said I wasn't doing anything for Christmas, but my family would probably be getting together for Chanukah.

"You're Jewish?" a classmate asked. "Then you're going to hell."

The teacher said nothing to her but told *me*: "It's not appropriate to talk about religion in school."

Two years later, on September 12, 2001, the day after the planes crashed into the Twin Towers, with my parents' friends and my classmates' parents unaccounted for and the smell of smoke still seeping southward through the windows of the "more liberal" high school I attended, my U.S. Government teacher said: "If they'd let me back in the army, I'd go to Iraq and Afghanistan and kill all the Muslims."

The classroom conversation protocol, I learned, enforced different rules for different people.

Even as an undergraduate student, I was advised to tread carefully in class discussions, such as when the professor of a lower-division required class asked about the symbolism of the rose in a text we were reading and I offered its resemblance to a woman's labia. In fact, until I entered graduate school, the only spaces where open, critical discourse was encouraged were my creative writing classes, where we talked about the construction of ideas and identities through language, and upper-division literature electives, where we studied the countercurricula to the canon.

Given my positionality, I think often about how my experiences, as well as the privilege my skin color affords me, have influenced the way I think about the work I do as a racial literacy researcher and educator. Going into this work, I had to wonder: Do I bring my white privilege to my resistance to trigger warnings? I cannot change my racial identification, but I can self-check my tendencies toward what Frankie Condon calls *whiteliness*, and I can ensure that through thoughtful research practices I make space for voices and perspectives other than my own in my scholarship.

I understand the motives of many of those who use trigger warnings. I choose not to, however, because as a trauma survivor and a racial literacy educator, who, despite her white privilege, has been othered and silenced in school settings, I have found that critical conversations, even if painful, are necessary and that despite even the best of intentions, the regulation of race talk and other counterconversations serves primarily to silence the already marginalized and maintain white cultural hegemony.

MAKING SENSE OF RACE TALK IN THE AGE OF THE TRIGGER WARNING

Open discourse around race and identity is a prerequisite to intellectual and emotional growth. Beverly Daniel Tatum suggested that curricula that heighten racial awareness can have a "ripple effect" by fostering an environment in which "students of color and other targeted groups" feel supported.[3] Over time and with practice, students who openly discuss race in the classroom may become more comfortable interrogating racism and other modes of identification and oppression, including sexism, homophobia, and xenophobia. To generate opportunities for transformative learning in the classroom, educators must create learning environments that "make students feel safe *and* invite them to tread bravely into less comfortable but necessary waters."[4]

There is no denying, however, that our schools—and our society—feel increasingly unsafe. From mass shootings and lockdown drills to sexual assault and harassment and police officers pulling students from their seats for using cell phones, schools and college campuses certainly are not the safe spaces we may idealize. Classroom time and professional development on all levels of education are increasingly dedicated to standardized and mandatory safety trainings, emergency preparation, and discussions of reporting procedures.

We have long known that our educational spaces are plagued by—and serve to uphold—the same racism, violence, sexual assault, marginalization, and alienation that prevails throughout the institutional structures of the United States. To combat and prevent these problems from within the classroom, we need to encourage transformative discussions that lead to intellectual and emotional growth and systemic reform.

Some scholars have argued that trigger warnings help teachers scaffold and unlock avenues for discussions centered on complex social and cultural issues. In practice, however, trigger warnings often have the opposite effect, shutting down or unintentionally demonizing complex conversations, both of which involuntarily promote fragility and reduced reflective functioning.

Just as problematic, while students of color are significantly more likely to endure trauma than White students,[5] trigger warnings often cater to what Robin DiAngelo has called white fragility. Labeling only certain texts as "safe" may unwittingly nudge some students and their stories to the margins of the classroom; in this way, trigger warnings ultimately serve not as protection for students of underrepresented populations and traumatic experiences, but as cushioning to protect the imagined fragility of the white student population. That trigger warnings seem to be more commonly used in predominantly white institutions highlights this problem.

In recent years, students, particularly those of educational, socioeconomic, and/or racial privilege, have received a "consistent message from adults: 'life is dangerous, but adults will do everything in their power to protect you from harm.'"[6] When it comes to race talk, however, that protection is problematic for two primary reasons: first, productive race talk necessitates that individuals practice racial literacy on analytical and emotional levels; second, the politeness protocol that is sustained by trigger warnings is directly tied to whiteness and privilege.

This latter problem has dire effects for white students and for students of color: while students of color have considerable experiential knowledge of race and racism, White students often lack experience in acknowledging and exploring their own whiteness and are shown to benefit most from cross-cultural encounters in the classroom. Even more troubling, silencing the emotional aspects of race talk means silencing voices and stories of people of color, stories that cannot be told or understood without emotion; in doing so, we risk exacerbating the marginalization of students of color in our classrooms.

While racist, patriarchal norms influence all parts of classroom discourse and interaction, classroom race talk provides a useful microcosm to examine the broader inequities that define U.S. education. Further, classroom race talk, given its dual potential to reify or challenge white cultural hegemony, requires great care be paid to students' emotional experiences and expressions. To be equitable, inclusive, and trauma informed, classroom race talk must be part of a larger approach to challenging, through discourse and action, the inherent patriarchy and white supremacy of academic notions of emotion and experiential learning and how classroom norms contribute to the traumatization and perpetuate the retraumatization of marginalized students.

A Conceptual Framework: Racial Literacy

The framework of racial literacy is derived from the ethnographic research of sociologist France Winddance Twine and the analytic paradigm developed by legal and civil rights scholar Lani Guinier. Guinier's analysis of the limitations of *Brown v. Board of Education* as a systematic response to the racial inequities intrinsic to American education necessitated a paradigm that enables us to "decipher the durable racial grammar that structures racialized hierarchies and frames the narrative of our republic."[7] This structural emphasis provides an important foundation from which to examine educational policies and practices that profess progressiveness yet which sustain racial hierarchies. Twine's emphasis on the "micro-cultural social processes in which racial hierarchies are negotiated"[8] offers a lens through which we can view interpersonal interaction, while my own explorations of racial literacy's discursive and rhetorical functions emphasize language in context.

The elements of the racial literacy framework—and the behaviors and habits of mind of those who practice racial literacy—include the recognition of racism as a contemporary, contextual, and intersectional problem rather than a monolithic or historical one; the understanding of the social constructedness of individual racial identity as well as the cultural value of whiteness; and the development of decoding practices through which to recognize and interpret racism on psychological, interpersonal, and structural levels and discursive practices through which to discuss race, racism, and antiracism, including sharing, labeling, confronting stereotypes, and hedging.[9]

If the contemporary classroom is intended to be a space where trigger warnings are used to address student trauma *and* where teachers and students engage in critical discourse around race and racism, those of us who engage racial literacy both as "a critical lens for the understanding of race and related variables and as a curricular goal for the courses we teach,"[10] must ask: Is it possible to teach toward racial literacy using the trigger warning?

Theoretical Influences

Though my work centers on racial literacy as a conceptual framework for rhetorical awareness, I draw heavily from the growing field of critical whiteness studies, which aims to decenter whiteness and reveal the ideological and institutional structures that maintain white supremacy and privilege. I am further influenced by feminist theories of emotion that blur the lines between the private, the arena to which women and feeling have traditionally been relegated, and the public, the politically governed spaces from which women and emotion have historically been excluded, thereby challenging the false division between these spheres and the ideologies those divisions uphold. "Feminists," as Megan Boler has written, "have a particular interest in critiquing binary divisions, because 'women' and everything associated with women falls on the 'bad' side of the binary."[11]

Popular racial discourse, too, has long set up a false binary. Discussions of race and racism in the United States have traditionally been framed as white versus black and excluded the racialized experiences of non-Black people of color. When non-Black people of color are included in discussions, language creates a new binary: White versus not White. This positions whiteness as the norm and everything else as a deviation therefrom, a binary that reifies the existing racist order. As someone who does this work, I readily admit that "it is quite difficult to talk about race through language that is itself a part of the problem."[12]

Because feelings are seen, erroneously or not, as part of the realm of women, what Kimberele Crenshaw has called *intersectionality* is an important additional to the conceptual toolbox for making sense of the trigger warning as it relates to racism and race talk. While explorations of race and gender in scholarship traditionally have focused on one dynamic of power and oppression (race or gender, for example), intersectionality encourages scholars to consider how the multiply burdened (economically disadvantaged women of color, for example) are affected by systemic inequity. Intersectionality can best be viewed as "an analytic disposition" through which scholars and researchers might conceive of "categories not as distinct but as always permeated by other categories, fluid and changing, always in the process of creating and being created by dynamics of power."[13]

Exploration of the trigger warning debate requires a theoretical framework that disrupts and complicates false binaries because public discourse already has framed the trigger warning as a binary that polarized educators: those for the trigger warning versus those against the trigger warning. These arguments are very often decontextualized and do not consider instructors' positionalities and the circles of influence, ideological and structural, within which the classroom is situated. However, as with all pedagogies, just as important as the conceptualization and the intention behind the trigger warning is its implementation.

TRIGGER WARNING AS APOLOGIA

If the goal of a trigger warning is to prevent students from reexperiencing trauma, it is necessary to consider which students are likely to benefit from the warning. Furthermore, as ought to be the case with any critical pedagogy, it is imperative that educators consider if and how trigger warnings might in fact perpetuate that retraumatization.

The politeness protocol of race talk, especially when combined with the academic protocol that undergirds all classroom talk, creates an environment that caters to white fragility. Trigger warnings contribute to that environment, but the effects of trigger warnings cannot be considered in isolation. The trigger warning is but one indication of a broader, more insidious framework for contemporary critical pedagogy.

In my previous research on the practice of racial literacy in the writing classroom, I found that one of the commonest discursive approaches in race talk is *hedging*, the prefacing or following of a statement with a clarification or apology meant to mitigate the effects of the statement and protect the speaker from criticism. A recognizable example of this is the use of "No offense" to proceed or follow a statement that might be considered offensive. Other scholars, including Eduardo Bonilla-Silva and Amy Vetter and Holly Hungerford-Kresser, have noted similar patterns in race talk by students, teachers, and others. In many cases, the statements that follow an instance of hedging are offensive, rendering the hedge useless; other times, the statements are innocuous but because of the speaker's impressions of racial discourse, are seen as inflammatory, rendering the hedge unnecessary.

The utterance of trigger warnings in the classroom may be seen as a form of hedging in which instructors couch their own critical pedagogies in uncertain terms. It can be argued that, when teachers preface conversations about racism or sexual assault with trigger warnings, they send a message that they themselves aren't comfortable with the materials they intend to introduce. Intentionally or indirectly, this discursive maneuver serves to shield instructors from student and administrative resistance; it therefore limits the extent to which students are encouraged to engage in transformative critical conversations.

The rhetorical genre of *apologia* is generally understood as a "speech of self-defense" and is usually precipitated by an accusation that asserts one's character or "worth as a human being."[14] Like hedging, apologia predominate in classroom dialogues about race; they are even more common in public and political arenas, generally serving as attempts by Whites in positions of power to defend against charges of racism and restore the respect of their audience or constituents. Consider, for example, the recent series of public statements made by Canadian prime minister Justin Trudeau following the discovery of old photographs in which he is wearing blackface and brownface. "What I did hurt people who shouldn't have to face intolerance and discrimination because of their identity," he said in one statement. "This is something I deeply, deeply regret."[15]

Paradoxically, these public apologies often exacerbate the effects of the original racist offense of which the speaker was accused. For example, in 2006, California's then governor Arnold Schwarzenegger commented during a meeting that Puerto Rican American assemblywoman Bonnie Garcia was "very Puerto Rican or the same thing as Cuban to me. They're all very hot. They have the, you know, part of the Black blood in them and part of the Latino blood in them together that makes it."[16] Schwarzenegger later said that "it was an off-the-record conversation" and "not meant to be in any negative way."[17] Regardless of the intent behind his statement or the setting in which it was made, however, Schwarzenegger's statement drew upon and reproduced essentialist stereotypes about Latin American women. By emphasizing his intent and the supposedly unofficial nature of the meeting rather than the problems associated with racial stereotypes, Schwarzenegger's apologia effectively minimizes the harm caused by his language.

Like any rhetorical or communicative genre, apologia relies on the interplay between the speaker's intent and the audience's expectations within a given context. Because audience expectations and context are collectively determined and socially situated, any instance of apologia tells us just as much about the social and cultural contexts from which it arises as it does about the individual using it. Similarly, critical race theory reminds us that specific incidents of racism are not isolated events but representations of larger belief systems and societal inequities. The function of any apologia, then, is the "way it is used in any given time to satisfy collective needs."[18]

Viewed rhetorically with a critical race framework in mind, the trigger warning, like hedging, is a manifestation of a larger ideology of racialized apologia that, under the guise of student responsiveness, serves to simultaneously limit critical discourse and reify existing racial formations. When used preceding race talk, the trigger warning allows instructors to introduce potentially controversial material (or material they fear will be seen as such) while at the same time defending their decision to do so.

On the surface, this sort of hedging apologia makes space for race talk; the implication, however, is that race talk is outside of the normal discourse of the classroom and therefore *requires* some sort of disclaimer. Even when instructors believe race talk to be a necessary part of critical pedagogy, trigger warnings label race talk as dangerous, controversial, and triggering. This apologia also sets the tone for the type of race talk allowed in the classroom: if the topic is triggering, the approach must be cautious, tentative, and conciliatory. These conditions reinforce the discursive norms of the classroom.

What does this mean for the faculty members teaching this new generation of college students? And the teachers who find this generation's younger siblings in their high school classrooms? In the age of the trigger warning, the challenge for educators is how to think about creating environments that meet our students where they are while at the same time productively challenging them and inspiring them to move forward.

ORIGINAL RESEARCH

During 2018 and 2019, I conducted a discourse analysis of the literature on trigger warnings to explore the ideologies that contribute to the arguments made by the teachers, researchers, and scholars. Sociolinguist James Paul Gee has suggested we understand language as a mode of saying, doing, and being that involves more than communicating information; what he has labeled *Discourse* (differentiated from pragmatic definitions of discourse by capitalizing the letter D) is communication using language, behavior, and "everything else at human disposal" that involves "enacting and recognizing socially significant identities."[19] Discourse analysis within this theoretical framework of d/Discourse can be understood as the study of both syntactic relations and their social and contextual significance.

In my examination of the literature, I drew upon seven *building tasks*, or components, of discourse Gee identified as integral to the understanding of discourse in *An Introduction to Discourse Analysis: Theory and Method*. Those building tasks include *significance*, what is prized or emphasized through not merely the content of the utterance but the construction thereof, including syntax and diction; the social *practice* that is implicitly acknowledged or rejected via a piece of spoken or written language; the *identities* established by the language in context; the existing or aspirational *relationships* the writer assumes or establishes with the intended audience; the *political perspectives* established regarding the distribution of social goods, including both concrete goods like currency and abstract ones such as legal responsibility and moral blame; the *connections* drawn or severed between people, concepts, and information; and the types of *sign systems and knowledge* emphasized or prized by the language in context.

To take up psychologist Guy Boysen's call to move beyond decontextualized "argument and rhetoric" in scholarship on trigger warnings,[20] in early 2019, I also surveyed and interviewed college-level composition instructors across the country about their experiences using trigger warnings. I elected to focus my research on the field of composition studies for three reasons. The first was a matter of access: though I have a background and considerable experience in teacher education and though much of my work focuses on faculty professional development, my home discipline is composition and rhetoric. As a result, I am active in many professional organizations wherefrom I was able to recruit research participants.

Second, though the amount of scholarship on trigger warnings is steadily increasing, much of it has come from the fields of psychology and women's studies. The work that has come from the field of English more broadly emphasized the potential or limitations of the trigger warning in literary study. I could find no empirical research originating from the field of composition studies, which struck me as a significant gap and therefore an important opportunity. This is especially interesting, given the third reason: because composition deals with the making of meaning through language and because writing classes, especially since the so-called social turn of the early 1990s, include a wide variety of thematic material that explores the connections between language and power, politics, identity, and representation, composition classrooms are spaces wherein the trigger warning is likely to play a significant role, whether or not teachers use them.

I draw upon the findings of these studies, as well as my previous research on trigger warnings, throughout this book.

WHAT TO EXPECT

In the following pages, I draw upon original research I have conducted into classroom race talk and the use of trigger warnings on the secondary and postsecondary levels to contextualize current educational trends in racial literacy, student responsiveness, emotional learning, and academic freedom. As I do so, I explore the potentialities, limitations, and abuses of trigger warnings, particularly in relation to race talk, racial equity, and critical pedagogy. When I include perspectives on the trigger warning and classroom stories teachers have shared with me, I use pseudonyms to ensure confidentiality.

Throughout this book, I offer curricular suggestions for high school and college instructors seeking to implement equitable pedagogies that simultaneously ensure student safety, provoke students' intellectual and emotional growth, and challenge cultures of silence on U.S. campuses.

Overview of Chapters

The chapters that follow explore the cultures of silence and marginalization from which the trigger warnings and the debates surrounding it emerge. In these chapters, I also direct our gaze forward by providing practical, equitable approaches to emotional learning, race talk, and difficult classroom conversations.

Chapters 1 through 3 provide a foundation for the rest of the book and aim to contextualize contemporary discourse and debates surrounding the trigger warning. In chapter 1, I examine the ways systemic racism and white supremacy historically have determined and continue to influence the structures, curricula, and practices in public, private, and higher education in United States. I also outline some of the many antiracist approaches to research, administration, and pedagogy presented by scholars across academic disciplines and educational contexts. My aims with this chapter are to both highlight the necessity of antiracist education and to demonstrate the many strides taken, particularly by scholars and educators of color, to combat white supremacy in educational and academic spaces. This chapter also serves to provide context and background for the arguments I make and the strategies I offer throughout this book.

Chapter 2 tracks the rise of the trigger warning: I discuss the various physical and virtual sites wherefrom the trigger warning arguably originated and the early content advisories and other precursors to the trigger warning that have served similar functions. In this chapter, I outline the debates surrounding the implementation of the trigger warning as well as the pedagogical problems it simultaneously raises and attempts to address. This chapter also features practical suggestions for educators considering using the triggering or working on campuses wherein the trigger warning is required or suggested.

In chapter 3, I explore contemporary, competing definitions of trauma as well as the types of trauma experienced by students on the secondary and college levels. I also narrow in on the disproportionate effects of trauma on racially marginalized peoples in the United States, including racial trauma and race-based stress.

Chapters 4 through 6 each address a different content focus, but all consider how classrooms can become "brave spaces"[21] where difficult and potentially emotional material can be learned addressed justly and sensitively. Chapters 4 and 5 address the inequities of the trigger warning as it is manifested in two related arenas: emotional expression and academic discourse. In chapter 4, I examine the trigger warning's relationship to Western modes of communication and classroom discourses of silence. In this chapter, I also address how the trigger warning caters to white fragility. Finally, I provide strategies for instructors to challenge the politeness protocol that maintains a marginalizing academic discourse.

In chapter 5, I explore how classrooms contribute to students' emotional socialization into a Western discourse that favors objectivity and Western ways of knowing over individual experience and inclusivity, and thereby perpetuates the othering of people of color, indigenous peoples, and white women. I offer teachers strategies for equitably exploring and attending to students' lived experiences and emotional learning in the classroom.

Chapter 6 offers a view of the classroom as a multidialectic, multidiscursive space wherein students can use their home languages and approaches to communication to challenge the white supremacy of traditional academic discourse. In this chapter I also explore how student writing can be a strategic site for managing individual and collective trauma and counternarrating marginalization, misrepresentation, and systemic injustice.

Chapter 7 shifts the focus of the book from the student to the instructor. In this chapter, I invite educators to consider how they ensure their own emotional safety in trauma-informed classrooms. I also address the potential risks to job security teachers face at a time when personal safety and intellectual freedom are being challenged both on the institutional and societal levels. I offer strategies with which teachers teaching toward racial literacy can anticipate and manage or prevent institutional or student-driven challenges to their autonomy. This chapter emphasizes coalition building and identifies and examines professional resources for teachers seeking like-minded colleagues and antiracist alliances.

Five of the chapters in this book feature special sections called Secondary Strategies and College Considerations. The Secondary Strategies section offers specific strategies that high school teachers can employ related to that chapter's particular content focus. I include this both because the secondary context and the age of students in the classroom directly influence students' emotional and intellectual development and because legal mandates, standardized assessments, and the involvement of parents and administrators pose particular challenges of which teachers must be aware and about which they are likely already concerned.

Though some may assume college-level educators have more freedom than high school educators, the neoliberalization of higher education and an ever-increasing reliance on contingent labor in higher education both has contributed to increased standardization of curricula and has led to limited job security for the majority of college instructors. As such, the College Considerations section addresses the particular legal, pedagogical, and institutional considerations that must be taken into account whenever instructors include potentially sensitive or controversial material in the course syllabus.

I intend to be provocative in this book. I provoke teachers to consider how trigger warnings and other critical pedagogical practices may indeed be far less critical than they seem. I provoke teachers to consider how their own positionalities with regard to race, past traumas, educational experiences, and patterns of emotional expression influence their ideas about, usage of, and attitudes toward the trigger warning. I especially provoke White teachers, researchers, and scholars (like myself) to critically examine the ways in which their research may unintentionally reinforce the white supremacy that dominates Western academic institutions and interferes with even our own attempts to offer equitable education to our students.

To equitably teach a diverse population of students—and to build teaching careers in educational institutions that may be inherently inequitable—teachers must interrogate structural racism and consider how to challenge complex racial and racist dynamics through their instruction. Teachers need to learn how to have difficult conversations in the classroom because students are *already* hearing and having these conversations, productively or not. Of equal importance, acquiring tools for engaging in these conversations enables teachers to better handle the emotional aspects of difficult conversations, a factor that plays a considerable role in the productivity of the conversation as well as students' individual learning and emotional well-being.

A Note on Terminology

Multicultural psychologist Derald Wing Sue defines *race talk* as "dialogues and conversations about race that touch upon topics of race, racism, 'whiteness,' and white privilege,"[22] and it is this broad conceptualization that I draw upon when I use the phrase throughout this book. In the classroom, race talk may arise organically as a response to course material or it may be introduced intentionally and systemically by an instructor. Race talk may be part of a curriculum designed to encourage racial literacy or it may be the result of microaggressions or marginalization. It may be respectful, disrespectful, emotional, impassioned, tentative, or awkward; more likely it will have many of these qualities, and more. Like language use and discourse more generally, race talk will evolve over time, ideally for the better, growing in complexity and criticality.

As in most of my work, including my previous book, *Teaching Racial Literacy: Reflective Practices for Critical Writing*, I have capitalized race labels in this book to highlight the formality and naming function of these labels "as social classifications rather than innate biological characteristics."[23] As a writer, my lexical toolbox is ever changing, and when I began writing this book, I intentionally decapitalized the term *white* in efforts to decenter whiteness.

Ultimately, I revised my approach for two reasons: First, I fear avoiding the capitalization may imply that there is an intrinsic, biological White identity, thereby naturalizing it and centering it as a normative identity in a racialized society. Considerable research has shown that, to develop racial literacy and an antiracist identity, White people must identify as White.[24] Therefore, even if there is no innate White identity, the socially constructed experience of being White is real and has real effects that must be acknowledged.

While it is integral for those of us who are White to see ourselves as racialized, it is equally important to decenter the cultural hegemony that allows us to ignore our own racialization. For that reason, I limit my use of capitalization to terms that identify a person or people (e.g., *White*, *White people*) and do not capitalize terms that refer to the broader constructs antiracism seeks to dismantle (e.g., *whiteness, white supremacy*).

When not referring to a specific racial or ethnic group, I at times use the terms *marginalized* (to emphasize the active work of racialization and its disproportionate effects on particular racial groups) and *people of color*. I also frequently use the term *POCI*, an acronym for *People of Color and Indigenous Peoples*. I use this term both because *POCI* acknowledges the marginalization and oppression of indigenous peoples in the United States and because many other terms too broadly group those who share the experience of marginalization in a society defined by white cultural hegemony yet among whom there are more differences than commonalities. For example, the terms *minority* and *minorities* are vague and, as the population of the U.S. changes, increasingly inaccurate; that I aim with this work to expose and decenter whiteness renders a term like *nonwhite*, which centers whiteness and perpetuates a binary view of racial identification, counterproductive.

I acknowledge the limitations even of *POCI*, especially the jargonish nature of acronyms, as well as the well-intentioned yet not necessarily effective terminological hedging of euphemisms.[23] As a scholar and teacher of composition and rhetoric, I reject the notion that any piece of language or terminology can be neutral. I am especially cognizant of the ideological functions of language, the subtext that lurks behind the words we too often use uncritically. Regardless of how critically we use existing terms or create new, perhaps better ones, language is referential and ideological and cannot be separated from the society that produces it. Put simply, it is exceedingly "difficult to talk about race through language that is itself a part of the problem."[24]

It takes more than words to challenge systems, especially when the inequities that maintain those systems are preserved by every facet of daily life and so deeply ingrained that, to many, they remain invisible. Social critique must be accompanied by a deep commitment to change in thinking, discourse, and practice. In the classroom, this requires that we reconsider the situated beliefs we mistake for universal truths and explore how, through our conceptual framing and our pedagogical practices, we can better attend to our students' emotional, experiential, and racialized realities.

NOTES

1. Mara Lee Grayson, *Teaching Racial Literacy: Reflective Practices for Critical Writing* (Lanham: Rowman & Littlefield, 2018), 63–64. See also chapter 5 of this book.

2. The term *snowflake* is recent derogatory slang for members of the Millennial generation, pointing to their (our) uniqueness and presumed fragility. Some credit Chuck Palahniuk, author of *Fight Club*, with the first pejorative use of the term snowflake.

3. Beverly Daniel Tatum, "Talking about Race, Learning about Racism: The Application of Racial Identity Development Theory in the Classroom," *Harvard Educational Review* 62, no. 1 (1992): 23.

4. Mara Lee Grayson and Adam Wolfsdorf, "Courageous Conversations in the Age of the Trigger Warning," in *From Disagreement to Discourse: A Chronicle of Controversies in Schooling and Education*, ed. Beth Duroyode and Rhonda Bryant (Charlotte: Information Age Publishing, 2019).

5. See Janice L. Cooper, Rachel Masi, Sarah Dababnah, Yumiko Aratani, and Jane Knitzer, "Unclaimed Children Revisited: Working Paper No. 2: Strengthening Policies to Support Children, Youth, and Families Who Experience Trauma," National Center for Children in Poverty, 2007, http://nccp.org/publications/pdf/download_204.pdf, and Nicholas J. Sibrava, Andri S. Bjornsson, A. Carlos I. Perez Benitez, Ethan Moitra, Risa B. Weisberg, and Martin B. Keller, "Posttraumatic Stress Disorder in African American and Latinx Adults: Clinical Course and the Role of Racial and Ethnic Discrimination," *American Psychologist* 74, no. 1 (2019). See also chapter 3.

6. Greg Lukianoff and Jonathan Haidt, "The Coddling of the American Mind," *The Atlantic* (September 2015).

7. Lani Guinier, "From Racial Liberalism to Racial Literacy: Brown v. Board of Education and the Interest-Divergence Dilemma," *The Journal of American History* 91, no. 1 (2004): 100.

8. France Winddance Twine, "A White Side of Black Britain: The Concept of Racial Literacy," *Ethnic and Racial Studies* 27, no. 6 (2004): 881.

9. Mara Lee Grayson, "Race Talk in the Composition Classroom: Narrative Song Lyrics as Texts for Racial Literacy," *Teaching English in the Two-Year College* 45, no. 2 (2017): 150.

10. Grayson, *Teaching Racial Literacy*, xv.

11. Megan Boler, *Feeling Power: Emotions and Education* (New York: Routledge, 1999), 6.

12. Mara Lee Grayson, "Race Talk," 161.

13. Sumi Cho, Kimberle Williams Crenshaw, and Leslie McCall, "Toward a Field of Intersectionality Studies: Theory, Applications, and Praxis," *Signs: Journal of Women in Culture and Society* 38, no. 4 (2013): 795.

14. B. L. Ware and Wil A. Linkugel, "They Spoke in Defense of Themselves: On the Generic Criticism of Apologia," *Quarterly Journal of Speech* 59, no. 3 (1973): 274.

15. Justin Trudeau, quoted in Paul Vieira and Kim Makrael, "Trudeau Apologizes Again as Another Old Image in Blackface Emerges," *The Wall Street Journal* (September 19, 2019).

16. Arnold Schwarzenegger, quoted in Michelle A. Holling, Dreama G. Moon, and Alexandra Jackson Nevis, "Racist Violations and Racializing Apologia in a Post-racism Era," *Journal of International and Intercultural Communication* 7, no. 4 (2014): 269.

17. Arnold Schwarzenegger, quoted in Associated Press, "Schwarzenegger Apologizes about Latino Blood," NBC News (September 8, 2006).

18. Sharon Downey, "The Evolution of the Rhetorical Genre of Apologia," *Western Journal of Communication* 57, no. 1 (1993): 43.

19. James Paul Gee, *An Introduction to Discourse Analysis: Theory and Method*, 4th ed. (London: Routledge, 2014), 18–19.

20. Guy A. Boysen, "Evidence-Based Answers to Questions about Trigger Warnings for Clinically-Based Distress: A Review for Teachers," *Scholarship of Teaching and Learning in Psychology* 3 (2017): 163.

21. Brian Arao and Kristi Clemens, "From Safe Spaces to Brave Spaces: A New Way to Frame Dialogue around Diversity and Social Justice," in *The Art of Effective Facilitation: Reflections from Social Justice Educators*, ed. Lisa M. Landreman (Sterling: Stylus, 2013).

22. Derald Wing Sue, "Race Talk: The Psychology of Racial Dialogues," *American Psychologist* (2013): 663.

23. Grayson, *Teaching Racial Literacy*, xvii.

24. For example, some disabled rhetoricians point to terms like *differently abled* as marginalizing, because their euphemistic nature minimizes the difficulty experienced by people with disabilities.

25. Grayson, "Race Talk," 161.

Chapter One

Racism, Antiracism, and Education

Classroom Spaces as Microcosms

> It is as if I had been looking at a fishbowl—the glide and flick of the golden scales, the green tip, the bolt of white careening back from the gills; the castles at the bottom, surrounded by pebbles and tiny, intricate fronds of green; the barely disturbed water, the flecks of waste and food, the tranquil bubbles traveling to the surface—and suddenly I saw the bowl, the structure that transparently (and invisibly) permits the ordered life it contains to exist in the larger world.—Toni Morrison[1]

Educational spaces are not immune to the racism and inequity (or violence, sexual assault, marginalization, or alienation) that plague the rest of the country.

In 2016, 1,250 hate crimes, "defined as offenses motivated by biases of race, national origin, ethnicity, religion, sexual orientation, gender, or disability," were reported on college campuses across the United States.[2] In 2017, 753 school-based hate crimes were reported to law enforcement agencies, an increase of 17 percent over the year before.[3] In January 2018 alone, 64 hate-based incidents at schools—more than two-thirds of which occurred in high schools—were reported.[4] In March of the same year, a unity-themed mural at the University of Iowa was vandalized and defaced with Nazi-inspired graffiti. In September, a White student in Louisiana placed a noose around the neck of a Black classmate. In November, swastikas were spray painted on a Holocaust scholar's door at Teachers College, Columbia University.

Campus inequity, however, isn't limited to hate crimes.

Students of Black, Latinx, and Native American racial formations drop out of high school at higher rates and enroll in college at lower rates than do

White and Asian American students. Many studies have shown that students of color, particularly Black males, are overreferred to special education for behavioral issues; paradoxically, however, some studies suggest that students of color with disabilities are less likely to receive necessary accommodations.

School suspensions and expulsions disproportionally affect Black and Latino males. In keeping with the increased likelihood for Black people to be arrested or incarcerated for the same infractions as White people, Black students are three times as likely as White students to be suspended from public school in the United States;[5] even when the infractions are similar, Black students are more likely to be disciplined. In fact, Black male students are likelier to be disciplined for "less serious, more subjective reasons."[6]

While racism and microaggressions, commonplace verbal or behavior slights, against Asian, Asian American, and Pacific Islander students are common, in many schools racism against those of Asian descent is ignored because it doesn't fit the Black/White binary that for generations defined American racism. The academic struggles of students of these populations remain unaddressed because such instances do not fit with the model minority myth, which emphasizes the academic achievement and successful assimilation of Asian Americans. Moreover, these broad racial categories do not take into account differences between Asian subgroups, a conflation that masks patterns of poor academic performance among Samoan, Hmong, and Cambodian populations, among others.

But these trends do not tell the whole story of racism in education.

"Since the earliest days of colonialism in North America, an identifiable racial order has linked the system of political rule to the racial classification of individuals and groups."[7] Racism, then, is not an aberration, but an American tradition. It is important to remember that "education systems in all societies are designed to serve as the primary institutions that reproduce dominant social and economic orders, customs, and beliefs systems"; as a result, schooling in the United States, public education in particular, is "a function of capitalism, white supremacy and their intrinsic restraints on democracy and social equality."[8]

If, as Latinx rhetoricians Iris D. Ruiz and Raul Sanchez suggest, colonization is understood "to include not only the taking of land but also the taking of culture and the defining of knowledge,"[9] it is not enough to say that schools suffer the same racism that prevails throughout the rest of the society. It would be accurate to say that schools are one of strongest forces—if not *the* strongest force—by which that racism is maintained and normalized.

EDUCATION AS ACCULTURATION

Schools, which ought to be sites of exploration and transformation, are also sites of oppression and acculturation—and they always have been. The history of schooling in the United States makes readily apparent its very raison d'etre: to preserve the cultural ideologies and hierarchical structures of American society.

Republican Education

In the early years of U.S. independence, the role of schools to promote active citizenship and republican values was widely celebrated, both nationally and within local communities. The size and the heterogeneity of the country, even in its earliest days, made the maintenance of order and the establishment of a cohesive populace difficult tasks for a new republican government. State-sponsored education, however, could prepare men to become informed voters and virtuous lawmakers and train women to properly raise sons who would become the same.

While some lawmakers claimed that education was a step in each citizen's pursuit of liberty, others, like Benjamin Rush, were far more motivated by fear of European influence than they were by justice: "I consider it as possible to convert men into republican machines. This must be done if we expect them to perform their parts properly in the great machine of the state."[10] In a country seeking to establish a strong, common national identity, free schools promised to turn citizens into "Americans," almost from infancy; in a 1783 textbook promoting an English separate from the British English of the old world, Noah Webster declared: "Let the first word he lisps be 'Washington.'"[11]

Americanizing the Immigrant Population

As the country expanded and as new racial and ethnic populations immigrated to the United States, particularly to growing urban centers like New York City, the schools were "the main institutions charged with the responsibility of homogenization."[12] One of the earliest official reports produced by the New York City Board of Education argued that students from all socioeconomic classes should attend public schools and learn the same curriculum. With language evocative of achievement ideology, the report stated that the poor, "due to their condition, are early obliged to form the habits of industry, effort, and self-reliance, which can alone secure success."[13]

The uplift of poorer students was not necessarily the purpose for this standardization, however; the report also states that by attending public schools, "the children of affluence may early learn that industry and effort will be indispensable to compete successfully, in the struggles of life, with the poor."[14] This statement articulates a common fear of the Protestant education reformers of the mid-nineteenth century that the populace of the poorer class, a large portion of which was made up of Catholic immigrants, would eventually, through industry as well as sheer population size, rise to threaten both the cultural values and the economic success of the Protestant majority.

By the early twentieth century, many immigrant groups had assimilated to the point that they became involved with public school teaching and administration—and took on the same roles of social reformers as those who had come before them. For example, while German Jewish immigrants to New York City had managed to assimilate not only into society but into the affluent elite by the late nineteenth century, the wave of Yiddish-speaking, Communist-influenced Russian Jewish immigrants, with whom they shared a religion but not a political ideology, at the end of the century threatened their social standing. As a result, a number of supplemental educational programs were implemented to provide vocational, cultural and language education to new Jewish immigrants.

The Educational Alliance, then known as the Hebrew Institute, was developed with "the expressed purpose . . . to Americanize the children of the ghetto."[15] There were significant overlaps between the public schools and these supplemental educational programs: one of the Alliance's directors, Julia Richman, also a member of the First Jewish Women's Congress, a meeting of established, highly educated Jewish American women with the mission to educate and civilize the Russian Jewish immigrants, later became a district superintendent of Lower East Side schools.[16] By the third decade of the twentieth century, Jewish people made up 40 percent of new public school teachers.[17]

In creating a more homogeneous American populace, the education system also helped to create a larger race of people who were considered White. As Italian, Irish, and Jewish immigrant children assimilated into American culture through schooling, their racioethnic identities were absorbed into the fabric of whiteness in which American culture is cloaked.

Exclusionary Schooling

Just as notable as the assimilation of some groups is the glaring exclusion of others. While European immigrants were expected to assimilate, African Americans were not expected to become Americans at all. When the earliest lawmakers landed on education as a method for unifying the citizens of the states and creating a national identity following the Revolutionary War, slavery was still common practice throughout the country. Early public schooling's emphasis on creating engaged citizens makes clear for whom the education was intended: African Americans, after all, were not citizens.

In some northern cities, public education was available for free Blacks prior to the Civil War. From the turn of the nineteenth century, public schools in Boston, Massachusetts, and New Haven, Connecticut, were open to Black students. In New York, free people of color could attend the African Free School.

In Baltimore, where the antebellum economy relied only partly on slave labor and where educated free Black workers were seen by White elites as cheap skilled labor, Black parents, activists, and teachers created an "an enclave of educational opportunity in the slaveholding South."[18] Publicly, these schools emphasized skills that would prepare free Black people to fill the posts most readily available for them. For instance, at the St. Frances Academy for Colored Girls, girls could learn sewing, washing, and other domestic chores. Religious instruction was common in the free schools, as was instruction in reading and writing; in fact, by the 1830s, in addition to holding jobs sweeping streets and delivering goods, Black men were hired in printing presses, newspapers, and bookstores. Baltimore was far from racially progressive, but so long as White Baltimoreans benefited from the education of free Blacks, the schools remained open.

While many Black people received education through public schools, it is important to remember that the early exclusion of African Americans from public schools was not an oversight; the schools did not intend to educate Black students. Likewise, the later inclusion of Black students was not in the best interest of Black individuals or the Black community but in the interest of the economy and the White elites who would benefit from an educated Black labor force.

Such patterns are not limited to the education of Black Americans. Native Americans and non-European immigrants had varying access to early public schools as well. Even when educational opportunities were available for these students, the goals of the education differed.

In the 1820s, mission schools oriented toward the "civilization" of Native Americans were funded by the federal government as part of the Indian Civilization Act (also called the Civilization Fund Act) of 1819. Schools were primarily set up on tribal land that abutted or interacted with White settlements. Students in these schools were taught English literacy and Christian religion. In 1868, the ironically named Peace Policy forced tribal communities onto reservations and removed tribal leaders, replacing them with Christian missionaries who taught religion, English reading and writing, and American ways of life in a systematic attempt to eliminate native cultures. One memorable motto of these so-called boarding schools was "Kill the Indian, Save the Man."

In the 1880s, so-called Mexican schools were created throughout the southwestern United States to provide limited, segregated education to children of Mexican-born parents. "Since Mexican Americans were considered nominally 'White,' they could not be racially segregated so their segregation was based on language and culture."[19] While language was forwarded as one official rationale for the segregation of Mexican-origin students, children in these schools were punished physically for speaking Spanish.

The conditions and curriculum of these schools bore little resemblance to those of nearby White schools. For example, the Baytown Mexican School, established in 1923 in Texas, was held in the Mexican Community Recreation Hall (owned by the Humble Oil and Refinery Company), where instruction was provided by female students from a local high school with the aim to transition Spanish-speaking children to English. The aims of these schools might best be summarized by the following remark made by a school board member in Garden Grove, California, in 1945: "If we educate the Mexicans better, who would pick our crops?"[20]

There are limited written histories of the education of peoples of Asian descent in the early United States. Laws passed during the nineteenth and twentieth centuries broadly excluded Asian and Asian American groups from American life as well as education. The Chinese Exclusion Act, passed in 1882, prevented the immigration of Chinese laborers; the Immigration Act of 1917 included a section barring immigrants from most of the rest of Asia and the Pacific Islands.

In San Francisco in the early twentieth century, Chinese children—even those born in the United States—were forced to attend segregated primary schools that served the express purpose of protecting White children from "association with pupils of the Mongolian race."[21] Japanese children (and children from other Asian and Pacific Island nations) were placed in the Chinese school as well. That immigrants from countries with different languages, customs, and belief systems were grouped together in American policy and education may provide context for the broad strokes with which Asian Americans are conceptualized in education scholarship, policy, and curricula today.

Though nonwhite students today increasingly graduate high school and attend college, the effects of their exclusion reverberate in schools. The ideologies foundational to American schooling, however, make it difficult to recognize, let alone rectify, the inequities that prevail in contemporary education.

Educational Inequality and the Meritocracy Myth

While much educational scholarship on the achievement gap between White students and underrepresented students of color and on, more broadly, race in education, emphasizes structural factors such as access to resources, school-based discrimination, and culturally insensitive instructional and assessment practices, the American Dream is so pervasive that individuals, including students, are more likely to use ideologies of achievement or meritocracy to explain patterns of high and low academic achievement.

In other words, individuals see success at the individual level: if a high school student receives a failing grade on an exam, the assumption is that the student did not study the night before, has poor test-taking strategies, isn't putting in the effort, or is struggling with the material. Perhaps, however, the student works after school to contribute to the family income or prepares dinner for a sibling while a parent works a second job or takes care of a sick parent; perhaps it is also the case that the student never learned test-taking strategies; perhaps the student is struggling with the material because the school doesn't have enough textbooks for every student; and perhaps that exam is written in a so-called standard dialect that the student rarely hears or speaks outside of the classroom.

However, the myth of meritocracy and the promise that those who work hard enough can obtain the American Dream do not allow for such systemic explanations. The ideology of achievement is so pervasive that even the most critically conscious, student-responsive instructors may not see the ways their own instruction reinforces it and perpetuates inequity. Because part of the purpose of schooling, intentionally or otherwise, is to disseminate ideology, students, too, often do not realize how they have internalized these myths of achievement and meritocracy. Moreover, education has been touted as the great equalizer for so long that, for many, its inherent systemic inequality has become invisible.

THE INVISIBLE WHITENESS OF U.S. EDUCATION

While individual acts of discrimination may be one way in which racism is made apparent in educational institutions, racism does not always make itself known through direct, vitriolic slurs or acts of violence. Often, it does not make itself known at all. In many educational spaces, racism is covert, implicit, and insidious, less the result of hatred than it is the consequence of an ideology of white supremacy that undergirds all aspects of the American educational system. This white supremacy, however, can be far more difficult to combat than individual acts of discrimination: its influence is so far-reaching and its entrenchment in our social, governmental, and cultural institutions is so deep that it is sometimes invisible, sometimes even to those who suffer as a result of it.

There are three primary modes by which white supremacy and racism enter the classroom: official governmental and administrative policies; school and course curricula; and classroom dynamics. None of these categories exists in isolation and there is considerable overlap: policies determine, directly or indirectly, the curriculum, which of course influences and is influenced by classroom dynamics; policies about class size and placement also determine classroom dynamics directly. Matters of policy, unfortunately, often feel out of reach of influence for instructors, especially those without administrative posts; separating these intertwined threads may make it easier for those whose work exists in the classroom space to identify and parse out the myriad influences of white supremacy and racism on the classroom.

Official Policies

Policies that influence education range from individual departmental and campus policies to larger-scale sociopolitical policies and laws under which schools operate. On the broadest scale, legal policy regarding the funding of public education dictates the allocation of resources to nearly 100,000 public schools across the country. Across the United States, public schools are funded by a combination, variable by state, of federal, state, and local monies.

In 2016, U.S. public schools received, on average, 10 percent federal funding, 45 percent state funding, and 45 percent local funding.[22] Local funding, however, is taken foremost from property taxes. This means that, on average, nearly half of the resources allocated to public schools are determined by the value of real estate in the surrounding school district. The almost too obvious result of this practice is that schools in wealthy neighborhoods with thriving businesses have ample financial resources while schools in poorer areas with lesser local economies have smaller institutional budgets.

More specifically, this means that schools in wealthy urban and suburban districts are better staffed, have newer facilities, and provide more elective instruction than schools in poor urban and rural areas. These schools are also likelier to offer advanced placement classes, college advising, and supplemental academic resources, such as tutoring, for struggling students. Poorly funded schools are often plagued by structural, curricular, and personnel deficits, such as old, structurally unsound buildings, limited copies of outdated textbooks, high student-to-teacher ratios, and an inadequate number of support and custodial staff, each of which compounds the problems caused by the others.

Because race and socioeconomic status are closely connected in the United States, the best funded schools serve a population of predominantly White students whose middle-class parents hold college- or even graduate-level degrees and work white-collar jobs. Schools with limited resources have higher populations of students from historically underrepresented ethnic and racial groups, more first generation and Generation 1.5 students, and more students whose parents work blue-collar or minimum wage jobs. While over the past decade some public school systems have created initiatives to strategically rezone districts for the purposes of ensuring greater racial and socioeconomic integration, since 2016 many plans for zoning reform have been dialed back or halted by the Trump administration.[23]

Despite great differences in resources, instructors and administrators in poorly funded schools are expected to achieve the same goals for students as those in well-resourced schools. Or are they?

Compounding the disparities among public schools are the increasing number of charter schools. Charter schools, which, though considered public schools, are overseen by private companies or organizations and accept funding from private sources, have higher teacher turnover and higher student attrition rates than traditional public schools. Despite the segregation that persists in public schooling, charter school students are even more likely to learn in highly segregated settings. Most problematically, because charter schools are privately run and are not required to meet the same standards as public schools, they do not have to uphold the same standards for instruction or staffing.

Charter schools are more likely than traditional public schools to hire uncredentialed teachers, and are less likely than traditional public schools to offer instructional supports for students struggling academically or to provide Individualized Education Plans for students with documented learning disabilities and differences. While proponents of charter schools argue that they offer parents and students, particularly those of underrepresented ethnic and racial groups, more choices when it comes to schooling, the addition of charter schools has done little to level the unequal foundation of public schooling.

Educational inequity on the elementary and secondary levels has long-term consequences: Black and Latinx students are less likely than their White peers to enroll in and graduate from college. White students are likelier to enter college with credit from advanced placement or early college courses while students of color and English learners are likelier to be placed in developmental or remedial courses (which, in many schools, come with fees but award no college-level credit). White and Asian students are likelier to attend research universities, while Latinx students are likeliest to enroll in two-year colleges. Fewer than half of Black and Latinx students who enroll in four-year colleges graduate within a six-year period.[24]

Policies on the postsecondary level, such as the Affirmative Action initiatives of the 1980s and 1990s, have been implemented with the express intention to increase student (and faculty) diversity. It is important to note that such policies, regardless of whether or not they are perceived as equitable, are additive rather than reformative. In other words, these policies function adjunct to existing practices and procedures but do not change the structures already in place. The preexisting policies that determine resource distribution, placement, admissions, and hiring practices are inherently inequitable, which is why they necessitate the addition of equity-minded initiatives. The creation of additional policies, however, in the absence of revisions to the underlying inequitable structures of schooling, serves as a temporary, incomplete solution.

The Curriculum

While individual teachers may—and often do—tailor course curricula to their students in creative, inclusive, and culturally responsive ways, the term *curriculum*, as more broadly used here, refers to the courses of study and learning objectives determined by the school, department, or university system. The curriculum includes content all teachers within a particular subject discipline are required, often by policy and other times by school culture, to cover as well as the goals set for that instruction. Even in educational spaces where instructors' autonomy and student-responsive differentiation are encouraged, the curriculum and educational objectives are expected to align with disciplinary, departmental, school, state, and/or accrediting body standards.

The debate over the standardization of the public school curriculum has existed for as long as there have been public schools. In major urban centers like New York City, public school curricula were uniform throughout the schools and emphasized republican values and Protestant ideologies. In New York City, though sectarian teaching was prohibited with the establishment of a central Board of Education in 1842, the Bible was a common course of study. While policymakers then argued that an unassisted interpretation of the Bible was a fair way to avoid sectarian interpretation, it is important to note that this argument is, in itself, a typically Protestant understanding of religious study; that Protestant editions of the Bible were used in the classroom further illuminates the school's cultural orientation.

Other standard texts in the early years of public schooling were also heavily weighted in the direction of Protestantism; for instance, the public school student might have had to read a biography of Protestant reformer Martin Luther. This orientation had much to do with the broader sociological goals of instruction. As early as the seventeenth century, when colonists arrived in what would later become the United States, "Puritans considered literacy key to the survival of their faith: Teach every child to read so that every child can read the Bible."[25]

More recent attempts at standardization have been less directly discriminatory but have not succeeded in their stated goals of leveling the field, so to speak, for all students. When the Common Core Curriculum was implemented in New York State in 2013, the gap between White students' eighth-grade English language arts (ELA) exam scores and exam scores of Black and Latinx students increased measurably from the year prior, before Common

Core–aligned exams were introduced: the fourteen-point gap between White and Black students' scores in 2012 increased to twenty-five points; the three-point gap for Latinx students increased to twenty-two points.[26]

Standardized testing, like most of the curriculum, is organized around hegemonic content and ways of knowing. Consider the history classroom: It is a commonplace that history is told by the victor. That dominant narrative, however, eliminates or diminishes the historical (and contemporary) contributions of those of nondominant cultures and belief systems, thereby reducing the complexity of American history to a single story of White American achievement.

When people of color are included in the curriculum, their accomplishments are lessened or sanitized; their actions and belief systems are reframed to fit the "master script" that legitimizes "dominant, White, upper-class, male voicings as the 'standard' knowledge students need to know."[27] For example, Rosa Parks becomes "a tired seamstress" who simply wanted a seat on a bus "instead of a long-time participant in social justice endeavors."[28]

Even when the accomplishments of people of color are celebrated, White resistance to those accomplishments is downplayed, as are the atrocities committed by Whites against them. Sacagawea is presented as an intrepid woman who accompanied Lewis and Clark on their expedition to the western United States; omitted, however, is that she did so alongside the French Canadian man to whom contemporary scholars believe she and another woman had been sold as wives years earlier. Martin Luther King Jr. is positioned as a nonviolent hero loved by all rather than "a disdained scholar and activist whose vision extended to social causes throughout the world."[29]

The muting of voices is most apparent when it comes to historical figures who challenged white supremacy in ways that did not conform to the standards of behavior expected of people of color. While King is reduced to a preacher of nonviolence, polite dissent, and civil disobedience, Malcolm X and the Black Panther Party (BPP), advocates of violent protest as a means of defense against racist violence and oppression, are often omitted entirely, despite their influence on contemporary schools and society.

For example, in January 1969 the BPP created, among other social programs, the Free Breakfast for School Children Program, which fed thousands of underserved children and paved the way for the free breakfast programs now commonplace in schools across the country, all while the party was the target of persecution, resulting most notoriously in the execution by Chicago police of national party deputy chairman Fred Hampton in December of that same year. That the federal School Breakfast Program was permanently authorized in 1975, shortly after the BPP's Free Breakfast for School Children Program was dismantled, makes clear that the party's efforts were paradoxically both undermined and co-opted by the U.S. government.

In short, the history taught in schools is not the complete history of the country; it is the history of white America.

In his research on Black history textbooks, antiracist history educator LaGarrett King found that even some course materials specifically dedicated to Black history address racist history passively, without offering a nuanced discussion of the sociopolitical contexts, macro structures, or intentionality of racism. Such approaches may be seen by teachers as "non-combative and safe" because they do "not challenge *common sense* racial thinking"[30] but they perpetuate the notion of racism as a collection of "individual acts and not based on continual systems of oppression."[31]

History may have some of the most glaring omissions of voices and stories of color but it is not the only discipline wherein whiteness dominates. The literary canon is filled with White, male, European authors. The names of White European men comprise most of scholars listed in science textbooks. Most of the philosophy studied in survey courses is Western philosophy. On the secondary and postsecondary levels, courses about nonwhite populations are typically elective, a term that implies they are not necessary for all students to know and which emphasizes their marginalization. Even the emphasis on objectivity and the scientific method that prevails in the hard and social sciences prizes White European ways of knowing.

Despite efforts by individual teachers and scholars to disrupt this whiteness by exploring more complex histories, authors of color, and non-Eurocentric ways of knowing and communicating, the broad school curriculum—itself influenced by policies, government officials, community pressure, and, to a lesser extent, instructor expertise and preferences—tells students what is important, what matters, and who matters. The voices and stories uplifted by the curriculum, as well as those that are marginalized or silenced, serve as daily reminders that, in the eyes of our educational system, it is whiteness that matters. This sends the message to POCI in the classroom that their "identity and history [are] unimportant" and their "racial experiences do not matter."[32]

Classroom Dynamics

Inside the classroom, racism and white supremacy play out in various ways and to varying degrees in the interactions between teachers and students and between students and their classmates. Because teacher-student interaction is strongly influenced by the individual positionalities of teachers and students, an important component of classroom dynamics is which bodies enter the classroom and which roles they play inside of it. While the ethnic and racial diversity of the student population in K–12 and higher education increases each year, the teaching force remains troublingly homogeneous. In 2015 in New York City, White students made up less than 15 percent of public school enrollment; 58 percent of New York City public school teachers, however, were White.[33]

On the college level, despite increasing diversity among part-time faculty in recent years, similar shifts cannot be found on the tenure track. While the number of underrepresented faculty of color increased between 1993 and 2013, Black, Hispanic, and Native American educators were no more likely to hold tenured or tenure-track positions than they were twenty-five years earlier; in fact, the percentage of Black women in tenured faculty position actually declined.[34] In 2016, more than three-quarters of full-time university faculty members were White.[35]

These imbalances play out in ways that are often unintentional but inequitable nonetheless, often in the form of *microaggressions*, subtle but commonplace verbal, behavioral, or environmental slights against minoritized racial or ethnic groups. Among the most commonly reported microaggressions committed by teachers are the following:

- Mispronouncing students' names, even after having been corrected
- Expecting students to represent or speak for the group with which they are assumed to identify
- Setting low expectations for students of color or for students from particular neighborhoods or socioeconomic backgrounds
- Scheduling exams or paper deadlines on significant cultural or religious holidays
- Assuming students have access to resources not provided by the school or university
- Assuming students do *not* have access to resources based upon their ethnic or racial identification

Some of the microaggressions students of color experience in the classroom come not from their teachers but from their peers. While the potential and problems of peer interaction differ greatly depending on the school context and the age of the students, a primary theme that emerges across contexts is the exclusion or isolation of students of color, particularly in predominantly White institutions (PWIs).

Since the late twentieth century, individual acts of racial discrimination have generally, though not exclusively, been less overt than in decades past. In the absence of covertly racist remarks, the daily experiences inside and out of the classroom of students of color, as well as emergent bilinguals and Generation 1.5 students, in PWIs may differ from the experiences of most of their peers. As one student explains: "I have been doing research about immigration because that is what I know the most about from my personal experience and from my research on the topic, often times I am able to offer/add an insightful idea about the subject. . . . My classmates are not exposed to the things I am exposed to as a bilingual, minority student here; therefore, we do not write about the same things."[36] For some students, these unique experiences may feel like and be seen as assets; the same student explains that "instructors saw the potential in me and my ideas, what I was bringing to the table."[37]

For other students, these experiences are isolating, and leave students feeling that they are "continuously being judged by and against the cultural and linguistic majority."[38] Based on previous experiences in classes or outside of the classroom, students who speak with an accent may fear being misunderstood or, worse, ridiculed for their language practices. Other students have difficulty collaborating on group projects with White, native English-speaking peers, who assume they will not be able to contribute fully due to their mother tongues.

CONCLUDING THOUGHTS

Popular rhetoric around schooling frames education as a liberatory, equalizing force by which those from marginalized groups can level the playing field of American society. At the same time, educational institutions have always been one of the primary venues through which inequitable ideology is disseminated within a society. Educators dedicated to the equitable instruction of all students are familiar with the popular narrative, its functions, and its limitations. Unfortunately, despite the best intentions, inequity is manifested through the oft-invisible institutional and pedagogical structures of the classroom, including the ways of knowing and speaking teachers may unwittingly encourage.

Though the school system may vocally celebrate pluralism, it rewards assimilation. In doing so, it prioritizes white European ideas, stories, and ways of knowing over more diverse others—and requires students to set aside significant elements of their cultural identities in order to achieve academic success. Even if this forced assimilation were not so intrinsically inequitable, it would still be exclusionary: while many ethnic groups, like Italian, Irish, and Jewish people, have been able to assimilate over time into white American culture, effectively becoming White in the eyes of the common racial binary, other groups, such as Black, Indigenous, and Latinx people, have not been afforded the same access.

Despite the intrinsic inequities of Western education and educational institutions, considerable strides have been made, particularly by educators of color, to challenge exclusionary epistemologies and design more culturally responsive, antiracist pedagogies. LaGarrett King teaches and studies antiracist history education. Science teacher educator Felicia Mensah studies and teaches culturally relevant science instruction and teacher training. Christopher Emdin, celebrated author of *For White Folks Who Teach in the Hood and the Rest of Y'All Too: Reality Pedagogy and Urban Education*, champions Hip-Hop pedagogies in urban science education. Writing studies scholar Asao B. Inoue is well known for his antiracist approaches to writing assessment. Jamila Kareem has offered a heuristic for creating antiracist program learning outcomes. Neisha-Anne Green, Michelle Johnson, Frankie Condon, Alexandria Lockett, and Allia Abdullah-Matta explore antiracist writing center administration and pedagogies. Some of these practices and perspectives, and many others, will be addressed throughout the remaining chapters of this book.

Scholars have long called out the ways in which disciplinary epistemologies and practices privilege whiteness and marginalize the ways of knowing and being of POCI, multilingual learners, and the disabled, and such efforts are increasingly garnering public attention. In March 2019, an informal, self-appointed working group was formed to create moderation guidelines for the Writing Program Administration listserv (WPA-L), a well-known professional listserv in the field of writing studies, following repeated incidences of racism and misogyny that betrayed the underlying white supremacy and patriarchy of the disciplinary space.[39]

In June 2019, the director of the National Institutes of Health announced that he would no longer appear on all-male conference panels.[40] Also in June, communication scholars boycotted a popular scholarly journal after its editor released a statement claiming that those pushing for more diversity in the field were "prioritizing diversity in place of intellectual merit."[41]

Racism silences, and silence perpetuates racism. For these reasons, antiracist educators encourage explicit discussion of race and racism both in scholarly discourse and in the classroom. Too often, however, attempts to address race and racism in the classroom are surface level and do not explore deeply or critically enough the ways racism and white supremacy are maintained by educational praxis. As Iris D. Ruiz points out, though there have been "honest attempts" to interrogate the concept of race, "the language of race and racism is regulated by mainstream publications,"[42] which shapes how instructors discuss and attend to race in the classroom.

In the language of social justice and antiracist pedagogy, there is a significant distinction between a *nonracist* stance and an *antiracist* stance: an individual taking the former abstains, whether intentionally or intuitively, from racist acts; an individual taking the latter stance actively challenges racism on both the micro and macro levels. In other words, while the nonracist individual may not personally discriminate, the antiracist individual critically examines, responds to, and seeks to dismantle racist institutions and systemic racial hierarchies. Antiracism is "an active process against racism that seeks to understand how racial ideology is manufactured and how it impacts the lived experiences of people daily."[43] Antiracism recognizes that racism is structural and ideological; antiracist education, therefore, must both acknowledge the complicity of educational systems and institutions in the maintenance of white supremacy and offer a counter hegemonic discourse to traditional (white) curricula and epistemologies.

Because the language of policy and pedagogy can catalyze or stall progress, and can illuminate or obscure truth, it is important that words like *antiracist* and *antiracism* not be used lightly or reductively. As happens with many other important critical frameworks once taken up in mainstream publications, *antiracism* has become a buzzword of sorts, and, as a result, there is potential for the word to be flattened, its meaning muted. Terms like *antiracism*, *social justice*, and *equity* abound in scholarship and program mission statements, but those terms do not necessarily translate to antiracist praxis. This is unsurprising, given that many educators themselves lack "a sufficient degree of critical antiracist knowledge."[44]

Education is a functionary of larger societal structures that maintain hierarchy and inequity, making it difficult for individuals within its systems to see the ways in which accepted educational practices (including those that seem culturally response and inclusive) serve to uphold the inequity that defines American society. It is imperative, therefore, that educational professionals, including but not limited to teachers, administrators, and counselors critically reflect upon their own assumptions and the ways in which they contribute, knowingly or unintentionally, to this process.

To ensure the development and practice of critical racial literacy, students should be encouraged to engage in such reflection and open discourse as well. The educational contexts in which these conversations are most necessary and ought to occur are often spaces of silence rather than racial literacy. In kind, even some of the pedagogical practices presumed most progressive contribute to the stifling and marginalization of such courageous conversations, and uphold rather than challenge the white hegemonic status quo.

It is from this culture of silence that the trigger warning has emerged.

NOTES

1. Toni Morrison, *Playing in the Dark: Whiteness and the Literary Imagination* (Cambridge: Harvard University Press, 1992), 17.

2. Dan Bauman, "After 2016 Election, Campus Hate Crimes Seemed to Jump. Here's What the Data Tell Us," *The Chronicle of Higher Education* (February 16, 2018).

3. Not all campus hate crimes are reported to law enforcement. More than half of those reported were based on race, ethnicity, or ancestry. See U.S. Department of Justice, Federal Bureau of Investigation, *2016 Hate Crimes Statistics*. https://ucr.fbi.gov/hate-crime/2017/tables/table-10.xls.

4. Cory Collins, "Hate at School: January 2018," *Teaching Tolerance* (February 7, 2018).

5. Erica L. Green, "Why Are Black Students Punished So Often? Minnesota Confronts a National Quandary," *The New York Times* (March 18, 2018).

6. Russell J. Skiba, "When Is Disproportionality Discrimination? The Overrepresentation of Black Students in School Suspension," in *Zero Tolerance: Resisting the Drive for Punishment in Our Schools; A Handbook for Parents, Students, Educators, and Citizens*, ed. William Ayers, Bernadine Dohrn, and Rick Ayers (New York: New Press, 2001), 182.

7. Michael Omi and Howard Winant, *Racial Formation in the United States: From the 1960s to the 1990s*, 2nd ed. (New York: Routledge, 1994), 79.

8. Deborah M. Keisch and Tim Scott, "U.S. Education Reform and the Maintenance of White Supremacy through Structural Violence," *Landscapes of Violence* 3, no. 3 (2015): 2.

9. Iris D. Ruiz and Raúl Sánchez, *Decolonizing Rhetoric and Composition Studies: New Latinx Keywords for Theory and Pedagogy* (New York: Palgrave Macmillan, 2016), xiii.

10. Benjamin Rush, "A Plan for the Establishment of Public Schools and the Diffusion of Knowledge in Pennsylvania; to Which are Added, Thoughts upon the Mode of Education, Proper in a Republic," in *Essays on Education in the Early Republic*, ed. Frederick Rudolph (Cambridge: Harvard University Press, 1965), 16–17.

11. Noah Webster, quoted in Carl F. Kaestle, *Pillars of the Republic: Common Schools and American Society, 1780–1860* (New York: Hill and Wang, 1983), 6.

12. Carl F. Kaestle, *The Evolution of an Urban School System: New York City, 1750–1850* (Cambridge: Harvard University Press, 1973), 158.

13. *Annual Report of the Board of Education of the City and County of New York, 1850* (New York: William C. Bryant, 1850), 15.

14. Ibid.

15. Stephan F. Brumberg, *Going to America, Going to School: The Jewish Immigrant Public School Encounter in Turn-of-the-Century New York City* (New York: Praeger, 1986), 65.

16. Ibid., 64.

17. Wendell Pritchett, *Brownsville, Brooklyn: Blacks, Jews, and the Changing Face of the Ghetto* (Chicago: University of Chicago Press, 2002), 26.

18. Hilary J. Moss, *Schooling Citizens: The Struggle for African American Education in Antebellum America* (Chicago: University of Chicago Press, 2009), 69.

19. Yolanda Chavez Leyva, "The Mexican Schools: An Invisible History," *Fierce Fronteriza* (May 23, 2017).

20. Claudio Sanchez, "Tougher Times for Latino Students? History Says They've Never Had It Easy," NPR.org (November 15, 2016).

21. Asia Society, "Asian Americans Then and Now: Linking Past to Present," Asiasociety.org. https://asiasociety.org/education/asian-americans-then-and-now.

22. Cory Turner, Reema Khrais, Tim Lloyd, Alexandra Olgin, Laura Isensee, Becky Vevea, and Dan Carsen, "Why America's Schools Have a Money Problem," NPR.org (April 18, 2016).

23. Michelle Chen, "How Unequal School Funding Punishes Poor Kids," *The Nation* (May 11, 2018).

24. Emily Tate, "Graduation Rates and Race," *Inside Higher Ed* (April 26, 2017).

25. Turner et al., "Why America's Schools . . ."

26. Valerie Strauss, "The Myth of Common Core Equity," *The Washington Post* (March 10, 2014).

27. Ellen Swartz, "Emancipatory Narratives: Rewriting the Master Script in the School Curriculum," *Journal of Negro Education* 61, no. 3 (1992): 341.

28. Gloria Ladson-Billings, "Just What Is Critical Race Theory and What's It Doing in a *Nice* Field Like Education?," in *Foundations of Critical Race Theory in Education*, 2nd ed., ed. Edward Taylor, David Gillborn, and Gloria Ladson-Billings (New York: Routledge, 2016), 25.

29. Ibid.

30. LaGarrett King, "Black History as Anti-racist and Non-racist: An Examination of Two High School Black History Textbooks," in *But I Don't See Color: The Perils, Practices, and Possibilities of Antiracist Education*, ed. Terry Husband (Rotterdam: Sense, 2016), 76.

31. Ibid., 75.

32. Adam Alvarez, H. Richard Milner IV, and Lori Delale-O'Connor, "Race, Trauma, and Education: What Educators Need to Know," in *But I Don't See Color: The Perils, Practices, and Possibilities of Antiracist Education*, ed. Terry Husband (Rotterdam: Sense, 2016), 31.

33. Hua-Yu Sebastian Cherng and Peter F. Halpin, "The Importance of Minority Teachers: Student Perceptions of Minority versus White Teachers," *Educational Researcher* 45, no. 7 (2016): 407.

34. Martin J. Finkelstein, Valerie Martin Conley, and Jack H. Schuster, "Taking the Measure of Faculty Diversity," *Advancing Education* (2016), 13.

35. National Center for Education Statistics, "Fast Facts: Race/Ethnicity of College Faculty," https://nces.ed.gov/fastfacts/display.asp?id=61.

36. Unnamed student, quoted in Kathryn Nielsen, "On Class, Race, and Dynamics of Privilege: Supporting Generation 1.5 Writers across the Curriculum," in *WAC and Second Language Writers: Research toward Linguistically and Culturally Inclusive Programs and Practices*, ed. T. M. Zawacki and M. Cox (Fort Collins: WAC Clearinghouse, 2014), 136.

37. Ibid.

38. Nielsen, "On Class, Race, and Dynamics of Privilege," 143.

39. The author of this book is a member of the WPA-L Reimagining Working Group.

40. See Pam Belluck, "N.I.H. Head Calls for End to All-Male Panels of Scientists," *The New York Times*, June 12, 2019.

41. Martin J. Medhurst, quoted in Colleen Flaherty, "When White Scholars Pick White Scholars," *Inside Higher Ed*, June 13, 2019.

42. Iris D. Ruiz, "Race," in Ruiz and Sánchez, *Decolonizing Rhetoric and Composition Studies*, 5.

43. King, "Black History as Anti-racist and Non-racist," 63.

44. Ibid., 77.

Chapter Two

The Rise of the Trigger Warning

> *Trigger warnings are one cursory method of acknowledging entrenched formal and informal marginalization—and a method that seeks to form an alternative learning and dialogue environment, a counter-classroom to the stigma imposed by the privileged objectivity of invading institutions that tell the violated to settle down or leave.*—Jane Gavin-Hebert[1]

> *Framed as an individualizing tool of equal access, discussions of trigger warnings center on the tool itself, rather than structural violence that trigger warnings name by way of a trace: trauma and its durable effects.*—Bonnie Washick[2]

Over just a few years, media attention to trigger warnings on school campuses has sparked a national (and, at times, international) public debate about academic freedom and student fragility. A strange phenomenon can be observed amid all this talk: While everyone seems to be talking *about* trigger warnings in academic settings, precious little research has actually emerged *from* academia. Even when faculty members have entered these conversations, they have done so primarily through popular media and news outlets. Though some scholars have begun recently to take up the call, there remains a dearth of scholarly theoretical or empirical research on the use of trigger warnings in classroom settings.

Does this mean that the hoopla surrounding trigger warnings is much ado about a few isolated incidents? This is probably not the case, since some of the research that does exist shows that trigger warnings are a common, often contentious, matter of discussion or policy on campuses and that educators, administrators, and students have strong feelings about trigger warnings, feelings that frequently are at odds with those of their colleagues or classmates.

Might it be that the relative lack of scholarship on trigger warnings is simply a matter of logistics and time constraints? Due to the rigorous peer review and periodic publication (often quarterly or biannual) of scholarly journals as well as the time it takes to conduct and report at length on a comprehensive, valid research study, the journey to publication is far longer for a work of scholarship than it is for a newspaper article or social media post. Add to the equation the backlog of submissions to the most renowned journals in a given field and the queue of accepted manuscripts already awaiting publication and it's no wonder that conversations of trigger warnings are happening more quickly in popular media, especially on social media platforms, where authors and readers can respond in real time.

This is a valid argument—but it is an incomplete one. After all, there *are* books, articles, and even dissertations on trigger warnings. (See the bibliography section at the end of this book for a comprehensive list of related resources.) There just aren't many. The problem, then, might be a little less logistical—and a lot more problematic. One of the reasons for the limited research on trigger warnings in educational settings may be the remarkable difficulty scholars have defining the trigger warning and identifying what it looks like in practice. Another reason may be the polarizing nature of the trigger warning and the contentiousness of debates about its usage: in this context, taking a strong stance for or against the trigger warning may feel risky, especially for educators with limited job security. (For more on job security and professional concerns, see chapter 7.)

WHAT *IS* A TRIGGER WARNING?

The trigger warning is difficult to define, and those who use trigger warnings, even within the same discipline, seem to use them in different ways and for different reasons.

In psychological terms, a trigger is a piece of sensory input that causes an individual with Post-Traumatic Stress Disorder (PTSD) to reexperience the traumatic event. For example, a truck that backfires and produces a sound similar to a gunshot might be a trigger for a military veteran who spent time in a combat zone. For a woman who has been sexually assaulted, a smell that reminds her of her attacker might be a trigger.

Triggers are often indirectly related to the original trauma, so while some situations may be more avoidable than others, one cannot always predict when triggers will arise or what stimulus might be triggering. Because experiences of trauma, like the traumatic events themselves, differ among individuals, a trigger for one person with PTSD is not necessarily a trigger for another. Responses, too, may differ: one individual may reexperience the trauma through physiological sensations like shaking or sweating; another may have intrusive, repeated flashbacks or memories of the event.

For psychologists, triggers—and thus trigger warnings—are connected to PTSD. Psychologist Guy Boysen defines the classroom trigger warning as "prior notification of an educational topic so that students may prepare for or avoid distress that is automatically evoked by that topic due to clinical mental health problems."[3] In this view, the trigger warning is intended for those with histories of PTSD and, ostensibly, other related mental health disorders.

Scholars and educators in other fields typically use the term more broadly. One such definition of the trigger warning is "a cautionary note that may be added to syllabi or online sites to alert readers, students, or casual browsers about violent or sexually explicit images and text in the materials on a site, in a course reader, or up ahead in a blind chain of internet clicks."[4] This definition implies that the trigger warning is not intended solely for the mental health sufferer; it also incorporates the cautionary notes used on the internet (the site where trigger warnings in their contemporary form arguably first appeared). It does, however, limit the triggering material to which the trigger warning refers to depictions of violence and those of a sexually explicit nature.

For some who use the term, there is a difference between the trigger warning and the *content note*, a more general statement that informs audiences of material of a less traumatic nature. Others use the terms synonymously. Similarly, while some believe all cautionary notes used in the classroom, such as broad statements on course syllabi, to fall under the definition of a trigger warning, others limit the definition of the trigger warning to specific statements made preceding particular course materials.[5]

The inability to come to an agreed-upon definition of the trigger warning may stem from the trigger warning's complex origins. Though often treated as a twenty-first-century phenomenon, trigger warnings are not exactly new. Content warnings, more broadly conceived, have been around for decades.

"Viewer Discretion Is Advised"

Though media ratings and advisory systems have been in effect in different forms since the late 1960s, television content advisories arose in the mid-1990s as a response to increased violence in media, increased violence in the United States, and what researchers and lawmakers found to be the correlation between the two. While many researchers suggested that media violence broadly impacted how individuals viewed and made sense of social realities, others believed there was a more direct correlation between watching violent acts on the screen and committing violent acts in real life. An official statement by the Commission on Violence and Youth of the American Psychological Association, one of the foremost professional organizations in the field of psychology, concluded that viewing violence on television led to "increased acceptance of aggressive attitudes and increased aggressive behavior."[6]

The Telecommunications Act of 1996, which mandated that all new television sets include a V-chip (for *viewer*) to enable parents to block particular television shows they might deem unsuitable for children, led to the development of the television ratings system currently used by most major networks in the United States. This rating system uses age-based ratings, such as TV-Y to indicate suitability for all children and TV-Y7 to indicate suitability for older children, as well as content warnings, such as V and S, indicating that the show features depictions of violence and sex.

Unlike movies, which are rated by a Motion Picture Association of America (MPAA) ratings board of full-time employees who are also parents, television producers and distributers assign these ratings to their own broadcasts. While ratings generally apply to television series as a whole, Viewer Discretion Advisories may appear at the beginning (and, in some cases, after commercial breaks) of a specific episode that features material deemed particularly inflammatory or out of character for the series.

Premium cable networks have their own, similar version of this ratings system, and streaming services like Netflix and Hulu generally, though not always, follow the same systems. Video games also have ratings, as do movies, music albums (which, since the 1980s, have included labels warning of explicit lyrics), websites, and, significantly, social media.

Trigger warnings, especially when used in school settings, differ in both nature and purpose from the content warnings that for decades have preceded television episodes. They are far more similar to the trigger warnings (now more typically called content warnings) that began to appear in women's online communities in the 1990s. Trigger warnings, as we know them today, may have emerged, indirectly, from the intersections of psychology, feminist cultural criticism, and the rise of the internet.

Online Eating Disorder Communities

In the 1970s, eating disorders, due to their apparent increase in prevalence, came to be seen as a social contagion, "spread via the channel of symbolic activity instead of a traditional biological route."[7] Anorexia and bulimia have since been treated through addiction models (as opposed to the treatment approaches advocated for traditional mental illnesses like schizophrenia); such models emphasize the danger of social networks associated with the addiction. It seems simple enough: heroin addicts should avoid both heroin and friends who continue to use. But how do those with eating disorders avoid food? Or friends who eat? For the eating disordered patient, triggers are everywhere.

Just as addicts are advised to join anonymous support groups, such groups are common in eating disorder treatment; however, treatment protocols often separate patients according to their level of illness or recovery (such as inpatient or outpatient) to prevent the possibility of spreading the contagion among members of the group. Accepted wisdom seems to be as follows: eating disorders can be spread from one individual to another; therefore, individuals with eating disorders must be quarantined to contain the epidemic. The result of such an approach, of course, is the stigmatization of the eating disordered individual, who comes to be seem not as a patient or victim, but as a perpetrator of its propagation. The individual is more likely to be blamed for her illness, even by those in medical and psychological communities, than is the schizophrenic or depressive, leading the bulimic or anorexic to isolate herself from others.

In the 1980s and 1990s, because many eating disordered patients were successful, high-achieving young women, the prevalence of eating disorders was attributed by some to societal pressures that provoke anxiety about appearance. The feminist scholarly community, critical of the representations of the female body in popular and commercial culture and the resulting insecurities and pressures such representations placed on young women, viewed eating disorders as a nearly direct result of those body image anxieties. Within this framework, a woman affected by an eating disorder was seen as having been brainwashed by the patriarchy, and though perhaps "unaware that she is making a political statement . . . hostile to feminism and any other critical perspectives that she views as disputing her own autonomy and control or questioning the cultural ideals around which her life is organized."[8] A young woman suffering from anorexia or bulimia in the 1990s, then, might have found herself both marginalized as a medical patient and viewed as antifeminist on her college campus.

Given the rise of internet culture around this time, it should come as no surprise that women in similar positions would find solidarity in online communities. In addition to recovery websites, *pro-ana* blogs and discussion forums, which simultaneously sought to destigmatize eating disorders and promote them as lifestyle choices rather than deviancies, emerged. Many young women found these forums to be safer spaces than those they occupied in their daily lives. However, because these sites enabled users to anonymously share tips for initiating or maintaining eating disordered behavior, which researchers and clinicians concluded increased users' body anxiety, many were shut down, on researchers' recommendations, by internet providers. Because many legal protections did not at that time apply to digital spaces, all of this occurred "with no due process and no consideration for freedom of speech," an action that "might represent the most extensive and underreported violation of the First Amendment in internet history."[9]

To keep from being blocked by moderators of recovery websites and forums and to prevent themselves from being viewed as agents of the patriarchy, for decades women with eating disorders (and, in some cases, scholars who study them) have employed trigger warnings on their own websites and blogs. For example, an artist who uses visual imagery to make sense of her struggles with anorexia might label the work with a disclaimer that states that she is not an expert in the field but simply an individual trying to create a space where others with the disorder might feel welcome. In this sense, "the focus upon safety in the eating disorder community is . . . an attempt to find safe haven from the discourse of trigger warnings itself."[10] In other words, in these online spaces, women use trigger warnings to identify spaces free from the marginalizing discourses that necessitate the use of trigger warnings in the first place.

Feminist Social Media

While examinations into the connections between the eating disorder and online trigger warnings highlight the use of the trigger warning as a defense against accusations of antifeminism, in many histories of the contemporary trigger warning, the practice's origins are actually traced to feminist online spaces, including blogs and social media. Explorations of such spaces suggest that the trigger warning is itself a uniquely feminist tool and practice in that it acknowledges the gendered experiences of PTSD and the prevalence of sexual trauma in contemporary society.

While trigger warnings were found in private online forums for women recovering from eating disorders as early as the mid-1990s, trigger warnings seem to have come into use in public feminist-oriented online spaces in the first few years of the twenty-first century. In the feminist blogosphere of the early 2000s, the trigger warning was conceptualized as a tool to enable women who had experienced sexual assault to assess whether they were prepared to engage with particular content rather than encountering it without consent. This approach to the trigger warning appears to serve as a kindness to individual audiences; more obliquely, it addresses the prevalence of sexual violence against women in American society.

For a long time, PTSD was foremost associated with military service, an association that, given the small percentage of women in the U.S. military, might lead some to believe that PTSD disproportionately affects American men. Recent studies in fact demonstrate the opposite: American women are nearly three times as likely as American men to suffer from PTSD in their lifetimes.[11] After all, one of the primary causes of PTSD is sexual violence, which disproportionately affects women. Until the 1970s, the stress response patterns of victims of sexual assault, which were consistent with PTSD, were labeled *rape trauma syndrome*, an identification that may explain why, to this day, the term *PTSD* often calls to mind male combat veterans rather than female survivors of rape. Given this popular misconception, by acknowledging the societal prevalence of sexual trauma, trigger warnings used this way are seen by some as "a form of activism."[12]

When social media sites Twitter and Tumblr were created in the mid-2000s, those authors who had used trigger warnings on their personal blogs began using the warnings preceding their tweets. Today, Twitter has systematized that practice: the site includes a feature enabling users to block material deemed sensitive—by the platform rather than users, it is important to note—or inclusive of graphic violence, pornographic images, or hate speech.[13] Should that material appear in a user's search, a warning will appear in lieu of the tweet's original content. The use of trigger warnings, then, seems to have spread in a grassroots, bottom-up fashion, from individuals to corporations.

Regardless of their origins, however, for more than two decades, content warnings, broadly speaking, have been part and parcel of mass media and digital spaces. Given the role media plays in contemporary daily life and learning, it shouldn't come as much of a surprise that such content advisories have made their way into educational institutions.

TRIGGER WARNINGS IN EDUCATION

"It is probably not coincidental that the call for trigger warnings comes at a time of increased attention to campus violence, especially to sexual assault. . . . Trigger warnings are a way of displacing the problem, however, locating its solution in the classroom rather than in administrative attention to social behaviors that permit sexual violence to take place."[14]

Though they had already provoked considerable public debate surrounding their efficacy and relevance,[15] trigger warnings as used in academia seemed to garner little attention until 2013, the year a *Slate* magazine article then dubbed "the year of the trigger warning."[16]

That year, on *Shakesville*, one of the popular feminist blogs on which, for many years, *Content Notes* had appeared regularly, Ruxandra Looft, an Iowa State University lecturer, addressed the need for something similar to the content note in the classroom: "When *writing* about these topics, one can preface articles with trigger warnings cautioning readers about the content ahead. . . . But what happens when a student is trapped in a classroom where a discussion brings up terrible and traumatic memories?"[17] Looft also articulated the difficulty in finding an appropriate use of the trigger warning inside the classroom: "But how does one work trigger warnings into the classroom lesson plan? . . . I'm still searching for that verbal equivalent of a written 'trigger warning' with which to give my students the agency to walk away when needed."[18]

Around this time, many of the calls for trigger warnings in college classrooms came from female educators, scholars, and student activists. This is unsurprising given that content notes have long been used to warn visitors to women-oriented websites of material that depicts or discusses rape and sexual assault and that, in the United States, more than 20 percent of women are sexually assaulted during their undergraduate career.[19] Some have argued that "it was students' advocacy of trigger warnings as a systemic solution that elevated trigger warnings to a topic of national debate."[20]

Student Activism

In early 2014, the Student Senate at the University of California, Santa Barbara, passed a resolution calling for the university to mandate the use of trigger warnings in the form of marks alongside material listed on the syllabus that might be upsetting for students with PTSD. Such a practice, the document stated, would allow such students to make informed choices about their education and "to avoid a potentially triggering situation without public attention."[21] The resolution noted that PTSD was already recognized as a disability by the university's Disabled Students Program.

It is important to note that this call for administrative and pedagogical awareness of student trauma did not exist in a vacuum. In fact, it occurred at a time of intense public attention to sexual assault on college campuses; while some of that attention came from campus safety and reporting initiatives launched by the Obama administration, much of it was the result of student activism.

One such example can be seen in the endurance art project "Mattress Performance (Carry that Weight)." In April 2014, Emma Sulkowicz, an undergraduate student at Columbia University's Barnard College whose allegations of rape against another student, Paul Nungesser, had been dismissed by a university inquiry, and more than twenty classmates, filed a complaint against the college and the university for violating Title IX, a federal law that prohibits discrimination on the basis of sex and which requires universities to protect students from sexual assault and harassment and to appropriately respond to allegations of gender-based violence on campus.[22] The case drew even more media and political attention the next year when Sulkowicz protested the university's (mis)handling of the case by carrying a fifty-pound mattress around campus as part of a senior art thesis. The activist art project led to the filing of another Title IX complaint against the university, this one by Nungesser, the student Sulkowicz had accused of rape.

University Mandates and Informal Policies

That student calls for trigger warnings came at a time when universities, often under pressure of public scrutiny, sought to improve the handling of sexual assault on campuses, cannot be overlooked. It is in this same context that some schools, like Oberlin College, offered the trigger warning as one such response.

In 2014, not long after the unsuccessful resolution penned by the UC Santa Barbara student senate, Oberlin College published on their website a guide, intended for professors, to protect students with histories of trauma. The guide explained that triggers were disruptive to student learning and suggested that professors exclude from their courses all potentially triggering content that did not directly relate to the course's learning outcomes. Seemingly emphasizing the structural nature of trauma, the document, though identified as the Sexual Offense Resource Guide, listed as potential triggers content related to "racism, classism, sexism, heterosexism, ableism, and other issues of privilege and oppression."[23]

While the guide labeled its recommendations as optional, many faculty members resisted the suggestions and perceived its publication as an attempt at creating university-wide mandatory policy. In light of this resistance, much of which was communicated to national media, the university removed the guide pending further deliberation.

"The Chicago Letter": Administrative Pushback

Shortly prior to the start of the 2016–2017 academic year, the dean of students at the University of Chicago distributed a letter to students entering the university, which quickly garnered national media attention. In the letter, Dean John "Jay" Ellison wrote that, due to the university's dedication to encouraging members of its community to "speak, write, listen, challenge and learn, without fear of censorship," the university did not support the use of trigger warnings.[24] While admitting that "freedom of expression does not mean the freedom to harass or threaten others," Ellison implied that trigger warnings allow students to avoid the discussions and debates that characterize the university's "commitment to freedom of inquiry and expression" because such discourse might challenge students and cause discomfort.[25]

Intriguingly, while Ellison claimed that safe spaces similarly allowed students to "retreat from ideas and perspectives at odds with their own,"[26] the university actually has many safe spaces on campus; in fact, Ellison was himself listed on the school's website as a campus safe space ally. This paradox illuminates the complexities of practices like trigger warnings and safe spaces and the challenges of simultaneously encouraging open discourse and protecting students from harm.

Many educators and administrators critiqued the letter immediately, some deriding what they saw as the dean's diminishment of the potential of trigger warnings and safe spaces to enhance students' well-being, thereby better preparing them to engage in difficult conversations. Others noted that academic freedom included faculty members' rights to use trigger warnings if they saw fit. Other educators and administrators celebrated the letter and applauded Ellison and the University of Chicago for voicing their own concerns. The presidents of Bowdoin University and Yale University professed similar commitments to open inquiry and intellectual fearlessness in campus talks directed to students later the same week.

One year later, Ellison released another letter to incoming students; this one reiterated the university's commitments but made no mention of safe spaces or trigger warnings. Ironically, it seems that despite the university's avowed resistance to censorship, Ellison (and likely other campus officials) thought it best to self-censor and thereby avoid the reactions the letter had elicited the first time around.

Points of Contention

Any mention today of trigger warnings is likely to produce strong reactions from educators, though those reactions are far from predictable; in fact, it seems that the same element of the trigger warning's rationale or implementation may cause one educator to support its use while causing another educator to reject it in its entirety.

For some educators and scholars, the trigger warning is an act of kindness that demonstrates awareness of students' experiences and honors individuals as people as well as students. For others, the trigger warning is evidence of a larger trend in academia of catering to students' feelings at the expense of their education. How appropriate a response to student trauma one believes the trigger warning to be seems to hinge upon two premises: first, how one defines trauma; and second, how one envisions the role of academia in responding to that trauma.

Infantilizing the Student Population

Greg Lukianoff and Jonathan Haidt's oft-referenced 2015 article in *The Atlantic*, "The Coddling of the American Mind," presents what is now a rather popular argument against trigger warnings: that they are evidence of the hypersensitivity of the liberal academy and the students inside of it. The authors place trigger warnings in the context of that they call *vindictive protectiveness*: the impulse to shield students from intellectual or emotional discomfort and to "punish anyone who interferes with that aim."[27]

This impulse relies upon an assumption, grounded in generational perspectives about safety, security, and ideology, that students are psychologically fragile and therefore in need of protection but that protecting students in this way impedes both intellectual progress and career development. In this view, the trigger warning is a uniquely Millennial phenomenon that has arisen in part from the confluence of late twentieth-century trends including school shootings and antibullying campaigns, which demonstrate that schools are dangerous places, and social media, which creates an intellectual bubble within which individuals encounter mostly thoughts and ideas that reinforce their own political and ideological perspectives.

Lukianoff and Haidt suggest that the trigger warning invites students to rely on *emotional reasoning*, wherein feelings direct one's interpretation of reality, rather than the critical thinking and empirical investigation education ought to engender. Seen this way, the trigger warning is problematic for students with trauma histories and students without trauma histories. For students with trauma histories, the trigger warning encourages avoidance, which violates accepted practices in trauma treatment, such as exposure therapy, a practice by which individuals are gradually introduced, in a safe environment, to triggering stimuli. For the broader student population, the trigger warning encourages avoidance of difficult or contentious subject matter and "prepares them poorly for professional life, which often demands intellectual engagement with people and ideas one might find uncongenial and wrong."[28]

Other writers, like lawyer and former *The Guardian* columnist Jill Filipovic, have sounded similar calls for schools to challenge students before sending them out after graduation: "College isn't exactly the real world.... It is, hopefully, a space where the student's world expands and pushes them to reach the outer edges—not a place that contracts to meet the student exactly where they are."[29]

Creating Student-Responsive Classrooms

While writers like Filipovic claim that college need not meet students where they are, others argue that universities do exactly that—or should. In fact, meeting students where they are is one of the primary tenets of student-responsiveness in classroom pedagogy, which aims to honor what the student brings into the classroom while at the same time helping the student move closer to course learning objectives. In fact, many advocates of the trigger warning see the practice as a move toward greater student-responsiveness in classrooms and on campuses.

Though PTSD is a recognized disability, many individuals with this and other seemingly invisible psychological and emotional illnesses find that when they share their struggles, they are met with resistance: "Often, when we mentally ill disclose our disability, we do so knowing that others may believe we are exaggerating our emotional pain."[30] In this context, the trigger warning serves to honor those disabilities that are often unseen and unacknowledged. As a result of this recognition, students with histories of emotional trauma may feel more respected and subsequently more engaged as members of the classroom community.

Moreover, while some educators are concerned that the trigger warning prevents students from engaging with difficult materials, others argue that it does just the opposite by creating conditions in which students with trauma histories can engage with potentially triggering material to the best of their abilities. This view contends that warnings allow students to prepare themselves emotionally and psychologically for such intellectual engagement. In this way, trigger warnings are "an additive and not a subtractive phenomenon: professors add a 'TW' to their syllabus or give a vocal trigger warning in class rather than excise material from a syllabus."[31]

Filipovic (and others) claim that the broad application of trigger warnings is problematic as a systemic solution but that individual students with trauma histories have every right to request trigger warnings from their instructors. Those who support the use of the trigger warning, however, criticize the onus this approach places on the individual student. Rather than meeting students where they are, requiring students with trauma histories to self-identify and request individual accommodations not mandated by the university also requires students to challenge their instructors' teaching practices. This approach may even force students into ideological battles with instructors who have power over students' academic success.

As one university student writes, "Although this was not my objective, I knew that when I asked the professor to consider the use of trigger warnings that I was implicitly challenging her pedagogy and subsequently her authority. . . . If met with condescending or doubtful attitudes, requests for trigger warnings within the existing student-professor power dynamic can be harmful."[32]

Fair Accommodations or an Inadequate Psychological Response?

Some proponents of the trigger warning suggest that because PTSD is an established illness listed in the *Diagnostic and Statistical Manual of Mental Disorders*, its usage falls under the category of fair accommodations for individuals with disabilities, and that, as a result, schools have not only an ethical obligation to meet students' accessibility requirements but a legal one as well, under the 1990 Americans with Disabilities Act (ADA). In this perspective, trigger warnings enable individuals with PTSD to receive the same education as their peers by providing an aid that assists them in engaging with course materials in healthy, productive ways.

Those who agree that educational institutions must attend to students' histories with trauma do not necessarily agree that trigger warnings are the way to do it. "Depression, anxiety, and PTSD are covered by the ADA in almost all colleges' interpretations of the act," and "because schools' interpretation of the ADA continues to evolve, it is feasible that trigger warnings could become an accepted accommodation."[33] However, there is presently little evidence that trigger warnings are in fact an effective accommodation.

Trigger warnings are thought to have variable success in mitigating trauma responses among those with PTSD: while in some cases the trigger warning allows individuals to choose when and how they encounter potentially triggering content, in other situations they may function as a self-fulfilling prophecy of sorts, providing individuals with a trauma-based lens for engaging with content. In fact, a recent psychological study by Benjamin W. Bellet, Payton Jeffrey Jones, and Richard J. McNally, likely the first study to "examine the effects of trigger warnings on individual resilience factors via a randomized controlled experiment," found that trigger warnings not only had no effect on anxiety responses to potential triggers, but they also "may increase perceptions of self-vulnerability by sending an implicit message about the long-term harm caused by trauma."[34]

Books that depict traumatic experiences, hate-based violence, and sexual assault are especially likely to be listed on course syllabi with trigger warnings, yet literary scholars and psychoanalysts alike argue that there is no evidence "that literature may re-traumatize our students."[35] The opposite has more often been found to be true: reading about individuals' experiences, including those with trauma, enhances students' capacities for empathy. Because emotional reactions arise from an aesthetic experience between reader and text, trigger warnings, which serve as a buffer of sorts, distance the reader from the text, thereby lessening the capacity for emotional connection and the potential "therapeutic aspects that can occur through intense literary engagement."[36]

Some argue that framing trigger warnings as fair accommodations does more harm than good for students in the academy who suffer from PTSD. Because triggers, psychologically speaking, affect only those with the disorder, their use in the classroom assumes that *all* students have the potential to be traumatized by course material; this presumption conflates potential intellectual or emotional discomfort and the legitimate struggles of those who suffer from PTSD.

Lived Experience and Course Curricula

Regardless of their efficacy in each individual situation, many proponents of the trigger warning suggest that there are broader implications of building warnings into the curriculum: "When students ask for trigger warnings, they are asking for people and institutions to recognize that their embodied experiences are not simply thought experiments, but lived realities that have left both visible and invisible damage."[37] Proponents of the trigger warning contend that, in a society wherein close to 20 percent of women have been sexually assaulted, trigger warnings make visible the trauma regularly enacted upon women, including on college campuses.

Some of those who resist trigger warnings have suggested that, unlike the political correctness of the 1980s and 1990s, which not only sought to restrict hate speech but also "challenged the literary, philosophical, and historical canon, seeking to widen it by including more-diverse perspectives," trigger warnings attend only to students' emotional well-being and do not challenge the structural ills of the academy.[38] However, many who support the use of trigger warnings see trigger warnings as doing just that: as a "cursory method of acknowledging entrenched formal and informal marginalization," they aid in the creation of "a counter-classroom to the stigma imposed by the privileged objectivity of invading institutions that tell the violated to settle down or leave."[39]

Neoliberalism and Academic Freedom

While some scholars believe that trigger warnings contribute to a more level playing field between students and instructors by enabling students to take an active part in their own intellectual progress and emotional well-being, others believe that trigger warnings pose a serious threat to academic freedom and instructor autonomy. Intriguingly, these concerns have very little to do with students at all; instead, they appear to be reactions to the neoliberalism and ever-increasing standardization of American education.

As educational institutions become more like businesses, educators are treated more like corporate workers than experts in their respective fields. As a result, instructors, the majority of whom are without the protections of tenure, are increasingly insecure about their careers. (See chapter 7 for a more comprehensive discussion of intellectual freedom and job security.) In this context, instructors may see mandates around trigger warnings as yet another top-down intrusion that devalues scholarly expertise and pedagogical autonomy in favor of efficiency and standardization.

While most of the faculty members who participated in surveys and interviews conducted in preparation for a report on trigger warnings by the National Coalition against Censorship (NCAC) were skeptical about the efficacy of trigger warnings, none believed it was fair to force individual students to engage with content that was retraumatizing or triggering for them. A large majority of those respondents, however, thought that the choice to use trigger warnings ought to come from instructors rather than administrators.

In fact, the NCAC reported that "supporters and critics of trigger warnings alike are opposed to administrators requesting or requiring their use."[40]

Beyond the Debates

Regardless of their debatable efficacy for individual students and the academy at large, there is no denying that trigger warnings start a conversation. Most notable, however, is what is not being said in that conversation: while some documents, like the UCSB student resolution, list racism among the topics that may potentially be triggering, with the exception of limited number of essays and blog posts,[41] very few arguments for or against the trigger warning address directly the impact of trigger warnings on the experiences of people of color in the classroom.

Reactionary Opposition to the Trigger Warning

Following their suggestion that the trigger warning perpetuates narrow-mindedness and political partisanship, Lukianoff and Haidt conclude that "a greater commitment to formal, public debate on campus—and to the assembly of a more politically diverse faculty" would improve students' openness to ideas that differ from their own.[42] One irony, perhaps, in this argument against partisanship and for political diversity is that such an argument is in no way an apolitical one, nor does it appear to be nonpartisan: founded on the erroneous premise that the university is *not* a politically diverse space, this argument replicates popular right-wing rhetoric that speciously positions academia as a space in which "conservative speech and scholarship is uniquely endangered."[43]

Another irony is that this call for faculty diversity makes no mention of the need for increased *racial* diversity among university faculty. Moreover, Lukianoff and Haidt, like many others who oppose the trigger warning, sidestep the fact that trigger warnings arose at a time when faculty diversity (with regard to race, ethnicity, and gender expression) is greater than ever before. Colleges and universities today also serve the most diverse student population in American history.

As such, arguments like the one made by Lukianoff and Haidt can be read as "antifeminist colonial backlash,"[44] part of a reactionary response to the very diversity for which they claim to advocate.

THE TRIGGER WARNING'S
PERPETUATION OF MARGINALIZATION

Similarly, many of the arguments in support of the trigger warning demonstrate the ways in which the trigger warning may uphold rather than deconstruct the inherent whiteness of the academy.

If trigger warnings are only predominantly in classrooms wherein potentially controversial material is discussed, they will more likely appear in classes that cover material society has typically deemed controversial. Trigger warnings are already most commonly used in women's studies courses and in other curricula that foreground discussions of individual and societal trauma, which disproportionately affect already marginalized groups, including people of color and White women. The students in those classrooms, however, are the ones who are already interested in and therefore likely cognizant of these societal inequities. While this may mean that these students are likelier to have experienced trauma in their own lives, such an emic approach does not reach the students outside those classrooms. Paradoxically, of course, it is likely those students who are most in need of the critical thinking and empathetic learning such courses engender.

Compounding this illogic is that determinations of what is and what is not controversial are made by comparison to the societally accepted norm. Courses like African American history, Chicano/a literature, and Black English, while necessary expansions of the white canon that for centuries predominated in academia, are electives rather than part of the required curriculum. Even their titles serve to distance them from traditional history, literature, and English; the assumption implicit here is that traditional means white. As such, using trigger warnings in these classes may further the notion that such topics are indeed controversial; in doing so, classes that address structural violence and marginalization will continue to be marginalized.

To point, while trigger warnings are often associated with the liberal university, their usage may be far less progressive than it initially seems. One study found that many university professors who used trigger warnings in humanities courses did so specifically for the benefit of conservative, religious students to avoid negative responses to sexual content, depictions or discussions of homosexuality, complex literary analyses of the Bible, or the use of nude models in art classes.[45] Rather than challenge normative notions of identity and knowledge, the trigger warning may in fact perpetuate such normativity.

SECONDARY STRATEGIES

As evidenced by the information provided in this chapter, discussions of trigger warnings in the public domain have centered, for the most part, on their role in postsecondary educations. However, these discussions appear to be trickling down to the high school teacher population, appearing in unofficial forums on the National Council of Teachers of English (NCTE) website and in official publications geared toward secondary educators, like the NCTE journal *English Journal*. Renowned English education scholar Peter Smagorinsky included a trigger warning in a 2016 article in the journal;[46] the September 2018 issue included a feature article questioning their usefulness.[47] Many high school teachers already use trigger warnings, especially in history and English language arts classrooms.

The challenges and debates surrounding trigger warnings on the secondary level are similar to those that have plagued higher education, but the truth is that the contexts of secondary education and the emotional needs of high school students differ in important ways from the context of the university and the needs of its students. Most significantly, students are younger and in the legal care of the school during school hours. Legal concerns mean that there may be more stringent guidelines for working with students placed on secondary educators than on their college-level counterparts. Additionally, depending upon the grade level she is teaching, a teacher may be working with students who are not yet comfortable with or cognizant of their own emotional capacities.

In many cases, however, because of the amount of time spent with students over the course of an academic year as well as varying levels of parental involvement, secondary teachers may be in a good position to recognize and respond to the individual emotional needs of their students. For this reason, unless the school has a specific policy or practice in place regarding trigger warnings, teachers should use their knowledge of the material, the school culture, and their students to determine whether trigger warnings are applicable.

It is important, however, that these judgments are neither sweeping generalizations nor absolutes; in other words, the use of a trigger warning with one class in the morning does not necessitate that it be used with another during the afternoon nor does it mean that the morning class will always need trigger warnings or that the afternoon class never will.

Finally, since one of the aims lauded by proponents of the trigger warning is to encourage students' participation in their own education, teachers should ask students what they know about trigger warnings and what they believe the role of the trigger warning to be in the classroom. Whether an individual instructor supports or rejects the practice of trigger warnings, few can deny that the questions they raise are significant for students. For example, what is the role of emotion in literary study or in history? What is the role of experiential knowing in the classroom? Whether they actually use them, teachers can assign readings about trigger warnings in classes on literature, media, cultural studies, or American history, or include trigger warnings as an option for a research project.

COLLEGE CONSIDERATIONS

If the educator feels strongly that some conversation needs to take place around triggering content and its potential for upsetting or triggering students with psychological trauma, our advice is to have a general conversation with the entire class up front at or near the beginning of the course. . . . If the professor makes this reality known to the students up front, then in a general sense the student gains a realistic sense for what the experience will be about, and thereby participates at their own risk. [48]

It is increasingly common for college-level educators to include content notes on course syllabi, either woven into the course description or listed as a separate policy. Like the prime-time television content advisory, which provides a general warning to exercise viewer discretion, the syllabus note typically informs students that they should expect to encounter sensitive, controversial, or potentially upsetting material throughout the semester. Rather than labeling particular materials as triggering, this statement instead places all materials in the context of the course, its learning outcomes, and the classroom or campus environment.

The broad content note begins to build teacher-student rapport in that being forthcoming demonstrates to students that their intellectual growth and emotional well-being matter to their instructor. This may make students more willing to engage in difficult conversations. The note can institute parameters for classroom conversation. So long as those parameters are equitable and student-responsive, including which approaches to conversation are encouraged in the course and why those approaches are favored can help students imagine how they might engage in discussion and prepare them to practice those discursive moves. Discussing these parameters with students is paramount in order to identify any disjunctions between instructor expectations and student perceptions of classroom protocol.

Instructors and students alike may find that interpretations of words like *respect*, *appropriate*, and *polite* vary considerably among members of the classroom. Most importantly, placing such a note on the syllabus makes clear that all course material may be challenging and therefore does not single out individual topics, texts, or conversations as controversial. This helps to normalize race talk and other difficult discussions rather than marginalizing them.

The statement also enables students who are unwilling to engage with such material to drop the course from their semester schedule without penalty. Instructors may bristle at this, especially because it may lead those most in need of critical race pedagogy to opt out, but at the college level, it is the student's choice to commit to or withdraw from the curriculum.

The primary challenge for instructors employing this approach is what to say in such a note and how to phrase it. If the statement does not address course material and student needs comprehensively and equitably, the statement may be of little use, at best; at worst, the statement may further silence conversations or exclude students from participation. The following are some suggestions for developing a broad syllabus content note.

DESIGNING A GENERAL CONTENT NOTE

When designing a general content note for placement on a course syllabus, careful attention should be paid to the content of and rationale for the note, the language used to describe it, and how students are expected to respond. Here are some tips:

1. **Consider the function of the note.** Is your goal to inform students that course material may be emotionally challenging? Are you trying to provide guidelines for ways to manage their emotions if they are triggered or are you trying to prevent students from being triggered in the first place? Is part of your goal to protect yourself should an uncomfortable situation arise? Whatever your reasons are, make them clear to yourself first so you can shape the warning accordingly.
2. **Consider the broader function of the syllabus.** The syllabus is a contract of sorts that sets the terms and expectations for the course and for your students. Once students have the syllabus, you're bound to the terms you've laid out (with the possible exception of the day-to-day course schedule). If an uncomfortable situation arises in the classroom or if a student challenges a grade at the end of the semester, you should be able to point to the policies on your syllabus to explain your decision or move toward a resolution.
3. **Spell out what is required of students in response to the content note.** Do you expect students to leave the classroom if they are triggered? Should they skip potentially difficult class

sessions entirely? If you expect students to contact you should they feel upset, tell them how and why you want them to do that. Remember that directness with a professor is difficult for many students; if they don't contact you, will you follow up? If you want them to make up assignments they miss should they excuse themselves from a particular class session, let them know what types of activities qualify as makeup work.
4. **Use clear, specific, inclusive language.** If you tell students to "be respectful," consider that students' notions of respect and how to show it may differ from your own and from each other's. Remember that phrases such as "remain calm" and "speak up" reinforce culturally situated codes of conduct that may be inequitable for many students.
5. **Be brief but comprehensive.** The note should include these elements—but it doesn't have to cover every detail or potential situation that may arise. The most important thing you can do is talk through the warning and related policies with students. Go over it in full during the first week and refer back should the need for clarification arise.

Sometimes these broad warnings come with guidelines for students to follow should they feel triggered by something shared in the classroom. The document should also refer students to on-campus resources, such as a (dis)ability resource center or a counseling office, as well as other policies that may be relevant, such as a departmental or university attendance policy that lists the number of excused or unexcused absences students will be allowed. In many cases, students are allowed additional absences in cases of health-related emergencies; instructors should check with their individual departments regarding the particulars of these policies and if or how they account for students' mental health. The syllabus serves as a contract of sorts and, as such, it is important for instructors to include all pertinent information and policies, in part to ensure self-protection should a student who does not follow procedures file a complaint or grade appeal down the line.

More important than the syllabus content note, however, is the discussion it introduces. Instructors should inform students about the type of intellectual and emotional work that is expected of them over the course of the semester. They should explain why specific materials, including texts, conversations, and assignments, have been included in the curriculum; why particular ways of learning and knowing are significant; and how students' emotional and psychological well-being have been taken into account.

Unless students share voluntarily and unprovoked, instructors should not ask about personal histories or experiences. They should, however, invite questions so that students can clarify any points they find vague or confusing. While no students should be forced to self-disclose trauma histories, some may use this opportunity to share their own experiences and perspectives.

CONCLUDING THOUGHTS

In terms of challenging the existing norms of academia and its institutions, trigger warnings do not do nearly enough. Framing the trigger warning as a response to widespread sexual assault, racial or cultural oppression, or contemporary violence is shortsighted, places enormous responsibility on individual instructors, and relieves institutions of the responsibility to address the ways in which institutional norms are complicit in creating a culture that marginalizes people of color and subjugates and victimizes women.

That said, inviting students to take part in conversations *about* trigger warnings (whether or not trigger warnings are actually used) can help teachers get a better sense of their students' needs and experiences while at the same time encouraging critical thinking and working toward curricular objectives. Moreover, by foregrounding discussions of sensitive material and sharing their rationale for that material's inclusion in the curriculum, instructors demonstrate that students' experiences have been considered, are valued, and will be respected in the classroom. These discussions provide students with trauma histories an opportunity to consider how best to approach their participation in the course. This, after all, is what the trigger warning is about in the first place: giving individuals the opportunity to make their own informed choices about their learning and well-being.

NOTES

1. Jane Gavin-Hebert, "Walking on the Shards of the Glass Ceiling," in *Trigger Warnings: History, Theory, Context*, ed. Emily J. M. Knox (Lanham: Rowman & Littlefield, 2017), 73.

2. Bonnie Washick, "An 'App' for That: The Case against the 'Equal Access' Argument for Trigger Warnings," in *Trigger Warnings: History, Theory, Context*, ed. Emily J. M. Knox (Lanham: Rowman & Littlefield, 2017), 89.

3. Guy A. Boysen, "Evidence-Based Answers to Questions about Trigger Warnings for Clinically-Based Distress: A Review for Teachers," *Scholarship of Teaching and Learning in Psychology* 3 (2017): 164.

4. Jack Halberstam, "Trigger Happy: From Content Warning to Censorship," *Signs* 42, no. 2 (2017): 535.

5. Mara Lee Grayson and Adam Wolfsdorf, "Courageous Conversations in the Age of the Trigger Warning," in *From Disagreement to Discourse: A Chronicle of Controversies in Schooling and Education*, ed. Beth Duroyode and Rhonda Bryant (Charlotte: Information Age Publishing, 2019).

6. Alison Bass, "Report on Youth Violence Urges Prevention," *Boston Globe* (August 10, 1993).

7. Stephanie Houston Grey, "Contagious Speech: Mediating the Eating Disorder Panic through Trigger Warnings," in *Trigger Warnings: History, Theory, Context*, ed. Emily J. M. Knox (Lanham: Rowman & Littlefield, 2017), 40.

8. Susan Bordo, *Unbearable Weight: Feminism, Western Culture, and the Body* (Berkeley: University of California Press, 1993), 176.

9. Grey, "Contagious Speech," 42.

10. Ibid., 47.

11. "Prevalence of Post-Traumatic Stress Disorder among Adults," National Institute of Mental Health, last modified November 2017, https://www.nimh.nih.gov/health/statistics/post-traumatic-stress-disorder-ptsd.shtml.

12. Washick, "An 'App' for That," 93.

13. "Twitter Media Policy," Twitter, accessed January 19, 2019, https://help.twitter.com/en/rules-and-policies/media-policy.

14. American Association of University Professors (AAUP), *On Trigger Warnings* (2014).

15. See Cottom, "The Trigger Warned Syllabus."

16. Amanda Marcotte, "The Year of the Trigger Warning," *Slate* (December 30, 2013), https://slate.com/human-interest/2013/12/trigger-warnings-from-the-feminist-blogosphere-to-shonda-rhimes-in-2013.html.

17. Ruxandra Looft, "How Do Trigger Warnings Fit into the Classroom Lesson Plan?" *Shakesville* (blog) (February 12, 2013), http://www.shakesville.com/2013/02/how-do-trigger-warnings-fit-into.html.

18. Ibid.

19. Rape, Abuse & Incest National Network (RAINN), "Campus Sexual Violence: Statistics," RAINN.org, 2019, https://www.rainn.org/statistics/campus-sexual-violence.

20. Washick, "An 'App' for That," 95.

21. https://www.as.ucsb.edu/senate/resolutions/a-resolution-to-mandate-warnings-for-triggering-content-in-academic-settings/.

22. Richard Perez Pena, "Fight against Sexual Assault Holds Colleges to Account," *The New York Times* (February 3, 2015).

23. *Oberlin College Sexual Offense Resource Guide*, quoted in Colleen Flaherty, "Trigger Unhappy," *Inside Higher Ed* (April 14, 2014).

24. John (Jay) Ellison, "Dear Class of 2020 Students," The University of Chicago, accessed February 10, 2019, https://news.uchicago.edu/sites/default/files/attachments/Dear_Class_of_2020_Students.pdf.

25. Ibid.

26. Ibid.

27. Greg Lukianoff and Jonathan Haidt, "The Coddling of the American Mind," *The Atlantic* (September 2015).

28. Ibid.

29. Jill Filipovic, "We've Gone Too Far with 'Trigger Warnings,'" *The Guardian* (March 5, 2014).

30. Sarah Orem and Neil Simpkins, "Weepy Rhetoric, Trigger Warnings, and the Work of Making Mental Illness Visible in the Writing Classroom," *Enculturation: A Journal of Rhetoric, Writing, and Culture* (2015). http://enculturation.net/weepy-rhetoric.

31. Ibid.

32. Jami McFarland, "On Privilege, Authority, and Abuses of Professorial Power," in *Trigger Warnings: History, Theory, Context*, ed. Emily J. M. Knox (Lanham: Rowman & Littlefield, 2017), 172.

33. Jordan Doll, "Gender Constructions and Trauma: Trigger Warnings as an Accommodation for Female Students in Higher Education," in *Trigger Warnings: History, Theory, Context*, ed. Emily J. M. Knox (Lanham: Rowman & Littlefield, 2017), 61.

34. Benjamin W. Bellet, Payton J. Jones, and Richard J. McNally, "Trigger Warning: Empirical Evidence Ahead," *Journal of Behavior Therapy and Experimental Psychiatry* 61 (2018): 139.

35. Adam Wolfsdorf, "Reflecting on Functioning in Trigger Happy America," *Changing English* 24, no. 3 (2017): 313.

36. Ibid.
37. McFarland, "On Privilege," 168.
38. Lukianoff and Haidt, "The Coddling."
39. Gavin-Hebert, "Walking on the Shards," 73.
40. National Coalition against Censorship (NCAC), *What's All This About Trigger Warnings?*, 3.
41. See Gay, "The Illusion of Safety/The Safety of Illusion" and Cottom, "The Trigger Warned Syllabus."
42. Lukianoff and Haidt, "The Coddling."
43. Sarah Jones, "Fed Up with Liberal Academia, Conservatives Call for Their Own Safe Space," *New York* (January 5, 2019).
44. Gavin-Hebert, "Walking on the Shards," 81.
45. NCAC, *What's All*, 5–6.
46. Peter Smagorinsky, "Huck and Kim: Would Teachers Feel the Same If the Language Were Misogynist?" *English Journal* 106, no. 2 (2016).
47. Adam Wolfsdorf, "When It Comes to High School English, Let's Put Away the Triggers," *English Journal* 108, no. 1 (2018).
48. Grayson and Wolfsdorf, "Courageous Conversations."

Chapter Three

Speaking Truth to Trauma

Schooling and Suffering in the United States

> No one is arguing for trigger warnings in the routine spaces where symbolic and structural violence are acted on students at the margins . . . Instead, trigger warnings are being encouraged for sites of resistance, not mechanisms of oppression.—Tessie McMillan Cottom [1]

Discussions of trauma in the classroom did not originate with the trigger warning, nor should they end there. Trauma is already a part of students' lives, course curricula, and the campus community—it always has been, whether it has been named or not. Too often, trauma is treated as an outlying experience, a departure from the norm, rather than as a common societal and personal occurrence with long-lasting yet varied psychological effects.

Providing effective education on any level requires seeing students as more than learners and instructors as more than repositories of information. Holistic education attends to the people who populate the classroom as whole persons who exist as individuals and as members of a community and who bring to the classroom as much as they take from it. Any discussion of trauma in the field of education that does not acknowledge its prevalence or its effects on students, teachers, and the classroom cannot be viewed as comprehensive, student-responsive, or equitable.

DEFINING AND IDENTIFYING TRAUMA

"*Trauma is exceedingly common, but clinically significant effects of trauma are not.*"[2]

The word *trauma* is derived from Greek and translates literally to *wound*. Historically and in its original language, the word was used to refer to physical wounding only; today, it is perhaps more commonly used to denote a distressing or disturbing experience.

The American Psychological Association defines trauma as "an emotional response to a terrible event like an accident, rape or natural disaster."[3] The American Psychiatric Association (APA) defines trauma more narrowly in relation to diagnoses of Post-Traumatic Stress Disorder (PTSD): traumatic triggers to PTSD include "exposure to actual or threatened death, serious injury or sexual violation."[4]

Though previously classified as an anxiety disorder, in the fifth and latest edition of the APA's *Diagnostic and Statistical Manual of Mental Disorders* (*DSM-5*) PTSD is listed under the category of Trauma and Stressor-Related Disorders. Other diagnoses in this category include Acute Stress Disorder, Reactive Attachment Disorder, and various adjustment disorders. Additionally, two subtypes of PTSD have been added to the *DSM-5*: the Preschool Subtype, which accounts for PTSD in children younger than six, and Dissociative Subtype, which identifies manifestations of PTSD with prominent dissociative symptoms.

Table 3.1 includes additional criteria for the psychiatric diagnosis of PTSD.[5]

Psychiatric and Psychological Conceptualizations of Trauma

As is apparent in the differing definitions provided by the American Psychological Association and the American Psychiatric Association, trauma is defined more broadly in the field of psychology than it is in psychiatric medicine. This is an important distinction to consider when addressing the role of trauma in the classroom setting, especially given that most research on trauma in education is informed by psychological rather than medical frameworks.

Additionally, it is worth noting that PTSD is a medical disorder that requires professional clinical diagnosis. It is estimated that close to eight million adults in the United States suffer from PTSD.[6] Although there is considerable research on the incidence of PTSD, many of the statistics offered are either estimates extrapolated from findings among representative populations or results drawn from self-reported data. It is likely that the number of Americans with official diagnoses of PTSD or related trauma disorders, or symptoms that align with those diagnoses, is actually much higher than studies demonstrate, due to the low incidence of reporting and treatment seeking, particularly among combat veterans and members of minoritized racial groups.

Table 3.1. *DSM-5* Criteria for the Diagnosis of PTSD

Diagnostic Criterion	Stipulation(s)	Potential Presentation of Criterion
A. Stressor	Exposure to trauma, as defined by real or threatened death, serious injury, or sexual violence Excludes exposure through media One required	• Direct exposure to trauma • Witnessing trauma • Learning that a loved one was exposed to trauma • Repeated or extreme indirect exposure to trauma, such as in one's professional capacity as first responder
B. Intrusion Symptoms	One required	• Recurrent, unwanted memories • Flashbacks • Nightmares • Intense distress when exposed to reminders • Intense physiological reactivity to exposure to reminders
C. Persistent Effortful Avoidance	One required	• Avoidance of trauma-related thoughts or feelings • Avoidance of external reminder of the traumatic experience
D. Negative Cognitions	Two required	• Inability to recall key features of the trauma • Negative self-view or worldview • Distorted blame of self or others • Negative mood or affect • Diminished interest in activities • Persistent feelings of isolation • Difficulty experiencing or expressing positive emotions
E. Arousal and Reactivity Responses	Two required	• Irritability or aggression • Self-destructive or high-risk behavior • Hypervigilance • Exaggerated startle response • Difficulty with concentration • Disturbance in sleep patterns
Additional Criteria	• Symptoms must persist for longer than 1 month • Symptoms create distress or functional impairment (e.g., social, occupational, or academic) • Symptoms cannot be attributed to other causes (e.g., medication, substance abuse, or other illness)	

The experience of trauma, however, does not necessarily result in the development of PTSD or another trauma-based disorder. In fact, while it is believed that 90 percent of people will experience a traumatic event during their lifetime (with more than half experiencing multiple traumatic events), fewer than 10 percent of people who experience trauma as defined by the *DSM-5* will develop PTSD.[7] The type of trauma likeliest to result in a subsequent diagnosis of PTSD is assaultive violence in the form of military combat or sexual assault.[8]

Secondary Traumatic Stress and Vicarious Traumatization

The reach of trauma extends beyond the individual who experiences that trauma firsthand. *Secondary traumatic stress* describes experiences that parallel the experiences of those with PTSD but which arise from indirect exposure to trauma. Those commonly affected include family members of a person who has experienced trauma and emergency providers who attend in the immediate wake of trauma to those directly affected. Those experiencing secondary traumatic stress tend to display physiological signs, like hyperarousal, and observable behaviors, such as avoidance, that are similar to those felt by direct survivors of trauma.

Psychologists and others who work regularly with trauma survivors may experience *vicarious traumatization*. Unlike secondary traumatic stress, which may arise gradually or rapidly, vicarious traumatization "is conceptualized as building over time in response to cumulative effect of working with multiple survivors of trauma."[9] While the specific effects depend upon each individual trauma worker's personal history, support network, and prior experiences with trauma, various traumatization tends to cause more cognitive changes than physical ones. For example, vicarious exposure to trauma may lead to shifts in one's beliefs and worldviews, perhaps causing the individual to become more cynical about the world or less trusting in intimate relationships. When physical symptoms are experienced, they are typically less intense than those experienced by trauma survivors.

In some cases, secondary trauma and vicarious traumatization may result as much from interaction and empathic connection with the trauma survivor as they do from the trauma itself. While some studies have suggested that even viewing media accounts of traumatic experiences can cause particular individuals to experience symptoms that align with secondary traumatic stress, the *DSM-5* has clarified that trauma cannot occur solely through media consumption.

Trauma and PTSD among the Student Population

The incidence of trauma among the student population is thought to be similar to the incidence within the general population. Types of trauma commonly experienced by college students include accidents, illnesses, and loved ones' unexpected deaths. At home, younger students may be exposed to domestic violence or experience abuse; at school, physical fights and bullying are common among children and adolescents. One study found that, over the course of a year, one-third of adolescents in the United States were involved in a physical fight; nearly one in ten were threatened or harmed with a weapon on school grounds.[10] Potential traumatic experiences that may affect the school community more broadly include natural disasters and, increasingly, school shootings.

Adolescents

Post-Traumatic Stress Disorder affects approximately 5 percent of American adolescents between the ages of thirteen and eighteen; these rates increase as teenagers get older, with 7 percent of adolescents between ages seventeen and eighteen suffering from PTSD. There are distinct gender differences in these statistics: 8 percent of adolescent girls in the U.S. suffer from PTSD compared to less than 3 percent of boys of the same age.[11] Girls who experience trauma are also likelier than boys who experience trauma to develop PTSD.

The incidence of trauma among adolescent students is likely to be greater in schools with substantial populations of immigrant and refugee students. Children with refugee backgrounds are likely to have experienced numerous traumatic events, including war, violence, loss, and separation from their families, the last of which often affects even immigrant students who are not refugees. In fact, "the process of immigration and acculturation can cause further damage."[12] Research has also demonstrated that past traumatic experiences have a negative impact on refugees' motivation to learn a new language.[13] Because immigrant and refugee children and adolescents often enter school with limited English proficiency, they are at increased risk of struggling academically as well as socially and emotionally.

Complicating the processes of identifying and attending to trauma in adolescents are the myriad emotional and behavioral responses students display in the aftermath of trauma. While many students experience symptoms like avoidance and hyperarousal, which may be recognizable as PTSD to the trained eye, many other students with PTSD and trauma-based stress "oscillate between withdrawing into themselves and acting out."[14] The latter component of this dynamic may emerge as aggression toward classmates, attention-seeking, or high-risk behaviors such as promiscuity and substance abuse.

Unfortunately, these patterns often lead students to be categorized as behavior problems rather than as vulnerable individuals who need help managing pain and distress. Given that nonwhite students are considerably likelier to be disciplined in or expelled from school settings, the lack of recognition of trauma-based stress patterns in children and adolescents has a disproportionate and potentially devastating effect on students of color.

Military Veterans

In the three years following the 2009 passage of the new GI Bill (officially called the Post-9/11 Veterans Educational Assistance Act of 2008) nearly one million veterans received financial aid to enroll in college, resulting in a student veteran population almost twice as high as just a few years earlier.[15] Eight percent of veterans enrolled in college reported a PTSD diagnosis.[16] Given that the annual incidence of PTSD among veterans of post-9/11 operations in Iraq and Afghanistan is estimated to be close to 20 percent and that veterans self-report at low rates, it is possible that a considerably higher percentage of veterans who attended college in the past decade did so with a diagnosis of PTSD or while experiencing PTSD symptoms. Some studies have estimated that in a class of 27 college students, at least one will be a combat veteran with PTSD or another disability resulting from military service.[17]

Many individuals, particularly POCI, enlist in the military initially in order to improve educational and financial opportunities for themselves or their families.[18] For these veterans there are increased pressures (both internal and external) placed upon the successful completion of a postsecondary degree. In many cases, however, veterans find that the credits they earned during their service, with which they expected to enter college, do not transfer to their civilian schools. This often results in disappointment and frustration as well as delayed progress toward graduation.[19]

Survivors of Sexual Assault

Sexual assault is one of the likeliest types of trauma to occur among the student population, particularly on college campuses. One in five college women experience sexual assault, making college women twice as likely to be sexually assaulted as robbed.[20] While discussions of sexual assault tend to focus on the increased risk women experience on college campuses, college men also experience sexual assault, though the incidence is far lower. Individuals who identify as gay, lesbian, or bisexual are at increased risk of rape and sexual assault, as are those of transgender and nonbinary gender identities.

Women in college report sexual assault at lower rates than do nonstudents in the same age group. While it is difficult to identify all reasons behind infrequent reporting, it is possible that the historically poor handling of sexual assault cases by colleges and universities has led many survivors to remain silent. The lack of reporting is especially troubling given that sexual assault is one of the likeliest types of trauma to lead to a PTSD diagnosis. In fact, more than half of women who experience sexual assault meet the criteria for PTSD regardless of whether or not they receive an official diagnosis.[21] Only a small percentage of survivors, however, seek help on campus, in clinical settings, or from victim services centers.

While a considerable amount of attention has been paid in governmental and educational policy as well as in the media to the prevalence of sexual assault on college campuses, half of women and 75 percent of men who are raped are raped before they turn eighteen.[22] While these assaults more commonly occur in the home than on school grounds, this patterns suggests that sexual assault is a concern in secondary education as well as in college. Further, because a prior history of sexual abuse increases one's chances of being sexually assaulted during college, it is imperative that middle and high schools address the risks and effects of sexual trauma.

Traumatic Events on Campus and in the Community

In the United States and around the world, children and adolescents are the largest populations affected by natural disasters such as wildfires, hurricanes, earthquakes, tornadoes, and floods. Even when lives are not lost, natural disasters may have long-term consequences for young people, including displacement and loss of housing and family financial struggles. Students may be forced to relocate and change schools, often leaving behind friends and other networks of support. These changes can compound the psychological effects caused by the initial experience of the disaster, increasing the likelihood of developing post-traumatic stress symptoms. Psychologists who work with youth survivors of natural disasters suggest that school supports will be increasingly significant in years to come, as climate change increases the frequency and intensity of natural disasters.

These natural threats are not the only traumatic events that may affect the public awareness of and concern with traumatic experiences in the school setting are increasingly common. Though not the first school shooting, the 1999 mass shooting at Columbine High School in Colorado sparked widespread public attention to school-based violence, bullying, the impact of media on adolescent psychology, and gun control. Mass school shootings in 2007 at Virginia Tech, in 2012 at Sandy Hook Elementary School in Newtown, Connecticut, and in 2017 at Marjory Stoneman Douglas High School in Parkland, Florida, have led to increased concern not only about the safety of the school environment, but also about the psychological effects of school-based violence on children, adolescents, and young adults. After the 2008 shootings at Northern Illinois University, nearly half of survivors experienced short-term post-traumatic stress symptoms and more than 10 percent experienced longer-term symptoms indicative of PTSD.[23] In addition to PTSD, school shooting survivors may experience major depressive episodes, generalized anxiety disorder, and substance abuse problems.

These school shootings (and countless others) contributed to the implementation of safety and security measures in schools and on college campuses nationwide. Today it is common to walk through metal detectors when entering a high school building; doors to classrooms at many schools and universities are equipped with automatic safety locks; children as young as five years old drop to the floor or hide under their desks during lockdown and active shooter drills; and local police departments lead safety trainings, many of them mandatory, for school personnel.

To some extent, these procedures serve the purpose of quelling parents' and, more broadly, society's fears that schools are unsafe places and therefore responsible for the violence that has occurred: "To implement something like an active-shooter drill was to signal to parents and the community that the school is being proactive—it was doing something."[24] For some students, lockdown drills are just part of the routine, similar to fire drills or the nuclear fallout drills of yesteryear. In fact, in some cases, teachers are the ones most unnerved by these practices.

For many students, however, the prevalence of school violence and these consequent safety precautions, amid a broader national sense of unsafety, bolstered by concerns about terrorism and other societal fears, have contributed to a heightened sense of risk. This sense of risk may lead to panic. In 2017, at New York City's Pace University, just a few blocks from where the Twin Towers once stood, some students and instructors hid under their desks in silence while others rushed to evacuate the building after a frightened student saw what was believed to be an ammunition belt and reported a possible shooter carrying a machine gun. Police and Emergency Services officers swarmed and closed off the area before determining the threat to be a false alarm. The ammunition belt, it turned out, was a fashion belt decorated with inert bullets worn by a student who identified as a punk rocker.[25]

The anxieties displayed by these students were real and founded, even if this particular threat was not. Some teachers have reported that their youngest students often wind up crying during lockdown drills, while young adults who experienced active shooter drills in the wake of the Columbine shooting share that the practice shifted their views of school and the world. As one scholar of public health rhetoric has noted: "Preparedness can be a good thing, but it has very real costs and consequences. For children whose personalities are just forming—who are figuring out what kind of world they live in—if this is the input they get, I think it will have a significant impact down the road."[26]

Disproportionate Effects of Trauma on Marginalized Racial and Ethnic Groups

Among almost all age groups, members of marginalized racial and ethnic groups in the United States are disproportionately affected by trauma. Individuals of marginalized racial groups are both more likely to experience trauma and less likely to seek help following a traumatic experience. Two major factors in this imbalance are the convergence of societal ills, such as poverty, around POCI living in the U.S. and the inequitable reach of systemic institutions, including child welfare and the criminal justice system, into the lives of POCI.

Systemic Factors

Individuals living in poverty, particularly in urban environments, experience trauma at higher rates than those of middle-class or high-income socioeconomic backgrounds; in many poor, urban areas, trauma is recurrent and chronic. Recent population data show that, while 13 percent of all Americans live in poverty, the rates are considerably higher for noncitizen immigrants and POCI: more than a quarter of Native Americans live in poverty, as do 23 percent of Black Americans and approximately 20 percent of Latinx people and immigrants without citizenship.[27] These statistics put people of color at increased risk of multiple types of trauma but especially assault-related violence.

Black, Native American, and Latinx children are overrepresented in state child welfare systems, wherein the risk of trauma is greater than in the general population. Within child welfare, Black and Native American children are likelier than children of other racial groups to suffer maltreatment and abuse. The incidence of trauma is also increased in the juvenile justice system, which incarcerates wildly disproportionate numbers of minoritized youth and wherein more than 10 percent of incarcerated individuals are diagnosed with PTSD.[28]

Racial Trauma

Another cause of increased rates of traumatization among POCI is the significant effect of racial trauma. Though not listed as a traumatic experience leading to PTSD in the *DSM-5*, racial trauma is recognized in the field of psychology as a major influence upon the psychological welfare of POCI and is an important consideration in the treatment of PTSD. *Racial trauma*, also referred to as *race-based stress*, denotes the dangers that result from the "real or perceived experience of racial discrimination," including "threats of harm and injury, humiliating and shaming events, and witnessing harm to other POCI due to real or perceived racism."[29]

Antiracist educators Adam Alvarez, H. Richard Milner, and Lori Delale-O'Connor have distinguished between *recognizable* experiences leading to trauma and *unrecognizable* experiences that lead to trauma. Recognizable experiences are those that "are often used as exemplars" because of their visibility and prevalence in existing discourse around trauma, such as the violence witnessed or experienced by military personnel.[30] Unrecognizable experiences are those that do not fit "the dominant view of trauma" and therefore often go unacknowledged and unaddressed.[31] Overt and covert racism are such traumatic experiences.

From an early age, children of color are exposed to messages of their devaluation that permeate all aspects of American life: The actors on network television are predominantly White, as are the characters in popular books; when there are people of color in mass-market media, they are likely to be portraying criminals, maids, or some other essentialist ethnoracial representation. Teachers are predominantly White, even when the students aren't. Police brutality, the industrial prison complex, hate crimes, and the anti-immigrant sentiment that pervades contemporary political rhetoric serve as reminders that American society is not just inhospitable but also unsafe. In the absence of direct, virulent racism, microaggressions draw attention to the fact that their bodies have marked them as different, other, or less than in society. Young POCI who experience repeated racial traumatization may internalize society's devaluation of their racial or ethnic communities and, as a result, their sense of self.

Due to ongoing exposure to discrimination, violence, and systemic racism, racial trauma is typically cumulative in nature. Historical traumas like colonization, genocide, and slavery, as well as the ongoing trauma of marginalization, also have intergenerational effects, as the wounds felt by the individual affect communities of color more broadly. Despite these long-lasting, wide-reaching effects, racial trauma does not conform to the *DSM-5* definition of a *traumatic event* in part because the definition and "the current definitions of trauma, traumatic stress, and trauma treatment are embedded in European perspectives."[32] As a result of this conceptual and terminological bias, the role of racial trauma is often omitted from psychiatric and psychological research on PTSD and related disorders.

Even if not conceived of as a direct PTSD trigger in current psychiatric practice, discrimination indirectly causes PTSD in that discrimination leads to traumatic experiences, including threats and physical violence, that can trigger trauma-based stress. Research has suggested that racial and ethnic discrimination put Black, Latinx, and Asian American college students at increased risk of developing PTSD symptoms and that discrimination may also slow the course of recovery or exacerbate symptoms of preexisting PTSD and other psychological disorders.[33]

Problematically, some of the most comprehensive longitudinal studies of patients with anxiety disorders researched almost exclusively White populations; as a result, there is a limited psychological "understanding of PTSD course in African American and Latinx populations."[34] In other words, though researchers have long noted the increased prevalence of PTSD among these populations, these populations are still too infrequently included in major research studies, a trend that prevents the development of equitable treatment options and, intentionally or otherwise, reinforces the marginalization and traumatization of Black and Latinx people. Because racial trauma exists within a sociopolitical context that perpetuates retraumatization, even in research, the traumatic experiences of POCI are often overlooked and undertreated.

The effects of racial trauma are variable, as racism and racialization function variably among different racial formations. Many African Americans instill racial literacy in even young children, in part to prepare them for the inequity and danger they may face; young children may be warned to speak with deference toward police officers, to keep their hands in sight, or to avoid asking for help even if needed. Many Asian American families, on the other hand, do not discuss race in the home, though the absence of race talk does not signify an absence of racial trauma but is likely the result of cultural communicative norms. Despite these differences, POCI share the experience of being not White in a society built on whiteness.

As functionaries of American sociopolitical ideology, schools are often ill equipped, at best, or unwilling, at worst, to address the socially and politically situated traumas that affect POCI among the student population. The rise in hate-based violence in educational settings since the 2016 presidential election as well as the symbolic and rhetorical violence of contemporary political discourse necessitate that school officials and educators pay particular attention to the traumatic experiences of youth from marginalized populations as well as the potential for retraumatization on campus and in the classroom.

Managing Trauma in the School Setting

Trauma matters in the school environment for many reasons: in addition to schools' legal and ethical obligations to provide sufficient care for students, particularly those under eighteen or who reside on college campuses, there is a clear pedagogical imperative: of the negative effects of trauma-based stress on students' academic performance. Students with trauma histories may experience impaired memory retention, difficulty with decision-making, and poor attention spans, all of which impact both psychological well-being and academic performance. In addition to increased anxiety and depressive symptoms, evidence suggests that, among children and adolescents, exposure to trauma may contribute to academic and behavioral problems, including poor school attendance, lower grade point average, and decreased rates of high school and college graduation.

Though high schools and colleges have procedures in place to address students' emotional struggles, including those that intersect with their academic performance, institutional approaches to trauma management demonstrate variable efficacy. Typical approaches to the management of trauma in the school setting are school-based counseling and mandated reporting policies.

School-Based Psychological Services

School counselors, psychologists, and social workers commonly comprise the team of health professionals on high school and college campuses. On the high school level, a counselor, whose work tends to focus foremost on students' academic goals and social functioning, may be the first person to whom a struggling student is referred, especially if those struggles manifest in the student's academic performance. When necessary, a counselor may refer a student to a school social worker or psychologist.

By federal law, school districts are required to employ psychologists for the purposes of evaluating students for referral to special education. School psychologists also meet individually with students who have behavioral, emotional, or social struggles, and consult with parents, teachers, and other adults in those students' lives. They may also lead support groups for students struggling with particular issues like grief or anxiety, or skills training groups for pregnancy prevention, drug prevention, or positive identity development. Following campus-wide crises such as natural disasters, acts of violence, or a student's suicide, school psychologists are an integral part of the school-wide or community response.

University-level counselors, social workers, and psychologists take on many of the same roles as their high school counterparts. In addition to individual counseling services and campus-wide interventions, counselors and psychological professionals may offer meditation, yoga, or stress-management classes. During midterms and finals weeks, counselors may work with departments like Student Affairs to run time-management workshops or drop-in counseling.

Larger residential colleges are likelier to have more robust counseling centers both because students who live on campus may have no local support network outside of the school and because some schools have medical centers that offer psychiatric as well as psychological services. (These schools typically require that all residential students are covered by institutional health care plans.) Some campuses also have round-the-clock hotlines for students experiencing suicidal thoughts, domestic abuse, or other crises.

Unfortunately, however, counseling centers on both the secondary and postsecondary levels are drastically understaffed. In the K–12 system, recommendations from the National Association of School Psychologists (NASP) call for "one school psychologist for every 500 to 700 students."[35] When budgets are cut, however, following the elimination of so-called nonessential programs like art and physical education, school psychologists are among the likeliest professionals to be let go. In public school districts, school psychologists often visit multiple schools each day.

On the college level, using a financially motivated strategy that parallels the hiring practices of the rest of the university, counseling centers frequently hire part-time therapists and social workers on a short-term contractual basis in the place of full-time professionals who can develop stronger ties to the campus community. In many cases, there simply are not enough staff members to handle the number of students in need and, despite the prevalence of mental health disorders among the college student population, school-based psychological services often are not the first point of contact for students in distress.

Recent data has shown that while more than half of American college students report feeling anxious or depressed, only 10 to 15 percent seek help at a campus counseling center.[36] While this discrepancy can be explained in part by some students' reluctance to seek professional help of any kind, limited resources may provide another explanation: Students who have called university counseling centers often report a long wait for an appointment. That appointments are often available only during business hours may necessitate that students choose between a counseling session and attending class; given the academic pressures with which students are already faced, many students do not see missing class as a viable option. When drop-in appointments are available, the wait lists can be even longer. In some schools, emergency appointments are only available to students when they are referred directly by faculty members.[37]

To provide service to as many students as possible, many college counseling centers offer talk therapy in the short term only; students needing longer-term treatment are required to seek professional therapy off-campus. For students with PTSD, a difficult disorder that often requires a longer commitment, this arrangement can be discouraging; students whose symptoms include difficulty trusting or confiding in others may find it especially difficult to open up to a school therapist only to be turned away after eight or ten sessions.

The limited psychological resources offered in schools and colleges disproportionately affect POCI. School-based counseling and psychological services are of particular import for adolescents from minoritized racial groups due to traditionally low rates of treatment seeking outside of school, yet schools often lack culturally responsive counseling resources. This is especially true in predominantly White educational settings, which means that in educational spaces wherein students of color are already likely to feel marginalized, they are also unlikely to receive adequate emotional and mental health support, which compounds that marginalization. The challenges are even greater for POCI with histories of trauma: the low rate of treatment seeking and the potential for ongoing discrimination to exacerbate the effects of PTSD and other trauma-based stress symptoms decrease the likelihood that POCI will recover from academic setbacks that occur in the wake of traumatic events.

When resources are available and responsive, they have significant potential to the increase emotional well-being and academic achievement of POCI. For example, high school counselors have been implicated as a major influence in the decision to attend college for Black and African American students and prospective first-generation college students.[38] College may feel out of reach for students who do not have access in their personal lives to adults with a U.S. college education; even for those with the desire to attend college, the application process can be daunting and confusing.

Other POCI may see postsecondary education as "white," and may feel that attending college will cause them to lose part of their individual or social racial identity. While too many institutional practices and policies serve gatekeeping functions, attentive, racially cognizant counselors and psychologists can play a powerful role in the emotional well-being and academic success of POCI. When those positions are eliminated, however, higher education may remain out of reach for students who have long been underserved.

Mandated Reporting

> *In my previous institution, a team of lawyers came to faculty council to list the things we were required to report. They said "when a student starts disclosing, you should interrupt and tell them you're a mandated reporter." Interrupt during a disclosure??*[39]

> *Yes! I've gotten that advice before, too. And it falls flat if you teach writing. How do we interrupt a student who writes about their assault?*[40]

During or following crises, teachers and professors are often the first point of contact for their students. Students may only meet a school psychologist once or twice, if ever, but they generally have more regular, sustained contact with their teachers. In the event of a crisis, a student may turn to a faculty member they trust, perhaps because the crisis has begun to affect their academic work or because the course material has covered something with which the student has personal experience or simply because the student feels a connection with that instructor.

There is no guarantee that student disclosures, however, will be kept confidential. Mandated reporting is increasingly required of college faculty members in postsecondary institutions. While the Clery Act mandates that crime statistics from universities receiving federal funding should be collected from school officials who have significant responsibility for campus activities, such as campus police and local law enforcement, faculty members are frequently called upon to be such mandated reporters. This pressure assigns to teachers duties for which they are neither compensated nor, with the possible exception of faculty in fields like psychology and criminal justice, comprehensively trained. It poses additional conceptual struggles for instructors of composition, creative writing, and performance arts: What happens if a student submits a memoir or gives a monologue about an experience of sexual assault?

Furthermore, mandated reporting can have dangerous consequences for students with PTSD and histories of trauma. If a student who has been raped discloses with the assumption that the professor will keep the information to herself, learning that the professor has made a mandated report to an administrator or campus police officer may feel like a terrible violation. If, on the other hand, the professor interrupts to warn her student that she is a mandated reporter, she has effectively silenced a trauma survivor during a moment of exceptional vulnerability. In additional to the hurt or disappointment the student may experience immediately, such an interruption may prevent the student from disclosing in the future, even to someone who is not a mandated reporter.

On the secondary level, teachers are already mandated reporters, but research has found that most teachers have "been given mandated reporting training, but little else in terms of dealing with trauma."[41] Disclosures are not the only incident that may result in the filing of a mandated report by a secondary schoolteacher. Laws in most of the U.S. require that teachers report any knowledge or suspicion, based upon student behavior, of child abuse or neglect. This means that, while the filing of a report is a mandate rather than a choice, the teacher is required to make a decision about what constitutes normal behavior for individual students. This relies on a teacher's subjectivity as well as his positionality.

That most American teachers are White while most American students are not makes it increasingly likely that behaviors deemed unusual or outside the norm by a teacher will be those that do not conform to white normativity. Whiteness norms are "ingrained in their theories and pedagogies of normative child development, learning, and mandated reporting, thus influencing how they are taught to read 'normal' and 'developmentally appropriate' behavior."[42]

Mandated reporting also places the teacher in the role of determining which bodies are subjected to government intrusion. While child welfare systems can and do save children's lives by removing them from homes wherein they are physically or sexually abused or severely neglected, child welfare's reach extends mostly into the lives of poor families and POCI. If a single mother of three living in poverty who works three jobs to pay rent each month and clothe her children yet who cannot afford childcare leaves the two younger children in the care of the eldest one afternoon when her neighbor is unavailable to babysit, and if, the next morning, the eldest child falls asleep in class and then, when questioned by her third-grade teacher, remarks that sometimes she is in charge with her siblings, her teacher may wonder if leaving an eight-year-old alone as a caregiver constitutes neglect and file a report. The teacher may even file a report not because he believes this to be neglect but because he fears for his own safety and job security should he fail to comply with the mandate.

Families, like this student's, that are in need of financial and childcare resources may instead experience government interventions such as mandated visits by a social worker or, worse, child removal. In this way, mandated reporting functions in part as a method by which educational institutions surveil and punish those who either do not conform to the norms of the classroom or who are already underserved by the systemic structures of society. Students with trauma histories, particularly POCI, very often are aware of these practices and "learn to shape their behavior and speech to reduce the potential for child welfare involvement. In this way, children often 'choose' to be silent about their experiences and act 'appropriately.'"[43]

CONCLUDING THOUGHTS

The trigger warning emerges as a response to trauma amid an educational environment that professes student-responsiveness yet mandates top-down, neoliberal practices that have more to do with legal liability than student welfare. It emerges from an educational environment that acknowledges the prevalence of sexual assault and rape culture on college campuses yet allocates more money to football teams than to counseling services. It emerges from an educational environment that celebrates diversity yet perpetuates the marginalization of many of the bodies in the classroom.

The trigger warning, of course, is not the problem—but it is not the solution either.

The implementation of the trigger warning relies on the assumption that the curriculum has the potential to traumatize students. This is not far-fetched: in many classes, the curriculum is defined by trauma. From history classes that address war, genocide, colonization, and slavery and English classes wherein students read real and fictionalized accounts of the same subjects to psychology, sociology, and even biology, learning about trauma is a central part of education.

There is little argument that these subjects are difficult and painful to talk about, let alone experience. But do they have the power to traumatize? Or to retraumatize students with PTSD and other trauma-based stress disorders? The psychiatric definition of PTSD excludes media as a potential trigger for the disorder. Research has found that youth is a risk factor for secondary traumatic stress and vicarious traumatization, which might lead one to believe that high school and college students (and those even younger) are in danger in the classroom. However, most research on secondary traumatic stress demonstrates that such stress results from exposure to the traumatized person, not from the trauma itself.[44] In this view, a student conducting interviews with sexual assault survivors would be at greater risk than a student reading about a rape, for instance. While some psychological perspectives suggest that media exposure to traumatic events can have adverse emotional effects on certain individuals, the brevity of lesson plan, unit, or semester in which a student studies particularly traumatic material makes it unlikely for students to suffer the cumulative effects of vicarious traumatization.[45]

To use trigger warnings, one must determine when a trigger warning is needed. In kind, to separate what requires a trigger warning from what does not require a trigger warning necessitates one determine what constitutes trauma and what does not. The *DSM-5* does not consider racism in its medical definition of trauma. Alvarez, Milner, and Delale-O'Connor note that, "while race-related traumatic experiences occur daily for many students of color, they may go unnoticed because they occur in a context where whiteness is still the dominant norm."[46] Paradoxically, racism is one of the commonest topics prefaced with a trigger warning in American schools. For some educators, the trigger warning may feel like a tacit acknowledgment of the racial trauma experienced by so many among the student population. Unfortunately, even when educators do see the link between racism and trauma, they may not see how their own classroom practices contribute to that trauma.

Generally speaking, the courses most likely to require the use of trigger warnings are those that deal with the identities, achievements, and treatment, including the historical and contemporary subjugation and marginalization, of POCI, White women, the LGBTQ community, and those who are intersectionally oppressed.

Some of this is very likely the result of increased awareness of trauma and marginalization among the scholars and educators in these fields. After all, teachers whose work deals explicitly with the destructive potential of racism, misogyny, and other bastions of patriarchy and white supremacy are more inclined to consider how their own classrooms resist or reinforce such oppressive normativity. However, even scholars who employ critical pedagogies and practices work within the ideological confines of their own experiences and sociopolitical positionality. As a result, it is necessary to question the efficacy of practices that are framed as critical yet might be less equitable than they seem.

To that end, it should be noted that most, though not all, of the calls for trigger warnings in contemporary education come from White-identifying students and educators. In fact, many educators of color have challenged the practice. Sociologist Tessie McMillan Cottom, like many others, has argued that the trigger warning is part of a "student-customer model" of education that serves "to rationalize away the critical canon of race, sex, gender, sexuality, colonialism, and capitalism."[47] The trigger warning, when placed before stories of marginalized cultures, reinforces perceptions of these stories as marginal, deviant, and in need of silencing.

In addition to a consideration of the material deemed trigger-worthy, one must also consider who is likeliest to be exposed to and affected by both those triggers and related trigger warnings. The students likeliest to take multiple classes in fields like women's and gender studies, Africana studies, and Chicano/a studies are those who personally identify with those marginalized groups. A very large body of research has demonstrated that these are in fact the students who experience the most incidences of and most cumulative types of trauma from childhood through adolescence into adulthood. Those students may be the most traumatized—but they are not the likeliest to experience vicarious traumatization in the classroom.

Research has also shown that the individuals most likely to experience secondary or vicarious stress symptoms are those who have little or no experience with trauma.[48] These students, therefore, have few coping strategies in place and, arguably, lower resilience in the face of potentially traumatic material. The most vulnerable students in the classroom, then, and those most in need of trigger warnings, are not students with PTSD or histories of individual or systemic trauma but instead but those who have not previously experienced trauma at all.

If trigger warnings are not for the marginalized and traumatized, for whom are they really intended?

NOTES

1. Tessie McMillan Cottom, "Should There Be Trigger Warnings on Syllabi?" *The Society Pages*, March 13, 2014. https://thesocietypages.org/socimages/2014/03/13/should-there-be-trigger-warnings-on-syllabi/.
2. Guy A. Boysen, "Evidence-Based Answers to Questions about Trigger Warnings for Clinically-Based Distress: A Review for Teachers," *Scholarship of Teaching and Learning in Psychology* 3 (2017): 167.
3. American Psychological Association, "Trauma," https://www.apa.org/topics/trauma/index.
4. American Psychiatric Association (APA), "Posttraumatic Stress Disorder," 2013.
5. APA, *Diagnostic and Statistical Manual of Mental Disorders: DSM-5* (Arlington, VA: American Psychiatric Publishing, 2013).
6. National Institutes of Health, "PTSD: A Growing Epidemic," *NIH MedlinePlus: The Magazine* 4, no. 1 (2009).
7. Boysen, "Evidence-Based Answers," 167.
8. Ibid., 168.
9. Eileen L. Zurbriggen, "Preventing Secondary Traumatization in the Undergraduate Classroom: Lessons from Theory and Clinical Practice," *Psychological Times: Theory, Research, Practice, and Policy* 3, no. 3 (2011): 223.
10. Sheryl Kataoka, Audra Langley, Marleen Wong, Shilpa Baweja, and Bradley Stein, "Responding to Students with PTSD in Schools," *Child and Adolescent Psychiatric Clinics of North America* 21, no. 2 (2012): 119.
11. National Institute of Mental Health, "Post-Traumatic Stress Disorder (PTSD)," updated November 2017, https://www.nimh.nih.gov/health/statistics/post-traumatic-stress-disorder-ptsd.shtml#part_155470.
12. Lauren M. Schmidt, "Trauma in English Learners: Examining the Influence of Previous Trauma and PTSD on English Learners and within the Classroom," *Current Issues in TESOL* (2018): 3.
13. Ibid., 2.
14. Ibid., 5.
15. Omar S. Lopez, Stephen B. Springer, and Jeffrey B. Nelson, "Veterans in the College Classroom: Guidelines for Instructional Practices," *Adult Learning* 27, no. 4 (2015): 144.
16. Boysen, "Evidence-Based Answers," 168.
17. Lopez et al., "Veterans in the College Classroom," 144.
18. Noreen M. Glover-Graf, Eva Miller, and Samuel Freeman, "Accommodating Veterans with Posttraumatic Stress Disorder Symptoms in the Academic Setting," *Rehabilitation Education* 24, no. 1–2 (2010): 47. See also Julia Melin, "Desperate Choices: Why Black Women Join the U.S. Military at Higher Rates than Men and All Other Racial and Ethnic Groups," *New England Journal of Public Policy* 28, no. 2 (2016).
19. Glover-Graf et al., "Accommodating Veterans," 47.
20. Rape, Abuse & Incest National Network (RAINN), "Campus Sexual Violence: Statistics," 2019, https://www.rainn.org/statistics/campus-sexual-violence.
21. Boysen, "Evidence-Based Answers," 168.
22. Janice L. Cooper, Rachel Masi, Sarah Dababnah, Yumiko Aratani, and Jane Knitzer, *Unclaimed Children Revisited: Working Paper No. 2: Strengthening Policies to Support Children, Youth, and Families Who Experience Trauma*, National Center for Children in Poverty, 2007, http://nccp.org/publications/pdf/download_204.pdf, 7.
23. Lynsey R. Miron, Holly K. Orcutt, and Mandy J. Kumpula, "Differential Predictors of Transient Stress versus Posttraumatic Stress Disorder: Evaluating Risk Following Targeted Mass Violence," *Behavior Therapy* 45, no. 6 (2014).
24. James Hamblin, "What Are Active-Shooter Drills Doing to Kids?" *The Atlantic* (February 28, 2018).
25. See Molly Crane-Newman, Graham Rayman, and Rocco Parascandola, "Manhattan's Pace University Evacuated after Studs on Student's Belt Get Mistaken for Ammo," *New York Daily News* (September 14, 2017).

26. Colleen Derkatch, quoted in Hamblin, "What Are Active-Shooter Drills Doing to Kids?"
27. Michael B. Sauter, "Faces of Poverty: What Racial, Social Groups Are More Likely to Experience It?" *USA Today* (October 10, 2018), https://www.usatoday.com/story/money/economy/2018/10/10/faces-poverty-social-racial-factors/37977173/.
28. Cooper et al., *Unclaimed Children Revisited*, 9.
29. Lillian Comas-Diaz, Gordon Nagayama Hall, and Helen A. Neville, "Racial Trauma: Theory, Research, and Healing; Introduction to the Special Issue," *American Psychologist* 74, no. 1 (2019): 1.
30. Adam Alvarez, H. Richard Milner IV, and Lori Delale-O'Connor, "Race, Trauma, and Education: What Educators Need to Know," in *But I Don't See Color: The Perils, Practices, and Possibilities of Antiracist Education*, ed. Terry Husband (Rotterdam: Sense, 2016), 28.
31. Ibid., 29.
32. Comas-Diaz, "Racial Trauma," 2.
33. Nicholas J. Sibrava, Andri S. Bjornsson, A. Carlos I. Perez Benitez, Ethan Moitra, Risa B. Weisberg, and Martin B. Keller, "Posttraumatic Stress Disorder in African American and Latinx Adults: Clinical Course and the Role of Racial and Ethnic Discrimination," *American Psychologist* 74, no. 1 (2019): 103.
34. Ibid., 102.
35. Kristen Weir, "School Psychologists Feel the Squeeze," *Monitor on Psychology* 43, no. 8 (2012): 34.
36. Nance Roy, "The Rise of Mental Health on College Campuses: Protecting the Emotional Health of Our Nation's College Students," *Higher Education Today* (December 17, 2018), https://www.higheredtoday.org/2018/12/17/rise-mental-health-college-campuses-protecting-emotional-health-nations-college-students/.
37. While most college counseling centers do not have official policies stating that students must be referred by faculty members, in my own experience as a university professor, I have had encountered many such informal practices. In one such instance, I contacted the school wellness center for a student in crisis and was told no appointments were available; once I identified myself as a faculty member, I was told to send the student over immediately to be seen.
38. Blaire Cholewa, Christina K. Burkhardt, and Michael F. Hull, "Are School Counselors Impacting Underrepresented Students' Thinking about Postsecondary Education? A Nationally Representative Study," *Professional School Counseling* 19, no. 1 (2015): 149.
39. Mara Lee Grayson, Twitter post, March 8, 2019, 8:14 a.m., https://twitter.com/MaraLee-Grayson/status/1104052837250551808.
40. Ruth Osorio, Twitter post, March 8, 2019, 10:41 a.m., https://twitter.com/rorhetorician/status/1104089840650543104.
41. Christine Mayor, "Whitewashing Trauma: Applying Neoliberalism, Governmentality, and Whiteness Theory to Trauma Training for Teachers," *Whiteness and Education* (2019): 200.
42. Ibid., 205–6.
43. Ibid.
44. Zurbriggen, "Preventing Secondary Traumatization," 224.
45. Ibid.
46. Alvarez et al., "Race, Trauma, and Education," 33.
47. Cottom, "Should There Be Trigger Warnings on Syllabi?"
48. Zurbriggen, "Preventing Secondary Traumatization," 224.

Chapter Four

Academic Discourse and the Inequity of the Politeness Protocol

> *Every educational system is a political means of maintaining or of modifying the appropriation of discourse, with the knowledge and the powers it carries with it.*—Michel Foucault[1]

Alana, a biracial (native Hawaiian and White) professor of rhetoric and composition, found it difficult to adjust when she accepted a new position at a public university in the American South: "I was Hawaiian enough in Hawaii, but in the Southern Bible Belt, no one seemed to know what to make of me." After two students complained about being asked to discuss an essay written in Hawaiian Pidgin English, Alana was reprimanded by her department chairperson for sharing a text that wasn't in Standard Written English.

Because her work explores the politics of language variation, Alana includes in every syllabus she creates a broad content note (which she identifies as a trigger warning) about the potentially sensitive nature of course material, followed by a policy stating how students should observe the warning. That policy includes the permission to leave the room at any time should course material result in unbearable discomfort and the direction that students should email Alana prior to the next class to discuss a makeup plan.

Early in her second semester at the school, in a writing pedagogy course for preservice English teachers, a conversation arose about who is authorized to teach African American texts—and who is not. Discussion quickly stagnated: as two of the class's three students of color insisted that Whites, who would "never understand the African American condition," had no right to "speak on behalf of minorities," some White students grew defensive, insisting that their classmates were being "too sensitive."

"You're White; you have no idea what racism feels like," an African American woman told a light-skinned classmate Alana knew to be Latina.

"I'm not White," replied the classmate. "I just don't agree with you."

"The conversation was fraught with problems," Alana later recalled, "and they were frustrated because it clearly wasn't going to be solved. No one seemed to be equipped to deal with open-ended debate." She suggested that everyone "remain calm" and "take a deep breath," then gave the class a five-minute break to collect themselves. "As a Hawaiian," Alana said, "I get upset sometimes when Whites teach Hawaiian literature because they don't understand what it's like to have your country overtaken and overrun. That's why it's important to talk about this. I felt like we'd opened a big can of worms and given my experiences at the school. . . . I realized it was not good for me to try to work with this."

When class resumed, she reminded the students "that this is a conversation, not a debate over who is going to be right or wrong." By the time class ended, Alana felt that she had lost some of the class, particularly the two African American students: "They seemed to withdraw from conversation over the rest of the semester." At no point in the semester, however, did any of Alana's students take her up on her trigger warning policy.

Much antiracist scholarship emphasizes the value of open cross-cultural communication in classrooms and on campuses. Exposure to ideas and experiences that differ from an individual's own may increase students' empathy; expand their understandings of identity, culture, and situated experience; and enable critical thinking and intellectual transformation. Open, critical conversations about race and racism are necessary both to challenge the ingrained white supremacy of educational ideologies and institutions and to encourage students to reflect upon their own roles within an inherently racist society.

Talking about race, however, isn't intrinsically equitable—and talking isn't enough, especially if the way race and racism are addressed places an undue emotional burden on students of color. In fact, because racism is "psychically damaging" and because "white hegemonic power often controls the directions and outcomes of race dialogues," race talk can be seen "as an inherently unsafe discourse" for students of color.[2]

Though racial literacy and racially cognizant curricula are increasingly prevalent, particularly on the postsecondary level, most classroom race talk is not introduced by the teacher, but instead emerges in response to curricular materials or preexisting in-class discussion. This often means that instructors, even those who are well versed in the dynamics of racial discourse and who have strategized in advance how they might handle such conversations should they arise, are unprepared in the actual moment that race talk emerges.

That isn't necessarily a problem, as conversations that arise organically in the classroom raise issues of curricular significance and are likely to be meaningful for students engaged in the conversation. However, when instructors are surprised by the content of the conversation and the manner in which students are communicating, a common response is to shut down or back away from the discussion. While sometimes that response is a knee-jerk reaction to a potentially uncomfortable conversation, in Alana's case, there are other factors at play, not least of which is Alana's concern about her job security.

Alana's fears have merit—having already been admonished by a supervisor in a new school, it isn't illogical for Alana to think that engaging her class in an already contentious debate might land her in more hot water. Her position, unfortunately, isn't an uncommon one: many educators like Alana, whose work addresses the political aspects of language and instruction, find that they have to defend the work they do to their students, colleagues, and administrators. That Alana herself identifies as biracial complicates the situation, as educators of color are likelier than their White colleagues to be rebuked for employing critical, antiracist pedagogies.[3]

Some educators may find it easy to sympathize with Alana, given the tenuousness of her position at the new university. Others may be frustrated with her refusal to engage her students further and think her withdrawal cowardly or the enactment of her privilege and power as the professor. Like the situation itself, the ethics of Alana's approach are far more complex.

Despite this popular narrative of the teacher as martyr, educators should not be expected at every turn to sacrifice themselves for the sake of their students. Given the frequency with which "politicians and administrators use stereotypical narratives of the devoted teacher to justify cutting funding, extending hours, and depriving teachers of wage increases," it can be seen as an act of political resistance to assert one's identity as a human being whose needs and desires aren't confined to the classroom.[4] The paradox here is that by asserting her right to security of resources, Alana deprives students, particularly students of color, an opportunity to share their feelings and experiences and engage with the complex critical education she wishes to provide—thereby feeding the institutional inequity that led to her insecurity!

At first glance, Alana's assessment of the situation seems accurate: given the students' lack of preparation to engage in difficult conversations, it is likely that further discussion would have led to no resolution. The class might need additional preparation in the form of self-reflection and critical inquiry before they are able to engage productively in nuanced conversations about education and positionality. The advice Alana gives her students (to take five minutes and a few breaths to calm down) also initially seems sound—they are upset, as is she, and it is possible that some time away from the discussion will allow everyone to return to class with clearer heads, prepared to have a calm, logical conversation using reason and rationality. The problem is that this advice not only ends the conversation but also is so mired in Western discursive norms and *whiteliness* that it reproduces the inequity it seeks to dismantle.

Frankie Condon defines whiteliness as a "constellation of epistemological and rhetorical practices rather than an ontological condition of raced-White consciousness."[5] In other words, whiteliness is more about hegemonic ways of knowing and modes of communication than it is about an essentialist state of being borne from the color and characteristics of one's physical body and position in society.

It stands to reason that one can perform whiteliness in the classroom while also self-identifying, as Alana does, as biracial, for her ways of knowing and being are influenced by ideologies and discourses that long have upheld educational inequity.[6] After all, most educators have been taught to emulate models of teaching that reflect the concept of "a single norm of thought and experience" that is presented as a universal condition; "this has been just as true for nonwhite teachers as for White teachers."[7]

THE POLITENESS PROTOCOL OF CLASSROOM CONVERSATION

In classroom discussion, educators tend to operate within the conventions of the Western conversation model, which emphasizes assertive yet polite verbal contributions and dispassionate logical reasoning. Academic protocol in general draws upon these conventions: students are expected to participate actively (which often means vocally) in class discussions, to the point that in many classes part of the final course grade depends upon their participation.

Because Western theories of cognitive development contend that speech is evidence of meaning-making, educators recognize students' in-class verbalization as evidence of both their effort as learners and their processing of class material. Similarly, students are expected to demonstrate respect for their teacher and classmates by raising their hands before they speak and by speaking calmly and politely.

Politeness is closely connected to etiquette, the code of behavior that stems from contemporary social and cultural norms. Given that etiquette arises culturally and contextually, however, what is polite in one cultural context may not be perceived as polite in another. Because race talk often involves cross-cultural communication, students are likely to operate from different understandings of conversational etiquette.

Moreover, as evidenced by the White students' defensive posturing and the African American students' withdrawal, race talk is deeply emotional, and emotion, like etiquette and other discursive norms, is a socially constructed and situated practice that derives its meaning from the public realm.

When Alana directs her students to remain calm, she assumes first that calmness is possible and second that calmness is preferable, thereby asserting that one mode of communication is expected and appropriate while others are unwelcome. While it can be argued that students ought to be prepared to operate within the discursive norms of a given societal context in order to succeed academically, professionally, and socially within that context, actions like Alana's serve to further marginalize students for whom those norms are not norms at all.

Alana ends the conversation because she finds it to be fraught with problems, many of which are common in classroom race talk: the White students' defensive accusations of hypersensitivity; the assumption of others' racial identifications; the essentialism of one's embodied experiences. She doesn't, however, address those discursive maneuvers, why they are problematic, or how they prevent critical explorations of race and racism in education—and she doesn't consider how her own discursive practices are equally inequitable. Without that metadiscourse, any classroom race talk is limited.

None of this is to say that it isn't possible to engage in productive race talk while being "polite" and staying "calm." It is possible and it does happen, especially in the classroom setting, wherein students are expected to simultaneously engage in difficult conversations and observe an (often unstated) academic protocol that emphasizes reason and rationality over emotional knowing. This ought to be a question not of possibility, but of equity: When an instructor demands that students speak calmly and politely, for whose comfort does she demand it? And what does it require from her students?

CULTURALLY SITUATED THINKING, FEELING, AND SPEAKING

Because language is inherently ambiguous, when communicating with others, individuals must draw inferences about meaning. Those inferences are informed by the language used in context and by that individual's knowledge of the world, which is itself based upon past experiences with similar language in similar contexts. As a result, how individuals communicate is reflective of the values particular to the cultural communities of which they are a part.

For example, the ideal of freedom often emphasized when conceptualizing Americanness stems largely from *possessive individualism*, a political and social philosophy closely connected to market capitalism. In possessive individualism, one's identity and worth are dependent upon one's freedom from or lack of dependence upon others. Being free, then, means being free from the will of others, a condition that can only be attained through possession—by possessing resources that limit one's dependence upon others, one can possess oneself, thereby becoming more fully human. Because in individualistic cultures, great emphasis is placed on the concept of the self and one's freedom of selfhood, a related feature in the United States and other Western cultural traditions is what psychologists call *expressive individualism*, the expression of one's inner thoughts and feelings as an expression of individual identity.

Collectivist cultures, on the other hand, emphasize the needs of the group over the needs of the individual. An individual's identity, then, is strongly relational and defined by one's connection with others rather than one's independence. Rather than defining oneself by fixed inner thoughts and feelings, people of collectivist cultures are more likely to see their desires and identities as changeable and context dependent. Because relationships and interactional behaviors are externally visible and recognizable, one's selfhood (here defined in relation to the group) is evident in their interactions with others and therefore does not need to be expressed verbally or emotively.

In individualistic societies, such as Australia, Great Britain, Switzerland, and the United States, directness in communication is typically viewed as an effective way of achieving one's goals; for instance, a speaker may present an idea and then explain the argument for the idea, providing support as deemed necessary based upon the response of the audience. In collectivist societies like China, Egypt, Russia, and South Korea, which prize indirectness and group harmony, individuals are more likely to lead up to a point, providing background information and their processes of reasoning before stating the primary assertion.

Due to contemporary globalization, most societies today fall somewhere within an individualist-collectivist spectrum, so do their members; because identities are plural, individuals may find that their own beliefs and practices do not align exactly with any one culture. Like most other aspects of discourse, patterns of cultural communication are quite complex.

DISCOURSE AND THE EDUCATION SYSTEM

Within broad cultural groups, there are many smaller social and cultural communities, all with their own value systems and related Discourses. Though colloquially the term *discourse* often is used synonymously with discussion or conversation, *Discourse* (differentiated from its homonym[8] by the capital D) refers to more than the words used in communication: Discourse refers to the processes and modes of meaning-making, including but not limited to language, within any social or cultural group. These modes include ways of talking, behaving, dressing, and thinking that align with the dominant norms and expectations for a person of a particular social position.

For example, in the classroom, students *act* as students by sitting at desks, raising a hand before speaking (often even if an instructor has told them that it is unnecessary to do so), and waiting to be dismissed before leaving the classroom. Similarly, the instructor takes on the role of instructor by initiating conversation or giving a lecture, acknowledging, verbally or otherwise, students whose hands are raised, and assigning homework.

Often, individuals intentionally and strategically take on these discursive behaviors, especially when they are unfamiliar. Consider, for example, the new teacher who only three months ago was a graduate student but who now stands before a classroom of her own students. She might be overwhelmed by the expectant gazes of the individuals before her and feel like an imposter. Likely, however, she nonetheless responds to the behavior of the students and the discursive expectations of the situation by initiating a conversation or giving a lecture and, for the rest of the class, doing as is expected of a teacher in the situation.

Eventually, perhaps even by the end of the first week, the new teacher might feel comfortable in that role. After all, while her position now differs from the one she occupied in the prior academic year, as a recent graduate student she is likely quite familiar with the discourse of the classroom. In this case, she may be familiar with the discourse of the classroom but unfamiliar with the power that accompanies her role as a teacher within it.

Any institutional Discourse is a *secondary Discourse* (as it is learned and practice outside the home, the site of the *primary Discourse*), and it is adopted through an apprenticeship of sorts: as one participates, one begins to adapt her speech, behavior, and even thinking to the new Discourse. Those who have spent much of their lives in classrooms like the one just described, participating in the Discourse of school and assuming teacher and student roles in expected ways, may feel very comfortable performing those roles and may appropriate the Discourse without a conscious attempt at performativity.

Other individuals, however, must work considerably harder and perform much more to meet the expectations of a secondary Discourse, either because they have had limited prior access to that Discourse or because that Discourse conflicts measurably with their primary, home-based Discourse. Within any society some Discourses are considered dominant Discourses while others are seen as nondominant. *Dominant Discourses* are "secondary Discourses, the mastery of which, at a particularly place and time, brings with it the (potential) acquisition of social goods,"[9] such as money, social or political power, or prestige.

DISCOURSE AND DISCOURSES

discourse (little-d): Extended pieces of language in context. Because language is referential and used to convey social and cultural meanings, discourse encompasses the words used, their form and function, and production and interpretation of communication.

Discourse (big-D): An "identity kit" of sorts that incorporates ways of speaking as well as ways of being, knowing, and behaving in a particular social or cultural group. An individual has many Discourses, and each is associated with a set of practices and values that may conflict with that individual's other Discourses.

Primary Discourse: The original, home-based Discourse. The primary Discourse is the earliest socialization via family, clan, or peer group and serves as a foundation for the later learning of other Discourses. Individuals may be least conscious of their primary Discourse because of its deeply ingrained nature.

Secondary Discourse: A Discourse learned after the primary Discourse. The secondary Discourse is generally learned through apprenticeship and grants access or membership to a social or cultural institution outside of the home such as a school, house of worship, club, business, or organization.

Dominant Discourse: A secondary Discourse of power that provides those who acquire it opportunities for social status, financial gain, and other social goods. Dominant Discourses are determined by social and cultural groups of power within a given society and most easily accessed by individuals already belonging to those groups. (In the United States, for example, the dominant Discourse is White, English speaking, and of middle-class or higher socioeconomic status.)

Nondominant Discourse: A secondary Discourse of less power that provides community and solidarity but does not provide access to power or greater resources within the larger society. Nondominant Discourses carry less weight in a given society, but they also may be overtly oppressed, marginalized, or minoritized.

> These definitions draw upon the works of James Paul Gee and Michel Foucault, as well as the linguistic methodology of critical discourse analysis.

Many individuals understand the power associated with the dominant Discourse and recognize that, in order to attain a certain level of success, they must acquire some ability to communicate using dominant discursive practices. However, because dominant Discourses stem from and are maintained by, respectively, people and institutions with power, dominant Discourses are inherently exclusive and inequitable in that they both uphold the values and ways of being of the socially dominant group and, given that individuals and groups within a society have unequal access to those Discourses, serve the function of gatekeeping, thereby prohibiting others from membership.

The Discourse of "Being American"

Education in the United States has always served, in myriad ways and to varying context-dependent degrees, to train students to *be* American. From an early age, one learns the country's history, its values, and the appropriate ways to speak, write, and act in its institutions. In other words, in order to succeed in school, students must acquire a secondary Discourse—in a process that is as much acculturation as assimilation. This process continues throughout students' educational careers. In her brilliant and controversial treatise on the requisite college-level first year composition course, Sharon Crowley writes:

> The continuing function of the required composition course has been to insure the academic community that its entering members are taught the discursive behaviors and traits of character that require them to join the community. The course is meant to shape students to behave, think, write, and speak as students rather than as the people they are, people who have differing histories and traditions and languages and ideologies.[10]

Both the concept of the student and what it means to be American, however, despite the diversity of the classroom and the country, remain tightly tethered to whiteness.

The history learned in schools is incomplete and told from the perspective and in the voice of the European White men who fought a violent revolution for freedom from the British colonizer while at the same time violently colonizing their new country and its native people. The freedom Americans value is one that historically excluded anyone who wasn't White, male, or landowning.

In terms of language, students learn that in school they must speak and write in what some refer to Standard English, regardless of the dialect or language they use at home; whatever the content of their writing, students are graded in part on their abilities to adhere to mechanical and formal conventions of a so-called Standard English.

There are two primary, related problems associated with this: First, while it is common for individuals to adapt their language use to particular settings, conceptions of Standard English are derived not from the diverse linguistic and discursive practices of students but from the practices of the people who made up the scholarly and student body generations before people of color were allowed, let alone welcomed, in schools. Marking this dialect as a "standard" equates white language practices with both the norm and the ideal and implies that any other, nonwhite English is nonstandard, lesser, and deviant.

Even more problematic is that there *is* no single standard dialect of English! There are no specific standards to define Standard English, and dialects referred to as such are those that are spoken by White speakers.[11]

The marginalization perpetuated by classroom discourse is not an anomaly. In fact it is upheld by the epistemological foundation upon which the entire system of education system is constructed. Western ways of knowing, the framework from which academic protocol is derived, draw upon empiricism, the scientific method, and objectivity. Because the scientific method is linear, it is also necessarily reductive; variables, such as the diverse experiences and ways of knowing students bring to the classroom, are explored insofar as they can be accounted for and controlled.

Critiquing whiteness and the social norms it upholds is exceedingly difficult because those norms, while largely "unmarked and unnamed," compose the "place from which White people look at [themselves], at others, and at society."[12] An often-drawn analogy here is that of the relationship of the fish to water—fish don't know what water is because all they've ever known is water. In the absence of critical literacy tools that enable White individuals to recognize their own positionality, the context (in this case the water) that maintains their privilege is only visible to those outside of it.

It has long been a commonplace in the field of literacy education that those who occupy oppressed, marginalized, or otherwise nondominant positions in society can, through acquisition of the dominant Discourse, occupy a position of agency from which to critique and challenge the practices of the dominant Discourse (using those same practices) and the inequitable structures of cultural hegemony it represents and upholds. There is no guarantee, however, that the acquisition of the Discourse will confer access or agency, in part because the ideological frameworks and institutional structures of U.S. society are designed to prevent rather than grant access and agency.

Even pedagogies intended to be inclusive may ultimately perpetuate exclusion and inequity. Practices, like the trigger warning, that aim to lessen classroom discomfort and increase students' emotional security do not necessarily achieve the ends they seek. Often, when they do, they do so only for select groups of students and in ways that disproportionately burden students who are already marginalized.

Why "Staying Calm" Is a Problem

When individuals communicate in ways that do not conform to the expectations of the audience or the etiquette of that particular setting, responses tend to overlook the content of the message and focus instead on the manner of expression. For example, many long-term couples are familiar with the experience of having an argument about a particular event or issue that quickly morphs into an argument about the way each partner is arguing; the original issue is rarely resolved and the argument may even escalate to the point that neither partner remembers how the argument began. All of this is to say that when a person is already upset, regardless of the cause of that upset, being directed to express that upset differently places a considerable responsibility on a person already experiencing emotional unease or, worse, dysregulation.

Similarly, because stories of race and racism are personal and connected to individual and group identities and experiences, race talk is necessarily emotional. Emotion, however, is typically discouraged in classroom discourse, largely because it is seen as oppositional to reason, despite the falseness of that binary. (For more, see chapter 5.) In this way, academic protocol already contributes to the broad silencing of race talk—but it more specifically silences the race talk and stories of racial trauma of people of color.

Because white perspectives dominate in the United States, POCI already do a considerable amount of work to be heard and to prove that their views and experiences are legitimate. When the topic of conversation in the classroom pertains directly to race and racism, POCI, whose contributions may be as experiential as they are empirical, often must reframe their stories and tell them in ways that fit the white cultural ways of knowing that predominate in academic institutions. To those used to such code-switching, the adaptation might feel almost automatic but the practice may have originated as a strategy to avoid accusations of being too sensitive or too emotional.

Because trauma, racial or otherwise, and trauma-based stress are highly emotional and unpredictable in nature, the idea that students can or should remain calm while recounting painful experiences or interrogating inequities they face regularly is unrealistic and inequitable. Responses directed at the manner of expression rather than the already emotional content invalidate the emotional weight of the experience and place an added emotional burden on the speaker.

Trigger warnings, which ostensibly enable individual students to remove themselves from painful conversations, reinforce the notion that classroom discourse should be calm, rational, and dispassionate. In doing so, they maintain the existing discursive norms of the classroom.

THE TRIGGER WARNING AS PART OF ACADEMIC DISCOURSE

Most educators who use trigger warnings do not suggest that they resolve the effects of trauma but instead that they mitigate the experience of *discomfort* that arises from exposure to the potential trigger. Such attempts to mitigate discomfort, however well intentioned, may do more harm than good, particularly when used in conjunction with critical pedagogies around race and racism.

Cognitive Dissonance

Communications scholars Joe C. Martin and Brandi N. Frisby suggest that trigger warnings can be understood via the psychological concept of *cognitive dissonance*. Cognitive dissonance describes the "existence of non-fitting relations"[13] between different thoughts and understandings simultaneously held in one's mind. Sometimes this dissonance leads to changes in behavior or attitude.

More often, when individuals are confronted with new information or beliefs that contradict existing ones, the "unpleasant state of dissonance motivates individuals to engage in cognitive work to reduce the inconsistency"[14] by adding or emphasizing *consonant* cognitions or actions (those that fit together) or by avoiding or decreasing the significance of *dissonant* cognitions or actions (those that are inconsistent with one another). In other words, the individual is likely to seek out information that conforms to one set of beliefs, typically those that are deeper ingrained and therefore more resistant to change, while denying information that challenges those beliefs and causes discomfort.

For example, if a student who believes herself to be a strong writer receives poor grades in her first college writing class, the dissonance between her self-conception ("I'm a good writer") and the new cognition created by her low grades ("My teacher doesn't think I'm a good writer") is likely to cause anxiety, not because her grades are low, but because those low grades contradict a belief she holds about her own talents and self-identity. To reduce that comfort, she might modify her behavior, perhaps by dedicating more time to writing or by visiting the university's writing center, or change her attitude by questioning her existing self-concept ("Maybe I'm not a good writer after all"). She is more likely, however, to soothe herself with consonant cognitions, such as "My teacher is an unfair grader" or "I didn't put enough effort into that paper," that allow her self-concept to remain intact. She might even avoid or postpone dissonant cognitions by dropping the class from her schedule.

Martin and Frisby suggest that triggers create dissonant cognitions: while the individual is physically safe, her emotional response tells her that she is not safe. As a result, the trigger warning, meant to *prevent* the emotional experience of being triggered, functions as a formal avoidance behavior intended to "reduce the experience of cognitive dissonance among students."[15]

Just as the students likeliest to experience secondary traumatization are those who have never experienced trauma and who, until this exposure, believed themselves to be safe, the students likeliest to experience cognitive dissonance are the students whose existing beliefs and ideas are not consonant with the new material. When reading about a sexual assault on a college campus, then, the student likeliest to experience cognitive dissonance is not the student who has been raped but the student who has never been assaulted, who perhaps even denies that sexual assault is a problem in the university. In this way, the trigger warning offers the most protection to the student who is both safest and most fragile.

There are actually some benefits to cognitive dissonance. Assuming that the trigger warning ought to be used to prevent cognitive dissonance demonstrates a lack of awareness of the potential for cognitive dissonance to function as a catalyst for intellectual and emotional growth.

White Identity and Disintegration

Cognitive dissonance plays an integral role in the stage of white identity development that psychologist Janet Helms identifies as *Disintegration*. Disintegration, the "conscious, though conflicted, acknowledgment of one's whiteness,"[16] results after a White individual comes into contact with enough people of color to recognize the differences between their experiences and their own.

Psychologist and antiracist educator Beverly Daniel Tatum noted that for White students, learning about racism "presents a serious challenge to the notion of the United States as a just society where rewards are based solely on one's merit."[17] To alleviate the cognitive dissonance this causes, White students may attempt to explain away the new information by seeking out support for their beliefs in the meritocracy (adding consonant cognitions) or they may withdraw from any discussion of racism, inside or outside of the classroom (avoiding dissonant cognitions).

While many White people avoid or repair the dissonance experienced in this stage (such as in the ways Tatum identified) and get stuck in *Reintegration*, the stage wherein White individuals attempt to reassert their supremacy and privilege, other White people move through reintegration and begin to actively question the superiority society has led them to believe is innate to whiteness. This questioning helps White individuals understand their role in either the maintenance or dismantling of racism and white supremacy.

When the trigger warning is employed prior to a depiction or discussion of racism, it provides a cushion for White students that may prevent the experience of cognitive dissonance. Because this dissonance is a necessary part of developing an antiracist White identity, the avoidance of dissonance allows White students to maintain their comfort, even if that comfort is based upon a limited whitely perspective of American society. As a result, it can be argued that the trigger warning caters to white fragility.

White Fragility

Antiracist educator Robin DiAngelo defines *white fragility* as a "state in which even a minimum amount of racial stress becomes intolerable, triggering a range of defensive moves."[18] That DiAngelo employs the word *triggered* to characterize the mechanism of white fragility is intriguing, given the word's connections to the psychology of trauma. One might be inclined to wonder if the intolerability of white racial stress qualifies as trauma and, if so, how that trauma manifests itself during race talk.

Because they are not subjected to racism, White people are not accustomed to racial discomfort; their threshold, therefore, for discomfort during race talk is lower than that of their peers of color. As such, during classroom race talk, White students are often quick to upset and, because cultural communication norms value self-expression, White students often express that upset. The expression of white fragility serves to restore the equilibrium to which those of white racial habitus[19] are inured.

While these behaviors certainly speak to the disequilibrium and dissonance Whites experience when confronted with their own privilege, and while they may certainly be accompanied by feelings of fear and helplessness, conceiving of these psychic effects as traumatic minimizes the realities of racial trauma. That White individuals often position themselves as victims unfairly attacked or blamed for racism, very often in the absence of actual attacks or ascriptions of blame, reifies conceptions of racism as a problem only for the person who experiences it rather than as a systemic reality of American life.

It is important to note too that, while the defensive moves Whites tend to perform during race talk serve as attempts, either direct or implicit, to reinforce their own privilege and societal racial inequity, those moves generally are acceptable within classroom spaces and align with the discursive norms of academic protocol.

Table 4.1. Triggers and Reactions of White Fragility*

Trigger Type	Example of Trigger	Potential Defensive Reaction
Challenge to Racial Comfort	A person of color is not careful to protect a White individual's feelings during race talk	Leaving the room or staying but crying, expressing anger, or asserting that they are being attacked
Challenge to White Centrality	A movie (or book or course curriculum) features a person of color in a central role or features no White people in central roles	Suggesting this is an example of "reverse racism"
Challenge to Authority	A person of color in a leadership role, such as a teacher or professor	Challenging the person of color's authority, doubting their expertise, or accusing them of "having an agenda"
Challenge to White Solidarity	A White individual disagrees with another White individual's perspective	Accusing the other White person of self-hatred or "White guilt"
Challenge to Objectivity	The suggestion that a White individual's positionality and frames of reference influence and limit their perspectives	Minimizing and deflecting by making generalizations, such as "Everyone is influenced by their own positionality" or "It's impossible to be someone else"
Challenge to Meritocracy	The pointing out of unequal distribution of resources or access among racial groups	Invoking the "bootstraps" argument to justify their own or another's status or success
Challenge to Individualism	The suggestion that community and group identification matter and influence one's beliefs and perspectives	Repeatedly asserting one's individualism or distancing themselves from systemic racism by claiming they "don't see color" or "treat everyone the same"
Challenge to Codes of Behavior	Any direct discussion of racialized experiences, especially by people of color	Criticizing the tone or manner in which people of color express themselves and ignoring the content of their messages
Challenge to Colonialist Relations	Refusal by a person of color to share stories or answer questions about racism or their specific experiences	Claiming that they won't understand racism if no one explains it to them or that the person of color is being rude by refusing
Challenge to Racial Liberalism	Feedback that a White person's behavior had a racist impact	Minimizing the impact by making jokes or claiming that people of color are "too sensitive"

* This table draws upon and expands Robin DiAngelo's framework of white fragility.

Working with White Students' Racial *Il*literacy

Antiracist educators Glenn E. Singleton and Curtis Linton explain that engaging in what they call "courageous conversations" about race in education "requires making race personal."[20] For White students, whose racial *il*literacy is maintained by societal structures and the racial privilege they confer, making race personal is often accompanied by emotional and cognitive challenges and considerable discomfort.

During race talk, however, the emotion-driven discursive practices of *white fragility* that serve to maintain White students' personal comfort turn the curricular focus on White students' experiences and thereby perpetuate the marginalization of students of color in the classroom. That the subject matter may be *about* questions intrinsic to the experiences and identities of POCI makes this othering especially troublesome. Further, because those practices typically align with affective and discursive norms, they contribute to the maintenance rather than the disruption of the status quo. In doing so, they obscure the systemic realities of racism as they play out through classroom race talk.

In a racial literacy classroom, however, students are asked to move toward discomfort rather than avoid it, even if cognitive dissonance moves them to resist. Moving toward discomfort is, of course, uncomfortable—for everyone in the classroom. During heated race talk, even when White students *don't* try to back away from the conversation, they may make comments or share ideas that are ignorant, offensive, and, to the antiracist educator, incredibly frustrating. As a result, some educators may themselves shut down the conversation, unsure how to proceed.

It is important to remember that if whiteliness is seen as a disposition rather than an innate quality, White people are not rendered permanently ignorant by their inability to step into the shoes of people of color. They are not bound to continually perpetuate the oppression of people of color via their communicative and behavioral patterns. Instead, they can, by recognizing their own whiteliness and reflecting on their positionality, work to challenge their individual behaviors.

Late racial literacy educator Amy Winans suggested that, rather than solely serving to uphold the status quo, White students' emotions may actually open up possibilities for growth. Racial literacy as practiced in the classroom requires students to grapple with ethical questions as well as analytical ones. Because White people are the most racially segregated population in the United States, many White students who employ rhetorics of colorblindness, professing that they don't see race and that they treat everybody the same regardless of skin color, are actually attempting to "define themselves as good, moral people in an environment in which direct interaction with people of other races is limited."[21] As such, it is important that teachers take

White students' "ethical motivations seriously—along with the emotions that inform their ethical views and their efforts to express and develop those views—even if their conclusions about race and racism are erroneous."[22]

Too often, however, the burden of explaining why those conclusions are erroneous is placed on the POCI in the classroom. For POCI, this results in what might be called *emotional labor*, a term used to refer to the processes of managing the experience and display of emotions, particularly in public settings, where one must conform to situated behavioral expectations. The term has also been used to characterize the additional, invisible work automatically and unofficially assigned to some people and not others in both work and home settings. During classroom race talk, that work is often assigned to students of color, the same population from whom considerable emotional labor is already required in the classroom.

For students of color, racism is *already* personal. Racial literacy scholars and critical race theorists have established that, for POCI, awareness of race and racism is a sort of *specialized knowledge* developed from firsthand experience as well as immersion in communities of color and interaction with other POCI. From one perspective, it may appear that by creating classrooms that address race talk, educators can place this lived expertise and the students who hold it at the center of the curriculum. This attempt to demarginalize marginalized students can quickly become problematic if the discursive practices of the classroom *use* the knowledge of POCI rather than expanding POCI's knowledge base or helping to further all students' broader educational goals.

While there is enormous potential in race talk for racial literacy, self-reflection, critical empathy, and transformation, in many settings, race talk is an uphill battle for people of color and the emotional labor required must be acknowledged and mitigated as much as possible. Student-responsive, antiracist teachers must ensure that POCI are not doing the lion's share of that work toward inequitable ends, such as the emotional comfort or the intellectual benefit of their White classmates. Put simply: students of color do not come to school to teach their White peers about racism.

To ensure White students can work through their feelings and experiences as they begin to understand the systemic nature of race and racism without dominating classroom conversation or placing an undue burden on students of color, teachers should provide White students with individualized, opportunities to work *through* their emotional discomfort rather than avoid it.

Unfortunately, even if the initial goal of the trigger warning is not student avoidance or disengagement, in many cases its implementation allows for students to back away from materials in the curriculum that they consider to be potentially harmful. Given that the students likeliest to experience—and attempt to avoid—such discomfort are those who enter the classroom with limited trauma histories and considerable racial privilege, mitigating that discomfort caters to white fragility and prevents White students from psychological growth.

Student Agency

While the trigger warning protects White students, it may actually contribute to the ongoing racial trauma students of color experience.

The broad trigger warning used by Alana, the teacher in the anecdote with which this chapter opened, requires students to be direct and open with her; in many places, however, aspects of school culture, such as the emphasis on maintaining a positive attitude, dissuade students from sharing negative emotions. In other situations, students may not display their discomfort because their culturally situated communication styles do not encourage or include direct displays of emotion or dissent.

Despite the Western emphasis on rationality, because of the cultural emphasis on self-expression, members of individualistic cultures are actually *more* inclined toward verbalization and more likely to base their behaviors and speech upon their emotions than are those from collectivist cultures, who are likelier to stay silent to avoid hurting another's feelings.

For students to be direct and open with Alana, they must also feel they have agency in the classroom space. Even some individuals who feel entitled to their emotions and are comfortable sharing them outwardly may not feel comfortable demonstrating their discomfort or disagreement with an authority figure like their teacher. The students most likely to respond to Alana's warning are those who *already* feel comfortable demonstrating dissent, expressing their emotions, and enacting agency in the classroom; to meet these criteria, students must have experience with the Discourse of the classroom, a Discourse that is most readily available to White European Americans occupying middle- or upper-class socioeconomic strata.

SECONDARY STRATEGIES

Prevailing cultural norms have considerable influence in secondary schools, and, very often, politically motivated and externally determined policies rather than educational theories or best practices determine what happens in the classroom. Standardized, top-down educational practices often leave teachers feeling powerless and restricted; adding discussions of equitable discourse to their curricula may feel impossible because the workload is already heavy, the schedule is too tightly packed, and the standards are too rigid. In some cases, teachers who do engage critical pedagogies around discourse may feel hypocritical given the inequitable standards and modes of assessment they are nonetheless required to employ.

While challenging structural inequities involves strategic planning and collaboration, teachers can take steps to make their own curricula more inclusive where language and behavior are concerned. Multiple identities and modes of communication should be represented in course texts, assignments, and lesson plans. The language of assignments should be clear enough to inform students of the teacher's expectations and comprehensive enough to provide context and a rationale for those expectations.

Of equal if not greater importance is the way discourse is addressed in the classroom. As preteens and teenagers may not be comfortable enough with the concept of discourse to jump into metadiscourse, it can be beneficial to introduce lessons on discourse/Discourse gradually in middle and high school classrooms. If the school culture mandates or encourages the use of trigger warnings, teachers can in fact use those warnings to introduce discussions of Discourse in the classroom.

When employing a trigger warning before sharing a particular text with students, a teacher can explain what the trigger warning is and why it is in use then ask students what they think about it. Some students may suggest that the trigger warning serves no purpose; others may think the trigger warning is useful to prevent students from getting upset in class. Students can be asked to consider why one might want a trigger warning, what "getting upset" consists of, and why one thinks upset should be avoided in the classroom. This opens lines of inquiry about the feelings individuals might experience in school, how students are expected to speak and act in the school setting, and what values those expectations symbolize. Eventually, a teacher can invite students to begin to make connections to their own communication styles by asking them to reflect in writing about their ways of feeling, being, and talking.

QUESTIONS FOR SELF-REFLECTION ON COMMUNICATION STYLES

Note: All of these questions can be tailored to meet curricular goals and standards as well as the particular needs and interests of the students in your classroom.

1. Are there words or phrases that upset you when you hear them?
2. Why do those words bother you?
3. How do you react when you hear those words?
4. Do other people you know react similarly to those words?
5. Do other people you know react differently to the same words?
6. Do you show your reactions to other people? Why or why not?

7. Are there modes of communication that upset you? For example, does it bother you if someone raises their voice, interrupts you, ignores you, or corrects you?
8. Do your reactions to situations change when you're in different places or around different people?
9. Do you know anyone who expresses their emotions differently from the way you do?
10. In what ways do you think body language matters in a conversation?
11. Do you think there should be rules for having conversations with other people? If so, what do you think those rules should be?
12. Were you ever explicitly taught how to have a conversation with someone? If so, who taught you?
13. What happens when you have a conversation with someone whose communication style is different from yours?
14. What might happen if you were to get into an argument with someone whose reactions were very different from your own?

This is best framed as independent work, and teachers should explain before students write that their answers are private: because of the personal nature of these questions and the culturally situated communicative practices to which they refer, some students may not want to share their reflections with their peers or their teacher. Given that the questions are *about* one's approach to conversation, if a teacher were to invite discussion and allow those who wished not to share to opt out, the act of opting out could itself be an act of sharing!

Teachers who are concerned about spending time on an activity that does not directly connect to the existing lesson plan can revise the questions by drawing upon existing course material. If students are reading *The Great Gatsby*, an English teacher might tell them to jot down some notes on Gatsby's way of speaking or Nick Carraway's comments on Gatsby's speech and then ask them to compare and contrast Gatsby's language use with their own. Once students have explored similarities and differences between monarchy, democracy, republic, and dictatorship in a unit on government, a social studies teacher can ask them to consider which forms of government bear the most resemblance to the school structure or their family structures and what effects that form has on their relationships, behaviors, and language use.

Beginning with their own discursive and emotional practices can ease students into the discussion and establish relevance. This self-reflection can also be seen as part of Social and Emotional Learning (SEL), which, if implemented equitably, is especially useful during adolescence. (For more on the potential and limitations of SEL, see chapter 5.) By connecting SEL to language practices, students develop the capacities to hear and respond to a variety of situated expressions of emotion. Becoming familiar with diverse forms of expression prepares young students to engage in cross-cultural communication; this base of knowledge early on will be especially useful later on in college or in the workplace, once the subject matter and nature of communication become more complex.

COLLEGE CONSIDERATIONS

By the time they get to college, students generally are expected to demonstrate familiarity with the discourse of postsecondary education by adhering to its norms, though, with the exception of some first year experience and first year composition courses, there are very few places wherein students explicitly learn that discourse. In the rare case that such norms are taught to students, they are often done so via a *banking* model of pedagogy[23] that provides information but little context and few opportunities to hone those practices.

The variation in classroom policies and protocol across departments and among instructors makes it even more likely that students will find themselves entering a conversation for which they are unprepared or to which they are uncertain how to respond. These situations are likelier on campuses with large populations of first-generation college students, emergent bilinguals, and international students. To prevent race talk and other critical conversations from becoming sites of misunderstanding or incoherence rather than engagement, instructors working on campuses or in departments where the trigger warning is encouraged can use the trigger warning to ensure that classroom protocol is clear to and inclusive of the students in the classroom.

Placing a broad content note on the course syllabus, as did Alana, the teacher whose anecdote opened this chapter, is a more strategic approach than prefacing individual class sessions or course material with a specific note. The content note does not address the particular potential triggers contained in the materials to be discussed but rather states that the material may be difficult, require courageous conversations, or necessitate critical engagement.

While Alana's syllabus statement could have benefited from revision, when instituted properly the broad content note has many benefits. First of all, it establishes up front the nature and requirements of participation in the course. Students see that engagement with the material is expected and encouraged. In most departments, the first day of the semester is dedicated at least in part to syllabus review, so students seeing this content note will have the opportunity to ask questions or express concerns they might have about the course or its curriculum. In addition to enabling instructors to clarify any confusion or alleviate potential discomfort before it arises, this helps instructors identify possible challenges that may come up throughout the semester. (For more on designing a syllabus content note, see chapter 2.)

While the content note may be useful in establishing classroom expectations, instructors also need strategies to ensure that race talk is critical and productive when it occurs. If a statement is made in the classroom that overtly or unintentionally reifies racist ideologies, instructors can use the statement to initiate a discussion of the situatedness of language use and communication protocol.

To ensure that students, especially those who have been subjected to insults or microaggressions, are not silenced, it is important that students be given the opportunity to react to statements made in the classroom before the instructor jumps in. It is also imperative that the earlier conversation resume following the discussion of language so that students can work through the challenge that led to communicative discord in the first place.

For instance, if a heated conversation arises in Professor Katz's British history class, James, a White male student, may tell Carla, a Black female student, to "calm down." This raced and gendered microaggression diminishes the weight of Carla's individual emotional expression, pathologizes what may be a culturally situated communication style, and asserts the superiority of white male communicative norms.

James may not understand why that piece of language is insulting to Carla, let alone why it might be perceived as racist or sexist. Carla may react by pointing out to James that he has no right to tell her to calm down. If the situation is not resolved or if students seem upset at that point, Professor Katz may ask the class: "Why don't we talk about what happened in this conversation?"

Professor Katz can connect the conflict to the broader course material by talking about the differences between British and U.S. American communication styles or by inviting students to imagine how people might have spoken in the historical time period they are studying. The instructor's involvement may not be necessary: if there is a women's studies or composition and rhetoric major in Professor Katz's class, that student may be familiar enough with feminist rhetorical theory to explain to James why his statement was considered offensive.

Taking advantage of such teachable moments makes clear to students that, sometimes regardless of intentions, miscommunications and microaggressions do occur. Students need to understand how and why they happen in order to work to prevent them. In transformative learning, individuals may be triggered and discord may occur—but it is possible to encounter, acknowledge, and work through such situations without derailing the progress students have made in the classroom. Exploring these moments provides additional opportunities for students to examine, critique, and dismantle inequity.

CONCLUDING THOUGHTS

There are emotional and psychological consequences to acquiring a dominant Discourse, especially when that Discourse not only is composed of patterns of communication and behavior that conflict with an individual's socially and culturally situated discursive approaches but also perpetuates their home Discourse's marginalization. To honor students' identities and home Discourses, instructors must ensure their own language practices in the classroom are inclusive and equitable. Teachers must also engage students in a critical examination of the Discourse and discourses that prevail in American education: doing so simultaneously supports students' acquisition of the dominant Discourse practices necessary to succeed in academia and provides them the tools to dismantle its white cultural hegemony.

French philosopher Michel Foucault believed that, despite its connections to social and political hegemony, discourse itself had the power to shape society. Speaking of the concomitant prudishness and sexual emphasis of public discourse in Victorian era society, Foucault pointed out that it was not the discourse itself but the fact that considerations of sexuality dominated discourse that was so intriguing about Victorian society. Foucault's work on discourse also shows that the rules of a given discipline or discourse community eventually "became epistemological enforcers of what (as well as how) people thought, lived, and spoke."[24]

In other words, the discourse, which may be derived from beliefs and practices within a particular culture or society, itself eventually shapes those beliefs and practices. Within this framework, there is potential in discourse for resistance as well as oppression—but to dismantle inequitable policies and practices around communication, instructors must ensure that their own pedagogical practices do not inadvertently perpetuate the same inequities they otherwise seek to challenge.

Being calm and polite in response to a single instance of discrimination may address the immediate situation, but it does not take into the account the broader societal inequities that are perpetuated by such etiquette. Engaging in antiracism via conversation necessitates challenging the *ways* individuals are expected to converse, the inequity intrinsic to those discursive norms, and the potential harm inflicted by students by pedagogies that intentionally enforce or indirectly reify those norms.

NOTES

1. Michel Foucault, "The Discourse on Language," in *The Archaeology of Knowledge* (New York: Harper, 1972), 227.
2. Justin Grinage, "Reterritorializing Locations of Home: Examining the Psychopolitical Dimensions of Race Talk in the Classroom," *Journal of Curriculum Theorizing* 30, no. 2 (2014): 92.
3. See Taiyon J. Coleman, Renee DeLong, Kathleen Sheerin DeVore, Shannon Gibney, and Michael C. Kuhne, "The Risky Business of Engaging Racial Equity in Writing Instruction: A Tragedy in Five Acts," *Teaching English in the Two-Year College* 43, no. 4 (2016).
4. Mara Lee Grayson, "Want to Connect with Your Students? Be a Person," *Education Week: Classroom Q&A with Larry Ferlazzo*, October 20, 2018, http://blogs.edweek.org/teachers/classroom_qa_with_larry_ferlazzo/2018/10/response_dont_just_teach_the_curriculum_teach_the_students.html.
5. Frankie Condon, *I Hope I Join the Band: Narrative, Affiliation, and Antiracist Rhetoric* (Logan: Utah State University Press, 2012), 76.
6. See Dae-Joong Kim and Bobbi Olson, "Deconstructing Whiteliness in the Globalized Classroom," in *Performing Antiracist Pedagogy in Rhetoric, Writing, and Communication*, ed. Frankie Condon and Vershawn Ashanti Young (Fort Collins: WAC Clearinghouse, 2017).
7. bell hooks, *Teaching to Transgress: Education as the Practice of Freedom* (New York: Routledge, 1994), 35.
8. This type of homonym can also be called a capitonym.
9. James Paul Gee, "Literacy, Discourse, and Linguistics: Introduction," *Journal of Education* 171, no. 1 (1989): 8.
10. Sharon Crowley, *Composition in the University: Historical and Polemical Essays* (Pittsburgh: University of Pittsburgh Press, 1998).
11. See Laura Greenfield, "The 'Standard English' Fairy Tale: A Rhetorical Analysis of Racist Pedagogies and Commonplace Assumptions about Language Diversity," in *Writing Centers and the New Racism: A Call for Sustainable Dialogue and Change*, ed. Laura Greenfield and Karen Rowan (Logan: Utah State University Press, 2011). For more, see chapter 7. To emphasize the constructedness of SAE (Standard American English) and the linguistic hierarchies that contribute to its presumed existence, all versions of SAE are referred to as standardized for the remainder of this book.
12. Ruth Frankenberg, *The Social Construction of Whiteness: White Women, Race Matters* (Minneapolis: University of Minnesota Press, 1993), 1.
13. Joe C. Martin and Brandi N. Frisby, "Institution-wide Trigger Warnings: A Case Study of a University's 'Common Reading,'" in *Trigger Warnings: History, Theory, Context*, ed. Emily J. M. Knox (Lanham: Rowman & Littlefield, 2017), 155.
14. Eddie Harmon-Jones, "Cognitive Dissonance," in *Encyclopedia of the Mind*, ed. Harold E. Pashler (Los Angeles: Sage, 2013).
15. Martin and Frisby, "Institution-wide Trigger Warnings," 155.
16. Janet Helms, "Toward a Model of White Racial Identity Development," in *Black and White Racial Identity: Theory, Research, and Practice*, ed. Janet Helms (Westport: Praeger, 1990), 58.
17. Beverly Daniel Tatum, "Talking about Race, Learning about Racism: The Application of Racial Identity Development Theory in the Classroom," *Harvard Educational Review* 62, no. 1 (1992): 6.
18. Robin DiAngelo, "White Fragility," *International Journal of Critical Pedagogy* 3, no. 3 (2011): 54.
19. For more on the concept of habitus, see Pierre Bourdieu, *The Field of Cultural Production* (New York: Columbia University Press, 1994).
20. Glenn E. Singleton and Curtis Linton, *Courageous Conversations about Race: A Field Guide for Achieving Equity in Schools* (Thousand Oaks: Corwin, 2006), 75.
21. Amy Winans, "Cultivating Racial Literacy in White, Segregated Settings: Emotions as Site of Ethical Engagement and Inquiry," *Curriculum Inquiry* 40, no. 3 (2010): 478.
22. Ibid.

23. Paulo Freire, *Pedagogy of the Oppressed*, trans. Myra Bergman Ramos (New York: Continuum, 2005), 72. For more, see chapter 6.

24. Edward Said, "Michel Foucault 1926–1984," in *After Foucault: Humanistic Knowledge, Postmodern Challenges*, ed. Jonathan Arac (New Brunswick: Rutgers University Press, 1988), 10.

Chapter Five

Coping in the Classroom

Emotions and Education

> Emotion is taught and learned at home and in school. It is an important, deeply embedded, site of social control.—Jennifer Siebel Trainor[1]

The call for trigger warnings is built upon a foundation of three related observations about education: (1) students experience trauma; (2) emotion plays a significant role in learning and schooling; and (3) pedagogical practices have emotional consequences. In light of these observations, as well as the inequities surrounding the conceptualization and implementation of the trigger warning, it is necessary to identify alternative strategies for acknowledging and attending to students' emotional histories and the role of emotional and experiential learning in the classroom. Whether or not it is acknowledged directly, emotion is an integral part of both schooling (as a system) and learning (as a process).

EMOTION SOCIALIZATION

Though emotion is generally theorized as personal, private, and idiosyncratic, it is actually deeply contextual and socially and culturally situated. In fact, the notion of emotion as individual rather than social or collective is the result of Western ideological frameworks.

Broadly, socialization is the "process of learning one's culture and how to live within it."[2] *Emotion socialization*, one aspect thereof, refers to the conditioning by which the environment shapes one's experiences with and understanding of emotions, as well as how one expresses and regulates those emotions. Though "infants enter the world expressing emotions that contribute to their own socialization,"[3] emotion socialization begins when children learn from their parents, guardians, or others in their immediate community which feelings and displays of emotion are acceptable for them and for others—and which are inappropriate.

Some factors that contribute to emotion socialization are direct, such as parents' emotional expressions to children, their reactions to children's emotions, and what they explicitly tell children about emotions. Indirect influences include parents' emotional expressions during other interactions and the global family climate. Children whose parents acknowledge their emotions and teach them strategies for emotional regulation demonstrate fewer emotional and behavioral problems in social settings than children whose emotional expressions are minimized or result in punishment. These socialization processes are contextual: children learn which emotions to express (and how) and which to suppress based upon particular cultural norms and social constructs. That said, "most research on emotion socialization focuses on two-parent, middle- and upper-middle class, low-risk samples with little ethnic diversity and mainly from Western cultures."[4]

Once children enter school, educational institutions are a primary and continuing sites of that socialization process—and the students who struggle most to meet the emotional expectations of the campus and the classroom are those whose cultural backgrounds differ from the dominant white norms of the classroom. For students to succeed in the classroom environment, this conflict is negotiated through socialization into the dominant culture as students learn both to confirm to its expectations and to see themselves as others see them. In this way, "the developing racial self reaches to one's emotional foundation."[5] Black men, for example, may learn as boys to "live lives of limited, restricted, controlled affect and expression" in efforts to prevent being seen as violent or aggressive.[6]

Emotion itself is a challenging concept to unpack, in part because it is tangled up in psychiatric discourse, which professes objectivity yet historically has pathologized experiences and ideas that deviate from White, Western, heterosexual, patriarchal conceptions of the brain and body. Even those critical pedagogues whose work challenges the dominant Discourse of the classroom tend to work within normative, ableist notions of emotion.

Disability rhetorics scholar Margaret Price identifies three patterns in pedagogical scholarship about emotion: the presumption of a "normal" subject by drawing a line, "either tacitly or explicitly, between the 'normal' and the 'pathological'";[7] the disclaiming of psychological expertise by explaining one's role as a teacher or scholar rather than therapist; and the othering of neuro-atypical and mentally disabled students. These habits "treat emotionality and intellectuality as adversaries,"[8] promulgate a deficit perspective of mental disability, and further normative notions about the role of emotion in education.

Emotion as the Curriculum

Social and Emotional Learning (SEL) is a framework common in American education and which has been integrated into curricula from kindergarten through high school. Originating in the 1990s, SEL is often used today as an umbrella term for school-based programs that aim to enhance emotional awareness and interpersonal skills. These programs draw from a variety of disciplinary perspectives, including psychology, public health, juvenile justice, and social work.

While SEL encompasses a wide range of emphases and programmatic approaches, SEL generally encourages five competencies: *self-awareness*, the recognition of one's own emotions, behaviors, strengths, and areas for growth; *self-management*, the ability to effectively regulate one's emotions, thoughts, and behaviors in a variety of situations; *social awareness*, the identification and acknowledgment of others' emotional and experiential realities; *relationship skills* like communicating effectively, negotiating conflict, and seeking help as needed; and *responsible decision making* about personal behavior that takes into account available options and potential consequences and aligns with one's beliefs and goals as well as social norms.

Despite claims that SEL leads to increases in students' emotional wellbeing and academic performance, a fair amount of research has shown substantial flaws in the design and implementation of SEL. The most notable of the limitations of SEL is that it relies upon a "universalist bias" based upon the "kinds of regulatory or expressive responses (such as talk) shared by the White, American middle class."[9] Because emotions are socially and culturally situated, students of different cultural backgrounds are likely to have different experiences with any understandings of emotion as well as varying comfort levels regarding the sharing or talking about emotion, especially among large, diverse groups, such as in the classroom.

Moreover, because SEL programs generally emphasize *recognizing* and *regulating* emotion rather than *experiencing* or *working with* emotion, curricula become codified into specific in-class activities and classroom structures and efficacy is assessed by surface-level measurables. As a result, many programs fail to attend to the various internal experiences of students, and, as a result, the complexities of their individual processes of emotional development.

When translated to specific classroom practices, "the language of caring often devolves to a discourse about control, rules, contracts, choices, activities, and organizational structures."[10] Without comprehensive attention to cultural relevancy, SEL may do little more than perpetuate the acculturation of a diverse student body into the dominant White Discourse of the U.S. education system.

Emotion as the Hidden Curriculum

Similar to Catherine Prendergast's labeling of race as an absent presence in the field of composition studies, philosopher and cultural studies scholar Megan Boler has called emotion an absent presence in theories of cognition, subjectivity, and epistemology: "Emotion—best kept silent—is nonetheless required as a foundational presence, the crucial counterbalance and reflective mirror-opposite to reason's superiority."[11]

In the false binary perpetuated by Western ideology and education, emotion and reason are not merely separate but diametrically opposed. In such a binary understanding, reason connotes intelligence, sanity, and progress. It is appropriate within the public sphere and is associated with men, who have historically occupied public life. Emotion suggests hysteria,[12] weakness, and primitivism. It is reserved for private spaces and is associated with women, the traditional caregivers and keepers of those spaces.

Just as language use is a way of ordering and making sense of information, emotions can be seen as *structures of feeling* by which worldviews held by social groups operate in the individual consciousness: the structure of feeling is "a social experience which is still in process, often indeed not yet recognized as social but taken to be private, idiosyncratic, and even isolating."[13] In other words, people see their emotions as individual when in fact they have been and continue to be constructed by the social, cultural, and political values and norms of the society of which that individual is a part.

Much of the work of upholding those norms happens in school via a hidden curriculum that teaches ideologies of feeling and rules of emotional conduct even in the absence of explicit emotional learning. Some less hidden parts of this hidden curriculum emerge via the regulation of students' expressions of emotion: Students who raise their voices, for example, are likelier to be reprimanded than heard or counseled, and the likelihood of being disciplined is far higher for students who are POCI.

Even in early education, students who cry are advised to buck up, cheer up, be less sensitive. In many cases, however, teachers and other authority figures don't have to say anything at all, for students' emotional expressions are regulated by the affective norms of their school communities. In schools that emphasize positivity and self-efficacy, students learn, without being told, that so-called negative emotions (like anger, sadness, and other forms of upset) have no place in education. Sensitivity becomes *other*, and students temper their emotional expressions to fit what they have now learned is the accepted norm; and now knowing that their own affective experiences are inappropriate or, worse, pathological, they begin, consciously or unconsciously, to dampen those feelings.

There are, of course, raced and gendered components of this process: sensitivity is gendered female and viewed as a marker of weakness because of that association. Accusations of "too sensitive" are also frequently hurled toward POCI who call out racial microaggressions and societal inequities. Socializing students to smile, be polite, and avoid conflict also socializes them to tolerate inequity, for calling out inequity is seen as complaining—or not working hard enough to overcome obstacles. The emphasis on positivity perpetuates the myth of meritocracy, the false belief that if people work hard enough, they will get what they deserve. This myth serves to separate individual experiences from the social contexts in which they occur and further obscures the inequitable social structures that contribute to individual experiences, successes, and challenges.

Another, more insidious, enforcer of Western ideology in the hidden curriculum is also the most hidden, as it is part of the foundation upon which Western education is built: objectivity. Objectivity, the reliance upon observable facts and the rules of logic for the acquisition of knowledge, assumes that logic and truth are static and universal, rather than dynamic and socially and culturally situated.

In schools, history is presented as a dispassionate record of what happened rather than a version of events told from the very particular perspective of the victor. And how often are students in high school writing classes warned to use unbiased language or to avoid using the pronoun "I" in order to sound more objective? Framing objectivity as a goal—or even assuming it is possible—teaches a worldview in which subjectivity is viewed as the antithesis of reason and therefore is relegated to the private realm. That the concept of objectivity was not intrinsic to the ancient philosophical and traditions that undergird Western notions of reason and argumentation, but rather may have originated with seventeenth-century Cartesian rationality, makes this "hyper-valuation" of objectivity even more absurd.[14]

When students learn not to show emotion or subjectivity or to behave in ways that downplay the role of feeling and experience in learning, knowing, and communicating, they are being socialized into a culturally accepted approach to the expression of emotion. After all, *not* showing emotion is as socially and culturally situated an emotional response as any overt emotional display.

At the same time, they are also being acculturated into a worldview that shapes and is reinforced by such approaches to feeling (and which either explicitly or subtly renders other approaches to emotion inappropriate). These ideologies *appear* natural, normal, and ordinary. They *appear* this way because they are deeply embedded in the social structures that undergird the cultural hegemony of the United States. They are so deeply embedded that often they become internalized and are assumed to be universal, which serves to minimize recognition and criticism of how those ideologies affect the lives of marginalized people.

System justification theory holds that "individuals are motivated to justify and rationalize existing social arrangements, defending and bolstering the status quo simply because it exists."[15] If one's experiences and interpersonal relationships exist within a particular social system, so too does one's psychological self-concept. To prevent the dissonance that may occur from the acknowledgment of the inequities within or the potential harm done by the social system, even individuals who are marginalized within a society may come to believe that the society works and that it is the individual, the self, who is inferior. This internalization works on both cognitive and affective registers.

As legal scholar and critical race theorist Lani Guinier explains, the work of racial literacy "is to make legible racism's ever-shifting yet ever-present structure."[16] It is necessary to call out the ways in which these false binaries uphold the White cultural hegemony that dominates all aspects of society in the United States, including the school system and the theories of knowledge it promulgates.

Emotion and reason are *not* oppositional: empirical observations and rational arguments are filtered through the senses and ideas about what is important or noteworthy (and what is not); judgments deemed objective are influenced by individual perception and social situatedness; and beliefs and affectivity factor heavily into interpretation and decision-making.

Emotion as an Integral Part of Learning

Feelings can have strong supportive or detractive effects on individuals' thinking, perceptions, recall, and academic performance, but it is not always the case that positive emotions lead to positive academic outcomes and vice versa. The matter, like most processes that involve multiple systems (biological, societal, and cultural, among others), is far more complex. In fact, even unpleasant emotions may have beneficial or unfavorable effects on an individual's academic performance. Recent research shows that "mild and acute stress facilitates learning and cognitive performance, while excess and chronic stress impairs learning and is detrimental to memory performance."[17]

Determinations of mild versus excessive, of course, vary depending upon the individual as well as the type of stress. Students who report learned-focused confusion prior to an exam are likely to perform better on that exam than on an exam that does not cause that negative emotional state, arguably because of their compensatory increase in focus on the task.[18] It seems, too, that some students actually thrive on learning-focused anxiety for this reason. Consider, for example, the student who, whenever she is assigned a paper, procrastinates for weeks then pulls an all-nighter before the morning the paper is due yet still receives a high grade.

When the anxiety is unrelated to the learning situation, however, the effects are less predictable—and often less positive. A student who suffers from a public speaking phobia may experience intense anxiety if assigned to give an in-class presentation. In some cases, students will cope with this anxiety by trying to avoid the situation by requesting an alternate assignment. If that isn't a possibility and the student is forced to stand in front of the class, the intensity of his anxiety and the complex nature of phobias may cause him to panic and either run or freeze. Some students in this situation will simply skip the assignment, resigning themselves to taking a hit on the grade.

Psychologists believe that emotion plays an important role in memory formation and recall and, typically, situations that are emotionally charged lead to longer-lasting memories. Emotions serve an important evolutionary function: fear alerts human beings of potential danger, which allows for adaptive behaviors to either avoid or manage the dangerous situation. This view of emotion, however, assumes a universal, normative psychological state that does not necessarily apply to all individuals. For persons whose mental disabilities involve chronic stress and anxiety, such as in PTSD and Generalized Anxiety Disorder, overactivity of the nervous system may actually lead to decreases in *neuroplasticity*, the brain's ability to form new synaptic connections, which, as a result, may impair learning.

Even if emotions are not placed at the forefront of the curriculum, the potential academic effects of psychological stress make a strong case for all educators to consider how their classrooms recognize and respond to the emotional needs of students, including in cases of trauma.

THE TRIGGER WARNING AS A RESPONSE TO TRAUMA

Theoretically, the trigger warning is not wholly without benefit. For students who do have histories of trauma, the trigger warning—theoretically—provides information and a moment to pause; theoretically, in that moment students can engage in thoughtful consideration of the benefits and drawbacks of partaking of the potentially triggering material. This makes sense—again, theoretically—but the efficacy has not been established. In fact, more research supports the case against its effectiveness, at least as a step toward the resolution of trauma. Because the trigger warning allows for students to *disengage* rather than engage thoughtfully, within the context of PTSD, the trigger warning can be perceived as perpetuating a strategic avoidance coping mechanism.

Avoidance Coping

Individuals with PTSD (as well as individuals without PTSD) commonly use *avoidance coping* as a way to reduce one's emotional arousal to a particular stressor and build personal capabilities to manage that stressor. Avoidance coping is an umbrella term that encompasses many strategies, including "seeking out other people as a social diversion, engaging in another task as a distraction, denial, repression, and suppression."[19] Avoidance coping requires an individual to engage cognitively in an appraisal of the potential stressor: she must first determine whether the stressor poses a threat and, if so, the extent to which that stressor threatens her own well-being; she must then determine how to prevent or manage the potential harm.

While avoidance coping typically refers to external stressors, *experiential avoidance* refers to one's attempts to avoid internal processes such as thoughts, feelings, and somatic sensations following trauma. The trauma survivor, in efforts to maintain a sense of control over their experiences and environment, may avoid experiences that have nothing to do with the trauma experienced. One may even restrict expressions of happiness—or avoid feeling positive emotions at all—for fear of losing control. Combat veterans with PTSD, for example, often set goals for themselves that include controlling or avoiding their own emotions.[20]

These attempts, however, do not translate to greater well-being. Theories of post-trauma processing maintain that individuals must integrate information related to the trauma into a model of the self, which often requires "some variant of exposure to aversive thoughts, emotions, and images related to the trauma."[21] To achieve that integration, typically one must engage in direct confrontation with the source of distress.

Attempts to regulate one's emotions via experiential avoidance, however, often lead the trauma survivor to behave in ways that are incongruent with one's own values and beliefs: Someone who has always had a deep connection with family, for example, may begin to isolate following the death of a loved one, while an avid runner may avoid running outside after being attacked in a public place. These avoidance behaviors actually "limit one's personal growth opportunities and diminish well-being"—and contribute to the maintenance rather than the resolution of phobias and trauma-based stress disorders.[22]

Trauma, Resolution, and Normativity

Though psychological research into the effects (or lack thereof) of the trigger warning emphasize its limitations as a resolution to trauma, very few educators who use the warnings have suggested that they are designed to *resolve* trauma. The focus of such research, therefore, exposes the limitations of psychological perspectives on trauma-informed pedagogies. In fact, an emphasis on the trigger warning as a resolution to trauma may reinforce notions that trauma and the psychological states it creates are extraordinary, problematic, and pathological.

When a student's mental state or disability is treated as something broken that must be fixed, educators and school systems more broadly frame the student as the problem rather than the classroom. In other words, marginalizing the experience of trauma allows educators to maintain the normativity of the classroom rather than adapting their teaching to include all students, including those with trauma histories and disabilities.

A parallel can be drawn here to other forms of othering in education, such as the racialization of the achievement gap. Though the achievement gap between White students and non-Asian students of color is well documented and grounded in myriad approaches to research, the rhetorical framing of that gap and the solutions posited promulgates a view of Black, Latinx, and Native American students as culturally deficient. The emphasis on the failure rates of students of color deemphasizes the failure of schools to address the needs of a racially and ethnically diverse student population. Responsibility, then, is shifted from the schools charged with educating the populace to the students (and their families or communities) for what they do or don't bring to the classroom.

Just as educators who advocate for culturally relevant teaching contend that it challenges such a deficit model of instruction, some educators who use trigger warnings suggest that the practice normalizes trauma, thereby destabilizing the intrinsic ableism of the classroom. Given that the trigger warning may simultaneously, if inadvertently, perpetuate the dominant White Discourse of the classroom, it becomes necessary to ask: How critical, then, is this critical pedagogy? And how can educators honor students' feelings and experiences without perpetuating the existing inequities of the classroom?

STUDENT-RESPONSIVE EMOTIONAL EDUCATION

Equitable, trauma-informed education necessitates consistent, broadscale pedagogical shifts that both challenge normative notions of academic discourse and emotive expression and attend to the ways students' internal lives, whether or not they are invited, enter the classroom.

Honor Student Experience

One of the foremost—and seemingly simplest—ways of attending to students' emotional histories is to shift the curricular focus to the students as experiencers and creators. Even in the classrooms of student-responsive educators, the focus is typically on the subject of learning rather than on the learners. This is often a practical matter more than a pedagogical one, especially on the upper secondary and college levels, where there is more curricular material to cover than in lower grades and less time to cover it.

Additional pressures like the need to prepare students for standardized tests and departmental scrutiny of instructors' passage and failure rates serve as frequent reminders to educators that they are there to teach the material and ensure students' timely progress toward graduation (rather than, say, their emotional welfare). Given these educational emphases, shifting the pedagogical focus to student experience may demand an ideological shift on the part of the instructor. This seemingly simple approach may not be so simple after all.

In what Paulo Freire described as the *banking concept* of education, teaching "becomes an act of depositing, in which the students are the depositories and the teacher is the depositor. Instead of communicating, the teacher issues communiques and makes deposits which the students patiently receive, memorize, and repeat."[23] This limited approach positions students as empty receptacles, teachers as lecturers, learning as memorization, and teaching as providing information.

The banking model represents not only a misunderstanding of the processes of learning but also an ideology of oppression, for while the teacher is conceived of as knowledgeable and powerful, an "absolute ignorance"[24] is projected onto the student. These educational power dynamics, of course, mirror the power dynamics of the society as a whole. Rather than experiencing true learning, students subjected to the banking model are indoctrinated into a power system that dehumanizes them.

While few contemporary educators would praise the banking model, much educational praxis does in fact frame curricular concepts, which are often already "alien to the existential experience of the students" as "detached from reality, disconnected from the totality that engendered them and could give them significance."[25] For example, college-level writing placement exams (which, in many schools, determine which composition course[s] students will take or from which they will be exempt) have been shown to be biased toward White, middle-class students not only because assessment of these exams places heavy weight on students' adherence to conventions of the standardized academic dialect spoken by the White, educated middle-class, but also because the topics students are typically asked to write about presume a knowledge base and cultural literacy accessible to a select few students of racial and economic privilege.

On such an exam, students may be asked to analyze and state whether they agree or disagree with a proposal to allow cell phone usage on airplanes. Because students who have experience with air travel can draw from memory and observation, they are better positioned to respond to this topic than are students who have never set foot on an airplane; for the latter students, the assignment requires greater levels of abstraction because they have less prior knowledge to build upon and must therefore theorize more.[26] If the exam prompt requires students to use concrete examples to develop their arguments, students who lack this experience are facing a considerably more difficult task. In fact, students who have never been warned that cell phone use could interfere with an airplane's navigational technology may not even understand the question posed to them!

Because readers of these exams might conclude, erroneously, that such students have problems with writing or reading comprehension, these students are likely to receive lower grades than their more privileged peers and, as a result, might be placed in a lower-level course. Asking students instead to respond to a question about commuting or transportation more broadly will allow those who lack the means or opportunity to travel by plane to draw upon their own experiences with trains, buses, cars, or bicycles, all of which are more readily accessible to a larger population.

This example may have broader, longer-lasting consequences than most, but students experience this sort of cultural irrelevancy regularly in the classroom. When the material students learn has no bearing on their lives—when their lives can have no bearing on the material—education becomes static or, worse, regressive.

To teach equitably, educators must honor the experiences students (both as a group and as individuals) bring to the classroom. Exploring "the interconnections between lived experience and theory" helps students "understand that what we talk about in the classroom is not separate from our everyday lives."[27] In this way, students begin to see their experiences matter in the classroom and that they are contributing to the intellectual environment as well as taking from it.

While in an ideal world students would possess the confidence and comfort in the classroom to, without encouragement, acknowledge and appreciate their own experiences as valid contributions to academic discourse, too often the voices and stories of students from marginalized populations are *other*ed even in the classroom. Comprehensively incorporating students' lived experiences in the classroom serves to both validate students' lived experiences, which is of particular importance for students whose voices and experiences have been marginalized, and to help students see knowledge as coconstructed rather than disseminated.

Pedagogical approaches to honoring student experience will differ depending upon the subject of the course, the educational level of the students, and other contextual factors, such as the campus community, the interests of the students, and the resources available, just to name a few. Textbox 5.1 includes a small sampling of the myriad opportunities available for including student experience in the classroom.

SOME STRATEGIES FOR INCORPORATING STUDENT EXPERIENCE

Assign a personal narrative.

A personal narrative can be a useful tool for encouraging students to make connections between the classroom and their lives outside of it. Personal narratives are also very useful for you as the teacher: they provide insight into who your students are as individuals and how they make sense of course material. (If the idea of a personal narrative seems like it doesn't fit the class you're teaching or your disciplinary expertise, it might help to know that many schools are moving toward a *vertical curriculum* of writing. This means that, even if writing is taught initially and primarily by the composition teacher, writing instruction continues throughout one's education and across the curriculum as students learn new approaches to and ways of thinking about writing in different disciplinary contexts.) Consider asking students to reflect in writing upon the following questions (or come up with some of your own):

- What do you already know about [topic]?
- What do you want to know about [topic]?
- When was the first time you experienced/felt/saw/heard/learned about [topic (e.g., racism/the American Revolution/a movie/classical music/capitalism/Aristotle)]?
- In what ways have you applied your knowledge of or experience with [topic] in your life? If you haven't, in what ways can you imagine applying this knowledge or experience?
- What associations do you make with [topic]? What does it make you think of, remember, or wonder about?

Don't **assign a personal narrative.**

Despite the benefits of writing across the curriculum, the personal narrative isn't always the most relevant genre, nor is the personal narrative necessarily the best way to encourage students to make connections between their lives and class material. In some cases, the assignment just doesn't fit the class or there isn't enough time in the semester. In those cases, it might be better to do a think-pair-share around the same questions (see below). There are other problems with the personal narrative as well: the assignment assumes that students are able to make connections between the class and their out-of-school lives and that they are willing and emotionally prepared to share those connections. *Honoring student experience also means understanding that students' stories are not always ready to be shared in the classroom.*

Think-pair-share to make real-world connections.

The think-pair-share works when you don't have time for the personal narrative or when you'd like to emphasize dialogue, pattern-finding, and problem-solving over self-reflection. In some cases, this activity works well at the beginning of the semester or school year because it helps students get to know one another. In other cases, particularly when the material is very complex or emotionally intense, it might be better to take some time to work up to this activity. The following are the basic steps of the process:

1. Ask students to consider the same questions as in the personal narrative during quiet, in-class writing. Tell students that they will be sharing these so they should exclude anything they aren't comfortable telling you or their classmates.
2. Pair students up (or have them find their own partners) to note the similarities and differences in their responses. What might account for those patterns or outliers?
3. *Optional but recommended, especially in large classes:* Pair up the pairs. Ask two pairs of students to come together to form a small group then proceed as in Step 2.
4. Ask pairs (or groups) to share the primary patterns they noticed with the class.

Encourage hands-on research.

While some disciplines emphasize quantitative research and controlled scientific experimentation, hands-on qualitative methods help researchers explore the experiential, human aspects of a concept or phenomenon. Inviting students to take on the role of researcher both introduces them to relevant research methods relevant to your discipline and helps them become active participants in connecting their experiences to the classroom. Students can try the following research-based activities:

- Interview someone who has experienced firsthand or who is an expert on the material of study.
- Create an anonymous survey to ask others about their experience with the material.

- Conduct field research by visiting a site that is relevant to the material and documenting (via jottings, photos, or video) what they observe.

It is important to remember that these cannot be surface-level approaches. In other words, if an instructor talks about the value of lived experience on Tuesday then gives an exam on Friday that presents the material as divorced from its humanistic dimensions, perhaps by requiring students to provide dates and facts devoid of context, students will see the falsity in the move and lose trust in the instructor. Educators should take care not to rush the creation of new curricula (or new approaches to existing curricula) and should check in with students along the way to see what connections they are making. Context is also important, and the classroom should not perpetuate the myth that the individual story can be understood universally.

When inviting students to use their experiences to make meaning of course material, it is important to acknowledge the limitations of individual experience, especially given the ways in which individual experiences are shaped by sociocultural contexts and positionalities. Experiences with trauma, in particular, vary depending upon the individual person and the external contexts, and students should not assume that what is true for them or one of their classmates is necessarily true for another. To explore their own situated emotional experiences, students need to develop capacities for thoughtful self-reflection, mindfulness, and somatic awareness.

Support Body-Mind Connections

Developing lesson plans that help students consider their embodied experiences in the classroom can be a useful way of encouraging awareness of the connections between emotions, ideas, and physiological reactions. Generally speaking, being *mindful* means paying attention to the present moment. Mindfulness practices can "slow down the cognitive thought process so that the individual is more open and able to learn new ways of perceiving, sensing, and feeling."[28] *Somatic awareness* involves listening to one's own body and affective responses to contextual stimuli. Because emotional and psychological challenges, especially traumatic experiences, often lead individuals to dissociate or disengage, somatic awareness and mindfulness-based activities can help people become more present in their bodies and in the moment.

Mindfulness has become a buzzword of sorts in recent years and, due to its origins in Eastern philosophies, it is often associated with the dedicated yogi or the transcendental meditator. Mindfulness, like somatic awareness, can also be an everyday practice. If a teacher while at dinner with her family begins to worry about her lesson plans for the next day, the practice of mindfulness might be as simple—or as difficult—as pausing during the worry-filled train of thought, noticing that the worried thoughts are there, and redirecting the mind back to the task at hand. The mindfulness is in nonjudgmentally noticing the movement of the mind and intentionally drawing it back to the present.

If after dinner that same teacher gets into a discussion with her spouse that seems to be turning into an argument, she can practice somatic awareness by noticing that her heart is racing and her muscles feel tense and acknowledging that she is angry. This awareness might encourage her to practice deep breathing before continuing the conversation.

In the classroom, mindfulness and somatic awareness practices can help students identify the bodily sensations of psychological discomfort, reengage in class activities, and explore the roots of those sensations. These practices can also provide an entry into important discussions about the differences between discomfort and trauma.

One of the problems of the trigger warning is that it allows students to withdraw from material that causes discomfort (yet does not re-traumatize); to prevent this from happening in the classroom, students must understand cognitively and somatically what might lead them to withdraw. By paying attention to their bodies during difficult moments—such as when reading a poem about sexual assault or during a heated discussion of racial inequity—students begin to recognize how their bodily responses to curricular material can inform them about their emotional reactions, especially those they don't immediately recognize. This can help students differentiate between the physiological warning signs of an oncoming panic attack and the discomfort of cognitive dissonance or frustration.

It is important to note that mindfulness and somatic awareness practices can be exceptionally difficult for students with trauma histories and anxiety disorders as well as for those with physical and mental disabilities. To ensure mindfulness activities are being taught in ways that are equitable and student-sensitive, activities should be customizable and brief.

No activity fits all students the same way; paying attention to one's breath can be relaxing for some and can cause anxiety for others. Teachers can offer options, such as assigning a sensory meditation that invites students to use any of the five senses. The goals of the activity remain the same whether the focus is on a sound, smell, sight, taste, or sensation. Even for students for whom these activities initially provoke little to no anxiety, spending too long on one practice can be counterintuitive. In many cases, leading students through two minutes of guided imagery will be more beneficial than asking them to sit for eighteen minutes in silent meditation.

One mindfulness-based therapeutic approach, *observe-describe-participate*, may be especially useful in the classroom due to the connections that can be made to classroom material and across curricula. Here's a description of the technique:

OBSERVE, DESCRIBE, PARTICIPATE

Step 1: Observe

Step back from the situation and notice what is happening, internally and externally. Watch without engaging or evaluating.

- What physical sensations do you notice?
- What is happening in the world outside of your body?
- What do you see, smell, hear, taste, and feel?
- If there are people around you, what are they doing?

Step 2: Describe

Provide words for what you are seeing and feeling. Use labels to identify sensations and emotions. Separate thoughts, emotions, and bodily states. Imagine you are the narrator of this story.

- What feelings are you having? If you feel fear, what do you fear? If you feel sad, what makes you sad?
- What thoughts are you having? If your mind is racing, where is it going? Is it in this present moment?
- What do you know in this very moment?
- If people are talking, who are they? Name them. If they are talking, what are they saying?

> "I feel a knot in my stomach. I'm very warm. I'm anxious about giving this presentation. Anxiety is just a feeling. I keep thinking that if I mess up this presentation, I'll get fired. It's just a thought. No one has threatened to fire me. I'm doing a good job. Jamie and Evan look relaxed. Jamie messed up a presentation last year and she didn't get fired. My coworkers are waiting for me to present. I am going to present."

Step 3: Participate

Begin to engage with the situation. Stay in the moment.

- Keep the mind focused on the situation at hand.
- If people talk to you, reply.
- If it helps, return to Steps 1 and 2 as needed.

Rather than being an end to itself (though its benefits for students with anxiety, stress, and dissociative behaviors are many), this practice can be a starting point for curricular activities in a variety of classroom settings.

- In a ninth-grade earth science class, a teacher can teach students the technique in class then for homework assign students to observe a local geological phenomenon like a rock formation and describe it in writing. In the next class, students can engage in a think-pair-share about the ways they participate in the development or management of geological phenomena.
- In a college sociology seminar, the technique can be used to teach some basic steps of ethnographic research (the study of culture), including participant observation (the method of both taking part in and studying a group or subculture to which one has insider access) and thick description (the detailed field notes, researcher memos, and qualitative depiction of data written by ethnographic researchers).

The extent and character of emphasis on bodily states and the mind-body connection vary across cultures and are demonstrated in multiple disciplinary contexts. In Chinese, Japanese, and West African languages, terms used to describe emotions derive from terms that describe the body and bodily sensations. Chinese Americans have been shown to use more somatic words to describe childhood memories and interpersonal relationships than European Americans.[29] Medically, people from non-Western cultures, particularly those with medical traditions wherein the body and mind are closely intertwined, tend toward somatization of psychological distress, reporting more bodily symptoms than emotional symptoms, whereas Europeans and European Americans demonstrate a greater tendency to report psychological symptoms.

This is especially significant given that SEL, taught uncritically, may uphold rather than challenge the normative White discourse of the classroom. When developing curricula that explore the mind-body connection, instructors should make space for individualization and student contributions. Assignments like the literacy narrative or the racial autobiography[30] or even a more research-based ethnographic inquiry can be tailored to SEL by asking students to describe how they or people in their cultures or communities tend to express emotion or examine how affective, psychological, and bodily states are represented in their home languages or dialects. Such inclusive mindfulness and somatic awareness practices and discussion thereof can open up spaces for complex cross-cultural learning in the classroom. Further, these narrative assignments can provide teachers with important insights into students' backgrounds and behaviors.

Interpret Behavior as Communication

Michaela, a composition professor, was teaching an upper-division writing class on a campus undergoing construction. Classrooms were limited during renovations, and noise from machinery was near constant. The class met twice a week in a short, wide classroom with thirty students. Desks stretched in three rows between the window and the door and, to address all students while teaching, Michaela had to walk side to side in front of the whiteboard.

At least one day each week, one of her best students, Sheryl, a graduating senior planning to go to law school in the fall, expressed what Michaela took to be annoyance: sometimes she sighed audibly and put her head on her desk. Other times she simply walked out of the room. Sheryl always sat by the window on the far left side of the room so whenever she walked out, she had to squeeze between desks and then walk between Michaela and the rest of the class to cross to the door. She always came back ten or fifteen minutes later. Michaela found Sheryl's behavior especially strange because, even when she looked upset, she participated in class discussions and her papers were strong.

One afternoon Sheryl sat in the middle of the classroom rather than by the window and, halfway through class, she got up and walked out. This time she didn't come back. Michaela planned to email her when she got back to her office but when she got there after class, Sheryl was already waiting outside the door.

"I know I've been rude," Sheryl said when she sat down, "and I wanted to explain myself. First of all, I'm pregnant. I've never been so tired in my life. I'm on edge all the time. The noise makes it worse. The smells make it worse. Everything irritates me. And that room! That room is so uncomfortable. I tried to sit by the window so I wouldn't get sick but it was louder there and it was hard to get out to go to the bathroom. So today I sat in the middle and it was worse. I really like the class but every minute I'm in that room I feel claustrophobic."

The idea that a person's actions tell others all that needs to be known about them seems legitimate; few people, after all, want friends who say they care but who talk behind another's back or refuse to help a friend in need. And how many people would go on a second date with someone who spent the first date texting during dinner?

There are limitations to the belief in judging action over all else, however. While the backstabbing friends in the first example might be worth ditching, there might be more to the bad date in the second example. Poor first impression aside, what if the person texting was talking to her younger sibling who has been struggling since their father died? What if she was concerned about her brother but didn't want to interrupt the date by taking a phone call? What if she didn't explain because she just didn't feel ready to talk about her father's death?

Because the actions are what we see, particularly in cultures wherein expression is valued as an indicator of the self, it is easy to rely on one's actions as the primary source of information about that person's personality. Individuals' impressions of others' behaviors are informed by their own culturally and socially situated expectations, so it isn't always easy to determine or understand why one behaves in a certain way. Body language, however, is an important form of communication (to varying degrees and in variable, culturally situated, context-dependent ways).

In the classroom, viewing behavior as a form of communication may help instructors at least identify when a student is uncomfortable but hasn't said so directly. In the above anecdote, it was obvious from Sheryl's behavior in Michaela's classroom that something was wrong, but it wasn't obvious what it was. While Michaela, perhaps influenced by her desire for all students to enjoy her classes, assumed that her student's behavior demonstrated annoyance, Sheryl's irritation and physical discomfort had little to do with Michaela and more to do with her own hormonal balance and the spatial conditions of the classroom. Sheryl demonstrated both agency and vulnerability by approaching her instructor and sharing very personal information. Many students do not demonstrate such self-efficacy—and many instructors don't inspire such trust in their students—so Michaela's original plan to email Sheryl after class to check in was a conscientious one.

In many ways, attending to students' behavior also requires that instructors acknowledge their own emotional realities. Consider, for example, what might have happened if Michaela, frustrated with the disruptive behavior, had called Sheryl out on her behavior in the middle of class. Though Michaela might have been justified in her frustration, calling it out likely would have prevented Sheryl from being open with her about her situation later on. If Sheryl felt she couldn't discuss her concerns with her professor, her attendance may have become sporadic, causing her academic performance to suffer. Instead, Michaela recognized, despite her irritation, that something was going on with her student and that reproaching her during class would not be productive. As a result, Michaela was able to provide support to Sheryl and they worked together to find ways to mitigate Sheryl's discomfort for the rest of the semester.

Model Self-Care

When Catherine first began teaching math at a small suburban high school, she was cautious about displaying her many tattoos. "The first time I wore cropped pants to school," she says, "two students in my morning class asked about the one on my ankle in the first five minutes of class. It went on like that for the rest of the day. Each time a student asked, I felt pressured to respond, but I was uncomfortable, and it derailed my lesson plans for the day."

Two of her male coworkers had tattoos peeking out from beneath the sleeves of their dress shirts, but, as a young woman who hadn't yet established herself at the school or earned the trust of her students, she decided it was best to hide them: "It was a pretty conservative school," she says. "Let's face it. People view tattoos differently on women." Plus, her tattoos are personal and talking about them can be difficult emotionally.

Early in her second year of teaching, with discussions of sexual assault and #MeToo dominating the news, social media, and the school hallways, the school mandated all students attend a workshop, led by the school psychologist, on sexual harassment, consent, and the right to say no.

Catherine, who had by then grown more comfortable in the classroom (even though she wore full-length pants, even in the springtime), attended the workshop with one of her classes. As she listened to the psychologist talk about personal space and privacy, Catherine realized that, if she wanted her students to honor their own bodies and respect others', she should try to practice and demonstrate the same.

"Now, on the first day of every semester, I talk with my students about respecting one another's boundaries. As an example, I tell my students that I have tattoos and that I don't like to talk about them. This way," she explains, "they understand that I have boundaries too and they know not to bring it up."

While many teachers struggle to conceive of themselves as authority figures, particularly in an educational environment that stresses standardization and top-down reform, structures that can make even the most experienced educator feel powerless, teachers are, for better or worse, authority figures to the students in the classroom. While systems of assessment reinforce instructors' roles as gatekeepers, educators' expertise may lead students to see them as role models. Though they differ ideologically, these are both authoritative roles, and without awareness of how one occupies those positions of authority, there is potential to abuse the power dynamic.

Both children and adults learn by imitating the behaviors and identities of those they admire. In addition to opening up venues for self-reflection and intellectual development for their students, equity-minded educators can use their positioning in the classroom to demonstrate approaches to working with, from, and through emotion in the classroom. Educators can model ways of connecting theory to experience (and vice versa) by sharing how they make sense of an academic idea. They can demonstrate listening to the body by noting how something makes them feel. Alternatively or additionally, they can model practices for honoring emotions by *not* sharing. Drawing a line between what one exposes and what one doesn't demonstrates that one has a right to maintain boundaries, in or outside of the classroom.

SECONDARY SUGGESTIONS

Because secondary curricula are already jam-packed with increasingly standardized units, teachers wishing to create trauma-informed curricula or place additional emphasis on the emotional elements of education may be overwhelmed by what can feel like the additive nature of the task. As such, it may be more beneficial to work individualization and mindfulness into existing units and lesson plans rather than attempting to expand those units and lessons to include the practices.

For example, during a unit on *The Catcher in the Rye* in American literature, teachers can design essay assignments that ask students to explore how the language in the narrative evokes Holden's emotional state at different points in the text or how emotion contributes to its tone and mood. They might then ask students to reflect upon how *they* feel while reading. (This can all be done in writing or for homework so that students aren't pressured to demonstrate emotional vulnerability in front of their classmates.) Such an assignment engages students in thinking and writing about emotion while at the same time practicing critical reading and learning to identify literary devices.

Teachers should also take advantage of the existing resources on their campuses. While secondary educators may already be working with SEL in their classrooms or on their campuses, teachers should explore what SEL programs are available in their schools and how those programs might support in-class curricula. School counselors may be invited to give short in-class talks on mindfulness or professional development workshops for teachers.

Where these programs are not readily available on campus, there are many supplemental organizations, some of them not-for-profit, that offer workshops and trainings for teachers and students. If funds are needed, teachers can apply for grants or support through professional organizations in their particular disciplines. These initiatives generally get off the ground more easily if teachers work together, so individual instructors may want to form alliances with other interested colleagues. Beginning by drafting a short proposal or presentation for a department meeting may spark interest and help instructors identify colleagues and administrators who are interested in collaboration. Unfortunately, in many educational spaces, antiracist educators can expect to be challenged by students, parents, and administrators, making collaboration an especially important part of initiatives related to antiracist education.

COLLEGE CONSIDERATIONS

The increased awareness of trauma among academic professionals is not limited to the instructional faculty on campus; some of the approaches outlined in this chapter may be available to students outside of the classroom as well. Yoga, for example, is increasingly offered on school grounds, often for course credit. While the wellness resources available on college campuses vary considerably among institutions and institution types, where applicable, instructors can use the resources on their campus to increase the connectivity between the trauma-informed classroom and the campus community. For example, in a class where mind and body awareness are significant (e.g., psychology or philosophy), instructors can create assignments that invite students to take and report back on a yoga, meditation, or Tai Chi class.

Yoga invites practitioners to be present, sit in meditation, hold asana, move in vinyasa, and lie in savasana with those same bodies they have tried or been forced to ignore or escape. In yoga, "embodiment becomes the means of knowing, feeling and making sense of the world and not just a physical enactment of social forces."[31] Yoga has been found to reduce symptoms of depression and anxiety and increase focus. Unfortunately, many of the populations most affected by trauma are not reaping the benefits of the practice.

Though the ancient art and science of yoga is traced back to India and China, in the United States it is often viewed as a White woman's practice. The practitioners featured on the cover of popular magazines like *Yoga Journal* are almost always White, thin, and female. This is not an issue of misrepresentation, however: More than four-fifths of American yoga practitioners are White.[32] In most major cities, yoga studios are concentrated in White, wealthy neighborhoods.

In light of these facts, instructors should take care to ensure that they are not asking students of color to enter spaces where they may feel marginalized. There are, fortunately, an increasing number of yoga studios and publications that cater to people of color, male military veterans, and religious populations (who might resist the spiritual practices of yoga class). While these targeted venues are a bit difficult to find, especially for outsiders to the communities they serve, instructors and students may be able to find those resources within their own communities or via affinity groups with which they are affiliated on campus.

In some classes, it also may be beneficial for students to explore more thoroughly the racialization of yoga in the United States. For example, a professor teaching an urban planning class or a sociology class can ask students to describe the neighborhood wherein the studio is located or, if students do opt to take a class, note the demographic makeup of the students as part of a larger discussion of gentrification.

Professors should always include options in this sort of assignment to ensure students are not directed to participate in activities that are inaccessible to them, whether because of social, cultural, financial, or mobility issues (among other challenges). This is especially important if students must leave campus to complete the assignment. In major markets, usually metropolitan areas like New York City and Los Angeles, and in very small markets that capitalize on low supply and high demand, like small college towns in otherwise rural areas, yoga classes can be cost prohibitive for many students. Instructors should locate more reasonably priced options: donation-based classes are available at some training studios in big cities and so-called *community* classes, taught by novice instructors and offered at a reduced or optional fee, are common at studios across the country. If those are not available, instructors should suggest an alternative, like viewing a free full-length yoga class on YouTube.

If physical limitations present an obstacle to such an assignment, it should be reiterated that meditation serves the same purpose as yoga. In fact, the *asanas* (poses) associated with yoga today existed in the ancient practice to prepare the body to sit in meditation. Most importantly, when options are offered, they should not be offered as alternatives only for the students who ask for them or outwardly demonstrate the need for them. Offering all options to all students helps to create an inclusive classroom that acknowledges, expects, and accepts difference.

CONCLUDING THOUGHTS

In response in part to the widespread use of the trigger warning, a problematic narrative has dominated discussions of trauma, education, and student-responsiveness. Students are too sensitive, or so says this narrative, and teachers and administrators are giving into the demands of overbearing helicopter parents and spoiled children who received too many participation trophies. Students need to toughen up, some say, because it's a harsh world out there after graduation. Many who promulgate this perspective group trigger warnings, microaggressions, safe spaces, and student protests under the same umbrella of practices that police free speech and cater to student fragility.

Despite the inaccuracies and biases of this argument, there may be some truth in it: it *is* a harsh world before and after graduation, and it is harshest for students without privilege. There are indeed threats to free speech, but there have always been threats to free speech, and they have most directly affected those who speak ideas of dissent in marginalized voices.

Regardless, this narrative decontextualizes students' supposed sensitivity, divorcing it from the capitalist, patriarchal, White hegemonic society that created it through prevalent racist violence, sexual assault, socioeconomic inequality, and the institutions that maintain these social ills. Another problem with this narrative is that "a depiction grounded in White, middle-class, suburban Americana has been universally (mis)applied to the most ethnoracially diverse generation in American history."[33] This erroneous universalization perpetuates the exclusion and marginalization of POCI in educational discourse.

To equitably address the role of emotion in classroom settings, educators must, as Michelle Payne writes, "stop seeing emotion, pain, and trauma as threatening, anti-intellectual, and solipsistic, and instead begin . . . to recognize them as ways of knowing."[34] While the trigger warning may appear to be an acknowledgment of student emotion, it does not account for the complexities of feeling or trauma: that emotions are felt and manifested differently by different people and in different social and cultural contexts; that the definition of trauma and its variable expressions are rooted in the ideological, epistemic, and discursive norms of society; that those expressions are regulated by societal norms and the institutional structures, like schools, that uphold them; and that, for many, such regulation may cause or perpetuate trauma.

Feelings, as a site of inquiry, open doors to discussions of the socialization and constructedness of experience and identity for both teachers and students. Like all other aspects of individual experience and social interaction, feelings are mediated by the ideologies and hegemonic structures of life in the United States. There are always feelings in the classroom, whether they are addressed or ignored. Considerations of feelings in curricular design and classroom practice can serve to destigmatize emotional expression, challenge normative notions of reason, encourage the practice of racial literacy, and create classrooms wherein students can feel secure enough emotionally to grow intellectually.

In the classroom, emotions matter because students matter.

NOTES

1. Jennifer Siebel Trainor, "From Identity to Emotion: Frameworks for Understanding, and Teaching Against, Anticritical Sentiments in the Classroom," *JAC* 26, no. 3–4 (2006): 647.
2. Carolyn Zahn-Waxler, "Socialization of Emotion: Who Influences Whom and How?" in *The Role of Gender in the Socialization of Emotion: Key Concepts and Critical Issues*, ed. A. Kennedy Root and S. Denham (San Francisco: Jossey-Bass, 2010): 102.
3. Ibid.
4. Ibid., 103.
5. James E. Smith, "Race, Emotions, and Socialization," *Race, Gender, and Class* 9, no. 4 (2002): 102.
6. Ibid., 103.
7. Margaret Price, *Mad at School: Rhetorics of Mental Disability and Academic Life* (Ann Arbor: University of Michigan Press, 2011), 47.

8. Ibid., 50.
9. Diane M. Hoffman, "Reflecting on Social Emotional Learning: A Critical Perspective on Trends in the United States," *Review of Educational Research* 79, no. 2 (2009): 540.
10. Ibid., 545.
11. Megan Boler, *Feeling Power: Emotions and Education* (New York: Routledge, 1999), xvi.
12. The word *hysteria* derives from the Greek *hysterika*, meaning *uterus*, and the term originally denoted an "illness" of emotionality only experienced by women.
13. Raymond Williams, *Problems in Materialism and Culture: Selected Essays* (London: Verso, 1980), 132.
14. See Susan Bordo, *The Flight to Objectivity: Essays on Cartesianism and Culture* (Albany: State University of New York Press, 1987).
15. Erin B. Godfrey, Carlos E. Santos, and Esther Burson, "For Better or Worse? System-Justifying Beliefs in Sixth-Grade Predict Trajectories of Self-Esteem and Behavior across Early Adolescence," *Child Development* 90, no. 1 (2019): 180.
16. Lani Guinier, "From Racial Liberalism to Racial Literacy: *Brown v. Board of Education* and the Interest-Divergence Dilemma," *The Journal of American History* 91, no. 1 (2004): 100.
17. Chai M. Tyng, Hafeez U. Amin, Mohamad N. M. Saad, and Aamir S. Malik, "The Influences of Emotion on Learning and Memory," *Frontiers in Psychology* 8 (2017): 3.
18. Sidney D'Mello, Blair Lehman, Reinhard Pekrun, and Art Graesser, "Confusion Can Be Beneficial for Learning," *Learning and Instruction* 29 (2014).
19. Todd B. Kashdan and J. Q. Kane, "Posttraumatic Distress and the Presence of Posttraumatic Growth and Meaning in Life: Experiential Avoidance as a Moderator," *Personality and Individual Differences* 50, no. 1 (2011): 85.
20. Ibid.
21. Ibid., 84.
22. Ibid., 85.
23. Paulo Freire, *Pedagogy of the Oppressed*, trans. by Myra Bergman Ramos (New York: Continuum, 2005), 72.
24. Ibid.
25. Ibid., 71.
26. For a more in-depth discussion of the abstract thinking required of student writers, see Cheryl Hogue Smith, "'Diving in Deeper': Bringing Basic Writers' Thinking to the Surface," *Journal of Adolescent & Adult Literacy* 53, no. 8 (2010).
27. Kari Storla, "Beyond Trigger Warnings: Handling Trauma in Classroom Discussion," in *Trigger Warnings: History, Theory, Context*, ed. Emily J. M. Knox (Lanham: Rowman & Littlefield, 2017), 193.
28. Mary Margaret Fonow, Judith A. Cook, Richard S. Goldsand, and Jane K. Burke-Miller, "Using the Feldenkrais Method of Somatic Education to Enhance Mindfulness, Body Awareness, and Empathetic Leadership Perceptions among College Students," *Journal of Leadership Education* 15, no. 3 (2016): 117.
29. Jeanne L. Tsai, D. I. Simeonova, and J. T. Watanabe, "Somatic and Social: Chinese Americans Talk about Emotion," *Personality and Social Psychology Bulletin* 30, no. 9 (2004).
30. For an example of the racial autobiography, see Mara Lee Grayson, *Teaching Racial Literacy*, 84–88.
31. Christy Wenger, *Yoga Minds, Writing Bodies: Contemplative Writing Pedagogy* (Fort Collins: WAC Clearinghouse/Parlor Press, 2015), 15.
32. Gurjeet S. Birdee, Anna T. Legedza, Robert B. Saper, Suzanne M. Bertisch, David M. Eisenberg, and Russell S. Phillips, "Characteristics of Yoga Users: Results of a National Survey," *Journal of General Internal Medicine* 23, no. 10 (2008). See also Rosalie Murphy, "Why Your Yoga Class Is So White," *The Atlantic* (July 8, 2014).
33. Mara Lee Grayson, "The Surreal World: Racism, Capitalism, and Complacency, Millennial-Style: Review of *Sorry to Bother You*," *The St. John's Humanities Review* 16, no. 1 (2019): 26.
34. Michelle Payne, *Bodily Discourses: When Students Write about Abuse and Eating Disorders* (Portsmouth: Boynton/Cook, 2000), 30.

Chapter Six

Reading Lives, Writing Lives

Languaging and Counternarrating Trauma

In general, members of every minority group continue to be measured largely by the degree of our assimilation—how closely speech patterns, dress, or demeanor conform to the dominant white culture—and the more a minority strays from these external markers, the more he or she is subject to negative assumptions.—Barack Obama[1]

Between my traditional Cameroonian clothes and lack of English, I stuck out like a sore thumb. Speaking English is a big deal in the United States. Well, speaking white *English is a big deal in the United States. Beyond my skin color, in order to truly fit in with my White friends, I had to learn to speak like them. This meant no accent, no mispronunciations, no French. The restrictions of communication left me silent for a long time.*—Veronique, 18[2]

Leah is a writing professor in an urban university that serves a predominantly African American and Latinx population. To graduate, all students at the university are required to pass a writing proficiency exam in their junior or senior year. Students who are concerned about passing the exam and those who have already failed the exam one or more times have the option of taking a writing class to fulfill the requirement.

When Leah taught that class for the first time, she found that students had considerable anxieties about writing and felt significant pressure about meeting the requirement for graduation. *I'm just not a good writer,* most of them confessed at one point or other. Usually, when Leah asked why they believed that about themselves, students provided one of two explanations: either their previous instructors had told them their writing needed a lot of work or English wasn't their first language.

Most of Leah's students were in their last semester and were concerned primarily with fulfilling the requirement so they wouldn't have to postpone graduation, but Holly, a junior, was especially interested in improving her writing. She attended office hours weekly, sometimes more often when an essay was assigned. Holly was thirty years old, married, had a ten-year-old son, and worked as a teacher at a daycare center. She was also an accomplished modern dancer locally and had received an associate's degree from the nearby two-year college before transferring to the university. She was very engaged and outspoken in class but tended to, in her words, "overthink everything" when it was time to write a paper. It was clear to Leah that Holly was thoughtful, engaged, and critically aware of the academic and affective challenges she and those of her classmates with similar backgrounds experienced at school.

One week during office hours, Holly told Leah that she really enjoyed the class but that she struggled to turn her thoughts into writing. She talked through her idea for the next essay with Leah then said: "Problem is, I can explain it to you here but when I try to write it down, I don't know what to say."

"Have you ever tried to write the way you speak?" Leah asked. "Just to talk onto the page?"

"Yeah. One of my teachers at the community college told me to do that, but . . . if I'm being honest, I don't think I should."

"Why not?" Leah asked.

"I don't want to sound, you know, ghetto," Holly said. "Even when I speak in class I feel that. I like to talk, I think I learn better that way, but I'm always nervous people will think I'm dumb."

Like many students, Holly struggles with putting her thoughts into writing. Though she claims that, when it comes to writing down her thoughts, she doesn't know what to say, it seems that something else is preventing her from expressing herself: the perceptions she anticipates her audience will have about her dialect, which she describes as "ghetto." For Holly, the challenge might not be in finding what to say so much as finding *a way to say it* that won't reflect negatively upon her.

The negative perceptions Holly anticipates from her teachers and peers have less to do with her intellect than with her racial and socioeconomic positionality. By equating ghetto with "dumb," Holly draws upon a racist conflation of dialect and intellect, one she appears to have internalized. Though *ghetto* is a bit of an "etymological mystery" thought to have roots in Italian and Yiddish, among other languages,[3] the term, which historically denoted a closed-off, segregated area to which Jewish people were restricted in European cities, for decades it has been used in the United States to identify a poor, urban area with Black residents. More recently, it has been used as an adjective, synonymous with *low-class* or denoting something "cobbled together from subpar materials."[4]

Holly's instructor, Leah, offers a piece of advice familiar to many writing instructors: *write the way you speak*. The problem is, however, that the way Holly speaks is not deemed acceptable in many academic settings. Leah seems to have good intentions here—she wants Holly to be able to express herself—but she doesn't acknowledge the ways that, in the educational settings of a racist society, Holly's language is likely to be used against her.

Language is one of the most significant ways through which individuals express their cultural identities. Because much of students' work from the earliest years of schooling through postsecondary education is conveyed via spoken or written language, language is also one of the primary criteria on which students are assessed. As a result, students' language is regulated and policed and their culturally situated language and rhetorical practices are marginalized and silenced.

LANGUAGING RACE[5]

Substantial bodies of work from the fields of linguistics, sociology, education, and rhetoric and composition have established that, in the United States, language practices that differ from *Standardized English*, the variations of English used in government, education, and other official institutional spaces, are devalued and vilified. Everyone who speaks a language speaks a dialect thereof, whether or not that dialect is the one seen as the language standard. In the United States there are many, many English dialects, influenced by region, ethnicity, and race, and in linguistic terms no dialect is inherently superior or inferior to another. Of course, the hierarchical valuation of dialect in the United States has little to do with language itself and much to do with those who speak that language.

Yet, despite the academic research, as sociolinguists H. Samy Alim and Geneva Smitherman have pointed out, there is "no national public dialogue on language that recognizes it as a site of cultural struggle."[6] As a result, language is one of the primary sites wherein white supremacy is maintained, uncritically and sometimes unwittingly, through formal educational policies and informal expectations (stated or unstated) grounded in a dominant language ideology.

Reading, Writing, and Speaking "White"

In the United States, so-called Standardized English is seen as a prerequisite for upward mobility and membership in the social mainstream. Standardized English is sometimes called *Standard English*, a problematic phrasing that uncritically establishes the dialect as the norm from which all other Englishes deviate. This normalization, however, has no natural basis and "is not identical with the language of any natural population of speakers; it is a very real institutional construct."[7] In fact, as antiracist writing center scholar Laura Greenfield explains, due to the fact that languages are always evolving, standard forms of languages don't exist, therefore there isn't actually a single standard English at all. What is assumed to be standard is "really nothing more than whatever is *not* designated as nonstandard."[8]

There have, however, been attempts at standardization. Shortly after the American Revolutionary War, the new nation's political and educational elite sought to establish and teach a codified American English that would, as John Adams put it, "strike all the world with admiration and Great Britain with envy."[9] Though the academy Adams envisioned for disseminating this particular English language never materialized, Noah Webster's *American Spelling Book*, published in 1783, and *American Dictionary of the English Language*, published in 1828, prescribed patterns of spelling and pronunciation that distinguished American English from the British variety, such as the omission of the *u* from words like *colour/color* and the replacement of the *c* with the *s* in words like *defence/defense*. Books by other authors, like grammarian Lindley Murray's *English Grammar*, published in 1795, sought to establish syntactical and stylistic norms for American English (many of which reflected British grammar).

Just as attempts at standardization of the school curriculum served to establish and disseminate an ideology of Americanness throughout the newly formed United States, the standardization of American English can be seen as an attempt to establish rhetorically and linguistically the legitimacy of the U.S. as an independent nation. Like the curriculum, which highlighted the achievements and spoke to the interests of the White male elite, these codified language practices were derived from those with the power of authorship.

Over the years, the style manuals distributed in schools disseminated a belief in a standard language and a set of practices (which actually differ from one style guide to the next) thought to be associated with it. Though no cultural group naturally speaks the standardized form(s) of English taught in classrooms, the form most closely resembles the language practices of those who are White, formally educated, and middle class or wealthy, leading some linguists to call it *White Mainstream English*.

Regardless of its origins, Standardized English as it is understood today is *prescriptive* rather than *descriptive*, meaning that it is framed as how one *should* speak and write rather than how one already does. These rules, of course, though they regard language, have less to do with language per se than with the function of language within a society. Language is shaped by and shapes the culture of a community, thus these prescriptions for communication can be seen as part of a forced assimilation process by which all speakers are expected to move toward the white mainstream and away from their own culturally situated speech, behaviors, beliefs, and epistemologies.

Students who enter school are acculturated into standardized language and, while the process may be relatively smooth for children from White, middle-class, and/or formally educated families, such acculturation may be difficult, demoralizing, and painful for students whose home dialects vary noticeably from the standardized school form. Students who speak Black English, for example, are likely to be corrected and criticized for speaking a dialect that linguists have long recognized as a unique English with systematic patterns of syntax, pronunciation, and usage. Such so-called nonstandard dialects are marginalized and criticized precisely because they are *not* deviant, because their very existence as functioning, culturally sustaining dialects threatens white cultural hegemony. As linguist and novelist Rosina Lippi-Green points out, Black English "is tangible and irrefutable evidence that there is a distinct, healthy, functioning African American culture which is not white, and which does not want to be white."[10]

Still, despite its underlying ideology of white supremacy and the challenges to one's cultural identity that accompany the acquisition of a school-based language form, for many students Standardized English carries with it promises of access, academic achievement, and financial success. Others may see this promise of assimilation as empty and hypocritical, for the acquisition of white language neither guarantees access nor equity nor prevents discrimination.

Speaking "Well," Being "Articulate"

Even when POCI demonstrate fluency with Standardized English, reactions to that fluency, often but not always from White people, make it clear that complete assimilation is impossible and that they will always be seen as, first and foremost, as other. For example, people of Asian descent may be told they *speak English so well* by White people who, judging solely by appearance, expect them to speak with an accent. Black people who speak Standardized English might be told the same or, as considerable research demonstrates, they might be called *articulate*.[11] Both of these comments are used as compliments by White people but in context carry a subtext of surprise and are, as a result, far less complimentary than they at first seem.

One implication is that a person of color speaking well—which in this case means speaking as White people are believed to speak—is unexpected, an aberration. Another implication is that speaking well is expected of and common among White people. Part of a discourse of exceptionalism, racialized and classed terms like *articulate* serve to distinguish particular POCI, typically those who are middle class and highly educated, from other POCI who presumably lack such capabilities. These terms are racial microaggressions, commonplace verbal or behavioral slights that, regardless of intent, "communicate hostile, derogatory, or negative racial slights and insults toward people of color."[12]

Microaggressions are not limited to race and language; slights may instead or additionally be based on gender, (dis)ability, sexuality, or religion, among other social classifications. (See chapter 1 for additional examples of microaggressions.) In many cases, those who have committed microaggressions are unaware of why and how they have insulted the person to whom they have directed the slight, lacking critical awareness of the connections between language and racism and of their own privileged positionality. As a result, they see only the compliment and do not realize the inequity of complimenting a person on their ability to conform to the linguistic and behavioral norms of the dominant culture.

Microaggressions demonstrate the pervasiveness of hegemonic ideology that positions the White, English-speaking, heterosexual, abled, male body as an unchallenged, universal norm. In the academy, linguistic microaggressions cannot be separated from the narratives of literacy and learning that reinforce cultural hegemony via educational policy and classroom praxis. Too many educators, however, diminish the impact of microaggressions for the same reasons they resist the trigger warning: it is, they claim, evidence of a too-sensitive generation of students. This reductive dismissal creates a false equivalency between the microaggression, a long-standing term for a well-researched discursive practice, and the trigger warning, a vaguely defined practice that is based on a narrow interpretation of psychological theory and limited empirical research.

WOUNDED STORIES AND STORIES THAT WOUND

Sociologists Bradley Campbell and Jason Manning point to microaggressions as a sign that, in the contemporary United States, victimhood is the overarching theme of *moral culture*, the prevailing ideological and ethical norms of social responsibility within a society. Greg Lukianoff and Jonathan Haidt, authors of "The Coddling of the American Mind," the infamous *Atlantic* article that arguably brought trigger warnings and the challenges thereto to the forefront of public discourse around higher education, in their book of the same title also point to the dissolution in recent years of *dignity culture*, a term used to describe an ideology, grounded in an ethic of tolerance and restraint, that positions all individuals as possessing of dignity. Campbell and Manning contrast dignity culture with the *honor culture* of the far past (which still prevails in parts of the world) and the *victimhood culture* of the present.

For these pairs of authors, dignity culture appears to be the ideal, though, as will be addressed here, it is not necessarily for the reasons laid out in the framework.

Victimhood culture, as per Campbell and Manning, is exemplified by the prevalence of complaints of microaggressions on college campuses. The authors claim that victimhood culture relies heavily on third-party involvement in that people react to insults, even those that, like microaggressions, may be unintentional, by bringing them to the attention of the public, an action the authors attribute to individuals' desires for sympathy. In their view, people who call out the microaggressions they experience "advertise their oppression as evidence that they deserve respect and assistance" and "rather than emphasize either their strength or inner worth, the aggrieved emphasize their oppression and social marginalization."[13]

Of course, what is seen as fishing for sympathy can also be seen as social activism: literacy scholars and critical race educators long have theorized that

Table 6.1. Three Models of Moral Cultures*†

	Honor Culture	Dignity Culture	Victimhood Culture
Marker(s) of status	Reputation Physical bravery	Individual inherent worth "Thick skin"	Public opinion Victimhood
Response to offense	Violent retaliation	Direct nonviolent action, such as compromise or problem-solving Legal system as a last resort	Public complaints, such as protests or social media campaigns Third party involvement Appeals to sympathy
Common beliefs and behaviors	Sensitivity to insult Aggressiveness	Self-restraint Tolerance Avoidance of confrontation	Sensitivity to slight Criticism of privilege
Context	Weak or absent legal authority	Stable, powerful legal system Cultural homogeneity	Cultural diversity Powerful systems of authority
Examples of societies	Early U.S. Enclaves of Arab world Street gangs	Mid to late twentieth-century U.S. Small towns	Contemporary U.S. College campuses

*According to Campbell and Manning and others
†These models are necessarily reductive and do not account for variation within cultures.

discourse itself and the critical examination thereof can effect social change. Given that the individuals likeliest to experience microaggressions are those who are marginalized, this argument is reminiscent of the decades-old calls for people of color to *be less sensitive* or to *stop playing the race card*, statements that speak to what Eduardo Bonilla-Silva has called colorblind racism, an ideology that claims racism is "no longer relevant" and "explains contemporary racial inequality as the outcome of nonracial dynamics,"[14] and which are, fittingly, microaggressions. Even if the calls for greater emphasis of inner worth are noble, it must be acknowledged that, though resiliency is an important trait among communities of POCI, inner strength does not create social change.

Like Campbell and Manning, Lukianoff and Haidt point to the child's "sticks and stones" retort ("Sticks and stones can break my bones but words will never hurt me") as evidence not that words cannot inflict pain but that, in a dignity culture, words can be dismissed with "contemptuous indifference."[15] Neither pair of authors, however, acknowledges the incongruity between demonstrations of contemptuous indifference and the supposed belief that all individuals have dignity, which would imply that all individuals ought also to be treated as such, nor does either pair of authors explore sociocultural situatedness of their assumptions about dignity.

Put simply, ideologies like "all people have dignity" have never accounted for all people in the United States. Lukianoff and Haidt briefly admit as much, conceding that "full dignity was at one time accorded only to adult, White men."[16] Their awareness of (in)equity appears to end there, however: that statement is followed in the very same sentence by the claim that "the rights revolutions of the twentieth and twenty-first centuries did essential work to expand dignity to all."[17]

Like Campbell and Manning's criticisms of discursive resistance as a method of attracting sympathy, this statement aligns with the rhetorics of postracialism and colorblindness that defined racial discourse during the last decade of the twentieth century and the first decade of the twenty-first century. By placing the action in the past tense ("did"), Lukianoff and Haidt imply that these revolutions have concluded and that dignity has indeed been extended to all people. In doing so, they elide the ongoing marginalization of and discrimination toward people of color, Jewish and Muslim people, immigrants, and indigenous peoples, not to mention the ingrained racism of U.S. legal, educational, and economic systems.

That the authors did not publish this book during the years in which Barack Obama was president of the United States, a time when many political pundits and social scientists pointed to the election of a Black-identified president as signs of American postracialism, but in 2018, a year marked by racist and anti-Semitic acts of violence across the country, renders this statement especially naïve, shortsighted, and insulting.

Campbell and Manning's conceptualization of victimhood culture appears to rely upon a similarly myopic view. Though they admit that those labeled as oppressors often seek to cultivate an image of themselves as victims, they, like so many conservative politicians and pundits, claim that "the narrative of oppression and victimization is especially congenial to the leftist worldview"[18] and make no mention of white fragility, reactionary responses to affirmative action, or the misogyny of so-called men's rights groups.

In fact, they gloss over the relationships between racism and microaggressions and between cultural hegemony and narratives of victimhood. It seems that, despite basing much of their conceptualization of victimhood culture on the prevalence of microaggressions, the authors would rather not talk about racism at all.

An exploration of the victim narrative through the framework of racial literacy, however, illuminates the possibility that that victimhood culture may not perpetuated by those who are oppressed in a society built upon white supremacy but instead by those who counter the legitimate social activism of marginalized groups with more white supremacy. Most commonly, the reactionary victimhood narrative emerges via self-serving claims of what some might call reverse discrimination.

None of these claims are new or unique to the twenty-first century. In fact, claims by conservative pundits that liberal students and activists are suppressing their freedom of speech rely on the very same rhetoric deployed by antebellum slaveholders and supporters of slavery. As essayist Eve Fairbanks has noted of antebellum proslavery rhetoricians, they "anointed themselves the defenders of 'reason,' free speech, and 'civility' . . . the most important thing to know about them, they held, was that they were not the oppressors. They were the oppressed."[19]

At its worst, this victimhood narrative of white supremacy leads to actual violence. The most frightening examples of the reactionary white fragility that may really define victimhood culture in the twenty-first century are the lengthy, self-pitying manifestoes written by white supremacists: those penned by the white supremacist who killed nine people at the Emanuel African Methodist Episcopal Church in Charleston in 2015, the white supremacist who killed eleven people at the Tree of Life Synagogue in Pittsburgh in 2018, the white supremacist perpetrator of a mass shooting at the Chabad of Poway Synagogue outside of San Diego in 2019, the Norwegian white supremacist who killed seventy-seven people in 2011, and the Australian white nationalist who traveled to New Zealand to carry out mass murders at the Al Noor Mosque and Linwood Islamic Centre in 2019, among others. Some of these white supremacist terrorists admitted to having studied the manifestoes of the others prior to committing mass acts of violence.

Again, this pattern harkens back to the white victimhood narrative of antebellum racism: before assassinating President Abraham Lincoln, John

Wilkes Booth "lamented that he no longer felt comfortable expressing 'my thoughts or sentiments' on slavery freely in good company."[20]

Rhetorical violence does not necessarily lead to physical violence but, at a time when mass murder is accompanied by propagandistic writing that positions already marginalized racial, ethnic, and religious groups as threats to the so-called white race, a model that points to students who call out microaggressions as exemplars of victimhood culture is rather limited. (That the term *racial microaggressions* was used originally in the 1970s,[21] an era preceding the emergence of the victimhood culture the authors condemn, further weakens their argument.) Regardless of their intentions, the arguments put forth by both Campbell and Manning and Lukianoff and Haidt appear to be built upon a foundation of their own situatedness in the dignity culture they praise and, it seems, wish to return. That dignity culture, however, is grounded in the white hegemonic status quo, and it perpetuates a colorblind racist narrative that blames the marginalized for their own marginalization.

TRANSFORMATIVE POTENTIAL OF THE TRAUMA COUNTERNARRATIVE

To challenge these narratives, students must be provided opportunities to share their own narratives, constructed in their own language(s) and told from their own perspectives. Equally importantly, students need opportunities to experience as readers others' stories of trauma, resilience, and resistance. Seen through the adult educational theory of transformational learning, which holds that through the taking on of another's perspective individuals are better able to examine their own interpretations and assumptions, sharing counternarratives in the classroom exposes students to perspectives that differ from their own, thereby making space for shifts in viewpoint. Racial literacy research in literature and writing classrooms has further shown that reading and writing counternarratives prepare students to think critically and reflectively, by both interrogating stereotypes and misrepresentations in media and examining their own internalized biases.[22]

Trauma narratives and related pedagogies are performative in that, directly or implicitly, both practices strive to create change. At times, that change is sought by and for the individual telling the story, such as the journaling done in a therapeutic environment. Other times, change is sought for the communities affected by the traumatic experiences depicted, such as the Vietnam War veterans who shared stories of trauma as part of the antiwar movement of the late 1960s and early 1970s. In the classroom, writers and readers of trauma narratives can also experience change. As writers, students have the opportunity to, through language, reconstruct the experience of trauma and experience the support and validation of their peers. For readers, the new information provided by the story and the experience of witnessing another's processes of trauma and healing can lead to personal transformation.

Shifting Rhetorical Contexts

In this way, also transformed by the use of trauma counternarratives is the traditional rhetorical situation that undergirds so much of school-based literacy. Most of the reading students do in schools is what Rosenblatt would have called *efferent*: just as in anatomical terms efferent blood vessels carry blood outward, an efferent reading is one in which students read for what they can carry out or take away from the text. In other words, they read for information. This often places the student, the reader, in a passive position, subjected to the text rather than making meaning with it.

When put in the role of the writer, students are told their purpose is persuasion: across the curriculum, students are assigned to write arguments that effectively convince a vague, hypothetical reader of a stance on a subject (about which the student is still learning) using reductive models of logical reasoning such as the five-paragraph-theme.[23] As the audience tends to be limited to the teacher or, on occasion, classmates with the same level of awareness of the material, the real goal of such writing is not persuasion but the demonstration of the student's knowledge and ethos. The former is often a mere regurgitation of information the instructor has provided. The latter, the student's assertion of credibility and authority in writing about a particular subject, is typically affected, for the establishment of ethos requires familiarity and membership in academic discourses in which students have not necessarily engaged as legitimate participants.

When taught as part of a *healing pedagogy* oriented toward the wholeness and well-being of the student, the use of counternarratives can build community in the classroom, invite students to critically explore the social and cultural factors that contribute to experiences of trauma, and help students both see themselves as cocreators of knowledge and reimagine their roles as writers.

Reading Lives

The pedagogical use of narrative to engage students academically, socially, and emotionally is grounded in decades of scholarship. In the late 1930s, English education pioneer Louise M. Rosenblatt explained that literature enlarges knowledge not because it provides information but because it provides additional experiences for readers: "New understanding is conveyed to them dynamically and personally. Literature provides a *living through*, not simply *knowledge about*."[24]

Developments in neuroscience and cognitive psychology lend support to this claim: meta-analyses of studies in cognitive science, many of which used magnetic resonance imaging to scan participants' brains while they were reading, have shown that the brain "does not make much of a distinction between reading about an experience and encountering it in real life; in each case, the same neurological regions are stimulated."[25] In other words, when a person reads a description of physical movement (such as "She kicks the ball"), the motor cortex of the brain is stimulated.

This might lead some to think that *reading* about trauma will *cause* trauma, but it is not likely for a number of reasons. For starters, the direct causes of trauma and the processes by which trauma-based stress disorders develop are far more complex than the stimulation of a small region of the brain upon reading. Research has also shown that secondary traumatic stress and vicarious traumatization tend to result from, respectively, a sudden trauma experienced by a loved one or prolonged exposure to others' experiences of traumas; in both cases, the traumatization stems as much—if not more—from intimacy with the traumatized individual(s) as it does from the originating traumatic experience. (For more on secondary and vicarious trauma, see chapter 3.)

In fact, it seems that there are far more benefits than drawbacks to reading about trauma, especially in classrooms wherein critical literacy and racial literacy are practiced by teachers and students. Literary scholars who study trauma literature have suggested that in the classroom trauma narratives, rather than victimizing students, actually invite students to take on more active roles as readers than the traditional textual encounter allows. Nearly a century's worth of scholarship has attested to the experiences, expectations, and interpretations readers bring to a text, thus contributing to the meaning-making of the narrative.

When reading trauma narratives specifically, students become witnesses both to the trauma experienced and the author's post-trauma self. As writing studies and trauma scholar Rachel N. Spear explains, by acknowledging that an author has lived past the experience of trauma and has been able to reconstruct that event through narrative, "students do not just validate authorial agency and the trauma stories; they assist in re-creating the author's very identity by recognizing the author as someone beyond the trauma, aiding in the reinvention of that individual's purpose."[26]

Catharsis and Critical Witness

Reading about trauma gives readers access to experiences and emotional realities that typically are kept private. As a result, when students read these trauma stories together as a community of witnesses, cocreators, and healers, it may lead to something akin to catharsis. Though sometimes used in clinical psychology to describe the reexperiencing of emotions related to past trauma, colloquially the term *catharsis* and its variants are used to refer to any sort of purging of emotion; after journaling about a fight with one's partner, for example, one might remark to a friend that venting on the page was "so cathartic." The term is most directly connected to the dramatic arts, however, wherein catharsis describes a shared experience of emotional release resulting, historically, from the viewing of tragic drama. When experienced in a carefully curated space, catharsis allows for a release of emotion that is communal, contained, and productive.

It would be naïve and irresponsible, however, to presume that reading about trauma can or should create a unified, universal understanding of trauma. The active role of reader in witnessing and recognizing trauma is accompanied by a social responsibility that requires the acknowledgment of trauma as a societal as well as individual phenomenon. In literature, creative writing, and English language arts classrooms, individual narratives are often said to illuminate larger ideas about the world. This claim is not without validity, but it paints too vague a picture using too broad brushstrokes and as a result, it is easy—too easy—for students to assume that every individual story can be understood universally. Because the white gaze is framed, consistently and problematically, as a sort of default in the United States, when students struggle to see the distinctions between experiences, it is usually the experiences of POCI that are omitted or ignored.

A critical witness stance "acknowledges commonalities of human experiences *and* inequities at one and the same time."[27] For this pedagogy to be truly critical, it is integral that students examine the ways trauma is manifested and managed differently depending upon cultural and social contexts. Instructors must create opportunities (assignments, discussions, cocurricular activities) for students to explore through a critical lens the complex power dynamics that contribute to the experience, impact, and interpretation of stories of trauma.

Writing Lives

Writing about trauma requires both reflection upon and reconstruction of the traumatic experience. An epistemic view of rhetoric sees writing as a means of arriving at truth and, ultimately, of creating reality; in this view, any attempt to put language to experience requires segmenting and ordering that experience and previous experiences to create a theory of the world in which those experiences have meaning. Language itself is a means of ordering, for through words, one chooses what to include or exclude, what to highlight or obscure. When put to language by an author, an experience is part of a world interpreted and represented by the writer. Through representation, the mirrored world becomes more than "the sum total of eardrum rattles, retinal excitations, and so on; it is a creation that reflects the peculiarities of the perceiver as well as the peculiarities of what is perceived."[28]

Because trauma in particular often manifests as unprocessed, overwhelming sensory input (such as flashbacks and intrusive mental images), in putting language to trauma, a writer can create a coherent story that conveys as much about the writer's worldview and self-identity as it does about the traumatic experience itself. During trauma and in its aftermath, an individual is stripped of control, but writing is an act of authority: through shaping the narrative the author takes on an agentive role that encourages the reclamation of power over one's own experiences.

When practiced in the classroom, there are pedagogical benefits as well as therapeutic ones: students who claim authority to tell their own stories can also see themselves as meaning-makers and cocreators of knowledge in the classroom setting. Moreover, any narrative re-creation of experience necessities the writer consider how an audience might order and interpret the same story and language. As such, the writing of trauma narratives encourages students to consider relationship between author and audience, thus further expanding the traditional rhetorical contexts in which students write in the classroom.

To determine how the audience might interpret a story, a student must explore who the audience is and how and why that audience might make sense of information in a particular way. Rather than relying on stereotypes and generalizations about imaginary audiences, students can actually talk to each other about the overlaps and departures in their culturally situated approaches to writing, communication, and meaning-making. In a critical classroom setting, this translates to inquiry-based discussion, greater peer-to-peer interaction, and, potentially, a more nuanced understanding of the challenges and benefits of cross-cultural communication.

Rewriting Trauma

Literacy educator Elizabeth Dutro, who identifies as a middle-class White woman, recalls that, after Sam, a poor, White student called *hillbilly* by his classmates, shared a story about missing his father who was in prison, she shared with Sam that her brother was in prison. While the sharing may have served Sam well in the moment, Dutro admits that their stories bear few contextual or rhetorical similarities. As she explains:

> There is very little connection in the ways our stories function for us. Mine has shock value—it shakes up my listener's assumptions. I get to see the double-take pass through my listener's eyes. Sam's story of his father can provoke

sympathy, even empathy, but no adult in his school would be surprised. He is more than one kid with a family member in prison.[29]

Dutro's story challenges traditional narratives about prison and who winds up there, while Sam's story does not.

It is no secret that race, gender, and economic status are determinants in the distribution of trauma among the student population. As a result, many students' stories will indeed demonstrate narratives of experience that prevail in popular discourse. While trauma narratives should never be filtered through an ideology of exceptionalism (through which, for example, an individual student's ability to overcome traumatic conditions is emphasized to the exclusion of any acknowledgment of the prevalence of those traumatic conditions), it is important that when students' stories enter the classroom they are not used in ways that reinforce popular narratives about trauma and experience.

In poor geographic areas, stories of student trauma already circulate widely in schools. That circulation in no way guarantees a critical stance of witnessing or narrating, however. Even when stories are met with empathy, they tend to "serve as evidence of already entrenched class-privileged assumptions about the deficiencies or deviance of students and families living in poverty."[30] This is even truer in schools wherein the student population is largely composed of POCI living below the poverty line. Too often, stories of students' difficulties inside or outside of school are told from a deficit orientation that, rather than acknowledge societal realities or critique institutional inequities, rhetorically places responsibility for those difficulties on the shoulders of young people, their families, and their communities.

It is not enough, therefore, to invite students to share personal stories. The ways their classmates bear witness matter, as do the instructor's responses, the broader curricular framing, and the lessons that precede and follow story sharing. For trauma pedagogies to challenge the inequitable structured perpetuated by traditional classroom practices, they must engage students in critical inquiry about trauma as an experience, a concept, and a rhetorical construction, about the political rhetoric and cultural ideologies surrounding it, and about the situatedness of traumatic experiences, including their own.

Writing *about* Trauma

Not every student in the classroom will have a history of trauma, though most have experienced emotional pain. Still, it is up to each individual student to decide whether writing about or sharing that pain is appropriate in a particular classroom space at a particular time. Students who have experienced traumatic events or considerable emotional distress but who haven't worked out the aftereffects on their own or in a therapeutic setting may not be emotionally prepared to put language to their experiences, let alone share those experiences with their teacher or classmates. Others may want to keep painful experiences private, perhaps due to the nature of the experience, their relationship or lack thereof with their classmates, their feelings of comfort or discomfort on the campus, their socially and culturally situated perspectives on emotion and emotional expression, or a combination of these and other factors.

With regard to racial trauma in particular, it would be inequitable and insensitive to demand that POCI speak from personal experience any time a conversation or assignment about racism is introduced. As one student studying a racial literacy curriculum has said, "How do I write about race and racism without writing about all the negative things I've experienced? I don't want to turn this into a list of traumas."[31]

Despite the psychotherapeutic benefits of trauma writing, the writing students do in a classroom that engages trauma narratives does not have to be personal in nature. To highlight the experiential expertise of POCI without demanding students expose their racial wounds, educators can create assignments that ask students to write *about* trauma as a concept or phenomenon. Such assignments provide opportunities for POCI to write from their experience-informed perspectives without sharing personal stories. For many students, this approach may encourage greater critical awareness of how individual painful events—including their own, whether or not they share them—are situated in a larger academic exploration of human experience. Whereas individual storytelling directs the curricular gaze inward, writing about trauma as a societal phenomenon directs students' critical gaze outward and toward the larger ideologies and institutions that mitigate or perpetuate trauma and resist or uphold inequity.

With scaffolding appropriate to the students and the classroom setting, instructors can use trauma as a framework through which to encourage the critical investigation of societal inequity. Initially, teachers can assign exploratory papers that ask students to describe or compare cultural perspectives on or responses to specific traumas: students might, for example, look at the ways particular societies conceptualize death and dying or ritualize mourning or how violent crimes are specified and victims compensated in different legal systems. Eventually, students can write research-based papers that explore the ways master narratives of trauma and experience are reproduced through media and reinforced by institutional structures and even educational praxis.

INCLUSIVE CLASSROOM LANGUAGE PRACTICES

If students *do* choose to tell their own stories, it is imperative that they be not only allowed but encouraged to do so in their own languages and dialects. This is not limited to narrative: encouraging students to use their own languages in the classroom is a necessary step toward creating more inclusive, equitable classroom spaces that resist white supremacy.

In the majority of educational spaces in the United States, teachers' instruction and assessment of language are still tied, sometimes obligatorily and sometimes unwittingly, to standard language ideologies. While the advocacy for the use of Standardized Englishes is often associated with political conservatism and English-only policies, the construct has been normalized in institutional settings to such an extent that many educators who are otherwise progressive do not realize that their attitudes about language are exclusionary.

As eminent writing studies scholar Victor Villanueva suggested more than thirty years ago, even those instructors who *do* recognize the legitimacy of languages like Black English often feel "torn between the findings of the linguists and the demands of the marketplace."[32] This may be even truer today, as organizations and corporations rely increasingly upon written communication (often in a wide variety of digital forms).

Many educators believe that learning Standardized Englishes is part of playing the game in academia and more broadly in the United States: if society places value on it, the logic goes, students must learn it to succeed. However, because discourse perpetuates ideology, the more educators require Standardized Englishes the more they legitimize that requirement and contribute to the white cultural hegemony that secures its domination over other Englishes.

Approaches to Assessment

It may seem that discussions of student language ought to be limited to classrooms that forefront literacy practices, but student writing isn't limited to English and composition classrooms. Students write in many classes and, especially in light of scholarship that attests to the importance of incorporating writing in the disciplines and across the curriculum, students' knowledge of course material increasingly is assessed based upon the written work they submit.

Literacy and writing studies educators are all too familiar with the lamentations from faculty in other disciplines that our students *just can't write*. What does this statement mean? To the compositionist, writing involves putting language to thought through consideration of the audience with whom one communicates and the context in which the written communication occurs; construction of argument; evaluation and incorporation of source material that may build, support, or complicate an argument; and choices of distribution of information, diction, and style. Writing is about more than the final product: students write to learn, to document, to explain, to evaluate, and to communicate. To those outside of the field (and, unfortunately, more than a few within it), writing often refers primarily to the surface features of language, such as grammar and punctuation.

Outside of the writing classroom—and, to a considerable extent, inside of it—students' grades should be based on the content of their writing, not the language with which it is composed. There is no reason in the world that a student who writes about the fall of Rome in a world history class should be assessed on her command of standardized grammar rather than on her analysis of the ancient empire's decline. Even if instructors intend to grade on content, implicit bias and the subjectivity inherent to the grading of student essays may prevent students who write in other dialects from being graded on their content area knowledge. For this reason, instructors seeking to create more equitable classrooms must assess their own assessment practices.

Writing studies scholar Asao B. Inoue has written at length about the use of *labor-based contract grading* as an equitable approach to writing assessment. In contract grading, students' final course grades are the result of an agreement, laid out in the syllabus but more specific than the syllabus itself, between teachers and students: if students do a set of specific things, they will receive a B. In their original form, grading contracts have reserved A grades for writing deemed "exceptional" by the instructor, a judgment of quality left to the instructor.[33] Given the dominant discourse of the academy, however, this sort of contract "still participated in white language supremacy," for it implies that "all students had a right to their own languages, just not a right to an A, not a right to have their languages valued most highly, unless that language matched a white racial habitus."[34]

The labor-based contracts for which Inoue is an advocate, however, emphasize the amount and rigor of the labor students do for the course. The default grade is still a B, but students can work their way up to an A by doing additional work: they can write additional papers, provide feedback on drafts of their classmates' papers, lead a class discussion or workshop, or expand an existing assignment through more substantive research, reporting, or reflection. By emphasizing student labor rather the final product students produce, instructors can both acknowledge the effort individual students put into the class and contribute to a broader antiracist project that challenges traditional grading practices, which, in their reliance upon the evaluation of quality, a criterion hopelessly bound with hegemonic beliefs about language and writing, uphold white supremacy in the academy.

Grading contracts, of course, are only one approach to antiracist writing assessment. As Inoue explains, "Doing grading well, either at the secondary or postsecondary level, is not simply about finding the best practice, method, or mechanism. It is about understanding the various ways that the nature and function of grades might be constructed in a classroom, and the variety of consequences to learning that are possible."[35] Instructors don't necessarily have to upend their entire approach to grading. Instead, they can look at their assignments and the rubrics they are already using to assess student work and explore where room for bias exists:

- How much of the grade is subjective?
- Are the criteria clearly stated?
- Are grading procedures broken down or is the paper graded holistically?
- What percentage of a student's grade is derived from the evaluation of the student's writing?
- If words like *clarity*, *style*, or *quality* are part of the criteria upon which students' writing is graded, are those terms defined?
- If terms are defined, have students played a role in defining them?

Instructors can then make changes to better acknowledge students' diverse linguistic moves and avoid penalizing those who resist or lack fluency in Standardized Englishes. Terminology pertaining to language should be defined and discussed with students—and revised to reflect their expectations and goals as well as the instructor's. Students have more to contribute than assessment practices typically allow, and when students feel supported and appreciated as individuals with rich cultural and linguistic backgrounds, they are likelier to succeed as writers and learners.

Multiple Academic Englishes

Students who speak Englishes other than a standardized academic form often face affective challenges as well as academic ones. They may have been subjected to ridicule and marginalization for their dialects. They may be very used to using different language practices at home and in school, but they may become frustrated by the constant struggle to turn their thoughts into language deemed appropriate by their instructors. Like Holly, the student with whose story this chapter began, they may have internalized societal attitudes toward so-called nonstandard dialects. Devaluing language, however, also devalues the speakers of that language, and the ongoing internalization of white language supremacy has potentially traumatic effects on POCI.

Part of the work of the instructor, then, is to validate students' home languages and literacies in legitimate, sustaining ways. If appropriate to the course, instructors can include lessons on or discussions of language and dialect. If that seems off-topic, instructors can assign students to read relevant scholarship that isn't written in Standardized English. For example, in his work on *code-meshing*, the blend of multiple dialects or discourses in one text, writing studies and rhetoric scholar Vershawn Ashanti Young frequently code-meshes himself.

H. Samy Alim and Geneva Smitherman take a similar approach (which they call *style-shifting*) in their 2012 book, *Articulate While Black: Barack Obama, Language, and Race in the U.S.* Smitherman, a world-renowned linguist, has used Black English in her scholarship since the 1970s. Writer and editor Lee A. Tonouchi writes both scholarship and fiction in Hawaiian Pidgin. Many other widely acclaimed authors of fiction use dialects besides Standardized Englishes, such as Junot Diaz, whose Pulitzer Prize–winning *The Brief, Wondrous Life of Oscar Wao* code-meshes English and Spanish.

These works, written by eminent scholars and artists in their respective fields, are just as academic as those written solely in Standardized English—and that point must be made explicit in the classroom.

To ensure that reading these texts with students amounts to more than lip service and that the classroom challenges rather than perpetuates linguistic hegemony, students should be encouraged to analyze not only their own language practices and the language practices of others, classmates and scholars alike, but also the white supremacist ideologies that uphold the erroneous notion that one dialect of English is superior to others. The critical analysis of how race is languaged and how language is raced is an important step in the challenging of white hegemony in education. After all, "schooling should not be about convincing students to play the game but, rather, about helping them understand how the game's been rigged and, more importantly, how they can work to change it."[36]

SECONDARY STRATEGIES

While best practices in education, particularly in fields pertaining to language and literacy, encourage educators to meet students where they are, teach the whole student, and invite students to bring their own literacy experiences and expertise into the classroom, too often writing plays a gatekeeping function for already marginalized students. The five-paragraph essay, a template upon which much standardized testing is based, is de rigueur in secondary education, particularly in schools that teach traditionally underserved student populations, but the template exists within a deficit model of education that provides strategies for testing rather than frameworks for learning.[37]

The pressures placed on teachers to prepare students for these exams, however, often leads to overreliance on reductive models like the five-paragraph essay and leaves little space for students to practice other genres of academic discourse, including narrative writing. That standardized assessments are heavily biased toward those fluent in Standardized English and, accordingly, against POCI further contributes to the emphasis on dominant discourse, often to the exclusion of students' home dialects. As a result, regardless of their individual beliefs about language and dialect, teachers willingly or unintentionally reproduce hegemonic ideologies of language and discourse.

To challenge the ever-increasing "routinization of instruction" and its detrimental effects on marginalized students, high school English teacher Ah-Young Song uses poetry with multilingual learners as part of a turn toward "creative writing and alternative forms of assessments."[38] Though poetry is not part of the Common Core State Standards, when writing poetry, a creative genre typically associated with self-expression, students have more freedom to use their own language and style to express their ideas than they usually have when assigned academic essays. The students in Song's classroom wrote poems based upon their own experiences speaking and writing in past English classrooms; in doing so, they were able to "disrupt deficit-oriented conceptions of themselves through the act of creative writing."[39]

Song's pedagogy is merely one example of an approach that challenges and moves beyond assessments that are reliant upon white language and dominant discourses. Her approach, however, has considerable implications for the rewriting of trauma: because traumatic memories are typically nonlinear fragments of sensory input, poetry, which conveys meaning through sensory description and figurative language, is well suited to the artistic expression of trauma and the post-trauma self.

Further, though the poem may draw upon the author's personal experiences and observations, unlike the personal narrative, it need not present itself as a personal story. The confessional aspect that defines much of writing around pain and trauma doesn't disappear but is mediated and cloaked in imagery. The self is conveyed not through plot but through voice.

For teachers in secondary settings who resist the use of personal narratives either because they know students have traumas they are unwilling to share or for fear that they will hear from students (or read in their writing) experiences they are mandated to report, poems may be a useful alternative. The use of poetry also connects well to the literary focus of secondary English language arts classrooms. Students can use their own poetry and the choices they make as they write to explore literary techniques like word choice, figurative language, and tone, all of which are included in the secondary level standards and likely to appear on standardized exams.

Chapter 6
COLLEGE CONSIDERATIONS

Students frequently enter college familiar not with the conventions of academic genres but with formulas meant to mimic those conventions, such as the five-paragraph essay. Even when they demonstrate some familiarity with the conventions, they often lack the rhetorical awareness to interrogate the efficacy of those formulas in a given situation and to determine what genre and conventions that situation calls for.

For example, students may know what a scientific lab report looks like, but they may not understand that it includes great detail to ensure experimental replicability or that it is constructed in passive voice to deemphasize the role of the researcher. Especially, but not exclusively, in courses outside of the English department or composition program, college instructors expect students to demonstrate proficiency in college-level writing without providing it, which reinforces its gatekeeper function, especially for marginalized and minoritized racial formations.

A great deal of research has demonstrated that students of underrepresented ethnic, racial, and socioeconomic populations experience difficulty adhering to the conventions of academic writing, largely because those conventions conflict with students' home languages and literacies. Particularly on the two-year college level, lack of familiarity with the mechanics and formal features of Standardized Englishes often leads students, particularly POCI, to get stuck, so to speak, in developmental or basic skills classes that precede general education composition and confer no undergraduate-level credit. As a result, these students are less likely to transfer from a two-year college to a four-year college, less likely to graduate in a timely fashion, and less likely to graduate at all. Though developmental English is in the process of being phased out of many U.S. four-year colleges, students whose home languages differ from Standardized Englishes are still less likely than their peers to successfully complete credit-bearing writing courses.

Instructors, both those who explicitly teach writing and those whose course assessments are based on students' written work, must consider and honor the "affective and ideological conflicts" students face when writing on the college level, especially the disjunctions between instructors' expectations of student writing and students' expectations of the same.[40] To do this, first and foremost instructors must find out what students' expectations are and what conflicts they have faced or anticipate facing in the college classroom.

The *Language and Literacy Autobiography* (also called the *Literacy Narrative*) asks students to reflect upon their uses of language, reading, writing, and communication outside of the classroom. This type of assignment is a staple in many writing classrooms. It is less often used in other course contexts, but it has merit for any classroom in which students are expected to communicate their knowledge of the material through written English. Textbox 6.1 includes some guiding questions to help students craft their autobiographies.

> ### QUESTIONS TO GUIDE STUDENTS' LANGUAGE AND LITERACY AUTOBIOGRAPHIES
>
> - What language(s) did you hear and speak in your home growing up?
> - What language(s) did you hear and speak at school? In your community? In other places?
> - How did you typically communicate with people throughout your childhood? Did you talk on the phone, face to face, via email or text message?
> - Who were your *sponsors of literacy*? How did the people/institutions/other forces in your life encourage or discourage you to read/write/communicate?
> - What is your first memory of reading?
> - What have been your most significant experiences with reading, writing, and communicating? Why were they significant?
> - What kind of reading and writing do you do today?
> - What language(s) do you currently speak? In what language(s) do you read and/or write?
> - How have your experiences with the spoken and/or written word changed over the years? What might account for those changes?

An assignment like this is useful for both students and teachers. Students who conceive of writing as something they do primarily in school settings may realize upon completing the language and literacy autobiography that they actually compose texts multiple times a day, including, for example, text messages, emails, and posts on social media.

For educators, the assignment provides key insight into the linguistic and rhetorical strengths their students bring to the classroom. Too many teachers simply don't put in the effort required to understand their students' languages or identify their linguistic and rhetorical strengths. Some even claim that they can't read papers written in dialects other than Standardized Englishes. If anything, this claim demonstrates a deficiency or, rather, a resistance on the part of the reader, not the writer.

CONCLUDING THOUGHTS

Simultaneously and paradoxically, in both scholarly and popular discourse around trigger warnings, trauma has been conceptualized amorphously and through a narrow lens. The proliferation of the trigger warning as trauma-sensitive pedagogy conflates trauma with discomfort yet condemnations of trigger warnings as anti-intellectual or ineffective rely upon definitions of trauma and psychological frameworks that are rooted in Western male heteronormativity. Multicultural psychologists and scholars of counseling education have challenged the definitions of trauma that prevail in educational discourse, emphasizing its situatedness in white Western perspectives on mental health and emotional socialization and suggesting that "the traditional conceptualization of traumatic stress needs to be reconsidered to incorporate other forms of pervasive psychological intrusions, such as systemic oppression."[41]

Despite the intentions of those who advocate for the trigger warning as student-responsive pedagogy, the practice plays into a master narrative that omits many students' socially and culturally situated experiences of trauma. (For more, see chapter 3.) To more effectively understand, recognize, and respond to student trauma, scholars and educators must listen to and learn from counternarratives of trauma that represent the diversity of the student population.

However, educators, even those who believe their pedagogies to be student centered, must be ever cognizant of the power relations of the classroom, especially when dealing with matters as complex, identity shifting, and contextual as trauma and language, and especially in environments wherein the power dynamics are multiply layered, such as high-poverty urban schools wherein the student population is predominantly Black and the teaching faculty predominantly White. Just as there is nothing liberating about professing the importance of Standardized Englishes as a tool for upward mobility then devaluing or depriving students from drawing upon their own linguistic assets, there is nothing equitable about creating a curriculum wherein marginalized students share their stories of marginalization for the satisfaction and validation of a White teacher.

To ensure classroom spaces they create are critical and equitable, educators must consider their own roles in those classrooms, the best interests of their students, and the purposes served by the writing students do and the policies of language and assessment instructors put in place. Regardless of the course content or the curricular scaffolding put into place, students should never be forced to share trauma or emotional pain but, if they do feel moved to share, they should never be silenced.

NOTES

1. Barack Obama, *Audacity of Hope: Thoughts on Reclaiming the American Dream* (New York: Crown Publishers, 2006), 235.
2. "Veronique" (a pseudonym) was an eighteen-year-old first-year college student who participated in a racial literacy–themed writing course taught by the author of this book.
3. Camila Domonoske, "Segregated From Its History, How 'Ghetto' Lost Its Meaning," NPR.com, April 27, 2014.
4. Ibid.
5. H. Samy Alim and Geneva Smitherman use the phrase *languaging race* to denote the examination of politics of race through the lens of language.
6. H. Samy Alim and Geneva Smitherman, *Articulate while Black: Barack Obama, Language, and Race in the U.S.* (Oxford: Oxford University Press, 2012), 3.
7. William A. Kretzschmar Jr. and Charles F. Meyer, "The Idea of Standard American English," in *Standards of English: Codified Varieties around the World*, ed. Raymond Hickey (Cambridge: Cambridge University Press, 2013), 143.
8. Laura Greenfield, "The 'Standard English' Fairy Tale: A Rhetorical Analysis of Racist Pedagogies and Commonplace Assumptions about Language Diversity," in *Writing Centers and the New Racism: A Call for Sustainable Dialogue and Change*, ed. Laura Greenfield and Karen Rowan (Logan: Utah State University Press, 2011).
9. John Adams, 1780, quoted in Kretzschmar and Meyer, "The Idea of Standard American English," 140.
10. Rosina Lippi-Green, *English with an Accent: Language, Ideology, and Discrimination in the United States* (London: Routledge, 1997), 179.
11. While these comments are used against people of various minoritized racial formations, the literature demonstrates that they are most likely to be used in the ways described here.
12. Derald Wing Sue, Christina M. Capodilupo, Gina C. Torino, Jennifer M. Bucceri, Aisha M. B. Holder, Kevin L. Nadal, and Marta Esquilin, "Racial Microaggressions in Everyday Life: Implications for Clinical Practice," *American Psychologist* 62, no. 4 (2007): 271.
13. Bradley Campbell and Jason Manning, "Microaggression and Moral Cultures," *Comparative Sociology* 13 (2014): 715.
14. Eduardo Bonilla-Silva, *Racism without Racists: Color-Blind Racism and the Persistence of Racial Inequality in America*, 5th ed. (Lanham: Rowman & Littlefield, 2017), 2.
15. Greg Lukianoff and Jonathan Haidt, *The Coddling of the American Mind: How Good Intentions and Bad Ideas Are Setting Up a Generation for Failure* (New York: Penguin, 2018), 210.
16. Ibid., 209.
17. Ibid.
18. Campbell and Manning, "Microaggression and Moral Cultures," 715.
19. Eve Fairbanks, "The 'Reasonable' Rebels," *The Washington Post*, August 29, 2019.
20. Ibid.
21. The term was first used by Chester Pierce in 1978. See Derald Wing Sue, *Microaggressions in Everyday Life: Race, Gender, and Sexual Orientation* (Hoboken: Wiley, 2010), xvi. See also Chester Pierce, *Television and Education* (Beverly Hills: Sage, 1978).
22. See Mara Lee Grayson, *Teaching Racial Literacy: Reflective Practices for Critical Writing* (Lanham: Rowman & Littlefield, 2018).
23. For more on the five-paragraph-theme, see Edward M. White, "My Five-Paragraph-Theme Theme," in *What Is College-Level Writing? Volume 2*, ed. Patrick Sullivan, Howard Tinberg, and Sheridan Blau (Urbana: NCTE, 2010).
24. Louise M. Rosenblatt, *Literature as Exploration*, 5th ed. (New York: The Modern Language Association of America, 1995), 38.
25. Annie Murphy Paul, "Your Brain on Fiction," *The New York Times* (March 18, 2012), SR6.
26. Rachel N. Spear, "'Let Me Tell You a Story': On Teaching Trauma Narratives, Writing, and Healing," *Pedagogy: Critical Approaches to Teaching Literature, Language, Composition, and Culture* 14, no. 1 (2013): 67.

27. Elizabeth Dutro, "Writing Wounded: Trauma, Testimony, and Critical Witness in Literacy Classrooms," *English Education* 43, no. 2 (2011): 206.

28. Richard L. Young, Alton L. Becker, and Kenneth L. Pike, *Rhetoric: Discovery and Change* (New York: Harcourt Brace Jovanovich, 1970), 25.

29. Elizabeth Dutro, "Writing Wounded," 207.

30. Ibid., 195.

31. Andre (a pseudonym), quoted in Mara Lee Grayson, *Teaching Racial Literacy*, 88.

32. Victor Villanueva, "Whose Voice Is It Anyway?" *English Journal* 76, no. 8 (1987): 21.

33. Asao B. Inoue, *Labor-Based Grading Contracts: Building Equity and Inclusion in the Compassionate Writing Classroom* (Fort Collins: WAC Clearinghouse, 2019), 62.

34. Ibid.

35. Ibid., 3.

36. Alim and Smitherman, *Articulate while Black*, 192.

37. UNC Charlotte Writing Project Collaborative, "The Five-Paragraph Essay and the Deficit Model of Education," *English Journal* 98, no. 2 (2008).

38. Ah-Young Song, "Voice and Experience: Forming Counter-narratives through Personal Poetry," *English Journal* 108, no. 3 (2019): 74.

39. Ibid., 77.

40. Mary Lea and Brian Street, "Student Writing in Higher Education: An Academic Literacies Approach," *Studies in Higher Education* 23, no. 2 (1998): 159.

41. Rachael D. Goodman and Cirecie A. West-Olatunji, "Educational Hegemony, Traumatic Stress, and African American and Latino American Students," *Journal of Multicultural Counseling and Development* 38 (2010): 184.

Chapter Seven

Career Considerations

Managing Challenges to Emotional Health and Academic Freedom

Larry is a part-time faculty member teaching composition and legal writing at a private research university in a major metropolitan area. Originally trained as a lawyer, Larry's experience served him well when he began teaching writing and rhetoric: his students appreciated what Larry calls his "real world" approach, which emphasized information and critical media literacies and practical persuasive writing, like cover letters and responses to political arguments.

A White man in his midthirties, Larry believes that his relative youth compared with his coworkers makes him accessible to students. He's the kind of teacher who hangs around after class to meet with students, who answers emails on the weekend, and who writes recommendation letters for past students during the summer.

One afternoon, a student approached Larry after the rest of the class had left. She explained that she had been involved in an altercation over the weekend: she had been out dancing with a group of friends when an acquaintance touched her in a way she wasn't comfortable with. She didn't say more than that, except to add that her father wanted her to press charges. She wasn't sure if she should pursue legal action.

"I know you went to law school," she said. "I thought you might be able to tell me what to do."

Larry was at a loss. For starters, he wasn't sure about what had actually happened to the student because she hadn't provided a lot of detail. He knew that, in general, sexual assault cases were difficult to prosecute. Even when the situation was clear, he knew that it could be a lengthy, painful process and that the process could be retraumatizing for the victim. He also knew that sometimes pressing charges was an important part of recovery.

But he couldn't, in his position as her instructor, provide legal advice, and as a relatively new faculty member, though he knew he was a mandated reporter, he wasn't sure about the extent of his responsibilities. He couldn't in good conscience give his student the answer she was looking for because the decision, however difficult, was hers to make.

"I felt like I just had to tiptoe while finding new ways of saying what little I could," Larry recalls. "So I said to her: 'I can only tell you basically that, in this kind of situation, no decision you make is the wrong decision. But it's not going to be me who tells you which decision that is.'"

"It was so brutal," Larry says of the exchange. He laments that it is sometimes difficult to be the kind of teacher he wants to be and to provide the support his students need, especially because it often feels like he's working a full-time job on a part-time salary. Of instructors like himself, he says: "You're compassionate but it means that you're staying late, you're taking their burdens."

Much of the advocacy for practices like the trigger warning seems to stem from concern that students will become victims of a classroom power dynamic that puts them at the mercy of instructors who may force them to encounter material for which they are emotionally unprepared. This view of teachers is a sad and limited one, promulgated perhaps by (mis)representations in popular culture: in one trope, the teacher is a power-tripping ogre whose primary source of happiness is the ridicule of students and the destruction of their youthful hope. Consider the rigid, tweed-clad college professor who refuses to answer students' questions in class or speak with students during office hours or the grumpy, aging high school teacher who takes pleasure in public mockery of teenagers.

Unfortunately, however, there are teachers who fit this stereotype. Just as many educators enter the teaching force inspired by powerful teachers in their schooling experiences, many educators who employ critical and culturally relevant pedagogies do so in part because of the uncritical, culturally insensitive curricula to which they were exposed at the hands of their own teachers.

There are just as many if not more educators who fit another problematic stereotype, one that is particularly dangerous in a healing-oriented classroom: the teacher as selfless savior. In this narrative, the teacher is a selfless martyr whose purpose in life is the education of students and whose happiness is dependent upon the ability to rescue those little lost souls in the classroom.

Countless popular culture narratives employ this trope: consider the university lecturer played by Julia Roberts in the film *Mona Lisa Smile*, who jeopardizes her career for the sake of a small group of students she's known for mere months, or the high school social studies teacher played by Gabe Kaplan on the 1970s television sitcom *Welcome Back, Kotter*, whose class of "remedial sweathogs" regularly climbed through the window of his Brooklyn apartment. This narrative feeds (and is perpetuated by) political rhetoric used to justify low teacher salaries, limited school resources, and teachers' out-of-pocket expenses. Even the news stories meant to challenge such rhetoric, like exposés about adjunct faculty members living out of their cars and heartfelt tales of schoolteachers who work two jobs yet use their limited income to buy books for their students, inadvertently feed it.

Worse, the teacher-as-martyr trope can morph quickly into a white savior narrative: consider the teachers played by Michelle Pfeiffer and Hilary Swank in, respectively, *Dangerous Minds* and *Freedom Writers*, White women whose stories center on their journeys to bring education to poor, Black, inner-city students. Unfortunately, to many would-be teachers, this trope is attractive. White women teachers and teacher candidates in particular may take on the white savior role: when beliefs about critical pedagogy are steeped in white hegemonic ideology and implicit bias, and accompanied by limited experience, White women may "profess liberal values and innocence from racist and sexist acts while accessing discursive repertoires which perform them as dominant and rational."[1]

These narratives lead to a public perception of educators in which those who teach are fitted into a false binary: they are either savior or oppressor, power-tripping stickler or lifelong buddy. They are committed to their work to the exclusion of all else or they are disinterested and burnt out, eager only to have the summer off. Obscured by these limited narratives are the actual, complex experiences of educators on both the K–12 and postsecondary levels, and the nuanced, deeply situated ways in which educators' multiple roles in the classroom can serve to challenge or perpetuate the inequities of U.S. schooling.

To understand how teachers can teach more equitably in the age of the trigger warning, it is first necessary to consider how the choices teachers make are influenced by contemporary political and public discourse as well as their own instincts for self-preservation. It is necessary to explore how educators experience grief and trauma, both as witnesses to the traumas experienced by the student population and as individuals susceptible to traumatic experiences of their own. It is necessary to identify the unpaid and unacknowledged emotional labor heaped onto teachers in the twenty-first century as well and to consider who bears the brunt of that labor on the departmental, campus-wide, and societal levels. Finally, it is necessary to come up with classroom practices and campus policies that respond equitably and comprehensively to the lived experiences of students, teachers, and communities while also ensuring that teachers can continue their work from one week to the next without fear of losing their jobs.

CAUTIOUS CLASSROOMS: CHALLENGES TO ACADEMIC FREEDOM

Some educators and scholars condemn the trigger warning as yet another way in which the oversensitivity of the student population is squashing open discourse in the classroom. It is from this perspective that one is likely to hear about threats to *academic freedom*, the idea that educators and students should be free to pursue scholarly inquiry, even if controversial, without institutional or administrative rebuke or censure.

Regardless of how one sees the trigger warning, it is impossible to deny that a major challenge to the efficacy of critical, trauma-informed pedagogies is the censorship of open conversation in the academy in general and the classroom in particular. The current U.S. political climate and recent suspensions of schoolteachers and university faculty members over politically charged public statements have made some educators question their institutions' commitment to academic freedom while others have increased self-censorship for fear of rebuke from administrators, students, or parents.

Personal Expression and Job Insecurity

In 2013, David Guth, a communications professor specializing in crisis communication, was placed on leave by Kansas University after he posted a tweet blaming the NRA for a mass shooting in Washington, DC. In 2017, George Ciccariello-Maher, then a tenured associate professor of politics and global studies at Drexel University, resigned after being placed on administrative leave for comments he made about white supremacy following the mass murder of fifty-eight people at a Las Vegas concert. Earlier that same year, Johnny Eric Williams, an associate professor of sociology, was suspended by Trinity College in Connecticut shortly after sharing an article titled "Let Them Fucking Die" and using the title as a hashtag in his retweet, which called for an end to white supremacy.

In May 2019, James M. Thomas, an associate professor of sociology at the University of Mississippi, almost lost his bid for tenure, despite the recommendations of reviewers, because of tweets he had posted the previous year. Weighing in on public debates over the interruption of Republican politicians' meals by critics, Thomas suggested that politicians whose policies are harmful to citizens don't deserve to be treated with civility, after which a Republican state senator publicly called Thomas "a low-life liberal" and demanded disciplinary action.[2]

In none of these situations did the faculty member's tweet lead directly to disciplinary actions by the university. Instead, disciplinary actions came only after the tweets were picked up by conservative media outlets that claimed the professors were inciting violence against White people.

To many in academia, attacks on faculty members by right-wing media are "smear campaigns"[3] orchestrated "with the goal of silencing academics."[4] The professional organization the American Association of University Professors (AAUP) has condemned attacks on faculty members, noting that "such threatening messages are likely to stifle free expression and cause faculty and others on campus to self-censor so as to avoid being subjected to similar treatment"[5] and has criticized the subsequent punitive actions taken by universities. The chair of the AAUP's Committee on Academic Freedom and Tenure called Williams's suspension a "clear violation of the professor's academic freedom."[6]

Some might wonder if these incidents are outliers, unique situations that have arisen from extraordinary circumstances; they are not. The publicity surrounding the incidents described in detail here is not the result of their singularity but an amalgamation of numerous factors including when and where they occurred; how, when, and by whom they were reported; and whether they went viral on social media or were picked up by media outlets. Plenty of other, similar incidents have received far less press, particularly those in which the faculty members involved lacked the protections usually afforded by tenure.

In June 2017, Lisa Durden, an adjunct professor at Essex County College, was fired after she defended a Black Lives Matter chapter event to which only people of color were invited. In July 2017, Ruthie Robertson, an adjunct instructor of international politics, was fired from Brigham Young University after declaring her support for LGBT rights in a private Facebook post. In August 2017, the University of Tampa chose not to rehire Kenneth Storey, a visiting faculty member in sociology who tweeted that Hurricane Harvey "kinda feels like [instant karma] for Texas. Hopefully this will help them realize the GOP doesnt care about them."[7]

Though these incidents may represent a trend of quashing free speech on the university level, secondary educators have been subjected to similar disciplinary actions as a result of their lives outside of school. In September 2016, Veronica Welsh, a foreign language teacher in New York, was assigned to administrative duty after posting on Facebook that students who supported Donald Trump were racist. In April 2017, Olivia Sprauer, a Florida English teacher who also worked as a bikini model (under a different name), was pushed to resign after her modeling photographs surfaced. In August 2018, Kandice Mason, a sixth-grade teacher from Georgia who teaches pole dance fitness classes, was suspended after photographs of her pole dancing were shared with school district officials.

Censorship and Self-Censorship

Fearing they will be held accountable for what they share or say on social media, many educators who are active on Twitter now profess in their profiles that their tweets are their own and are not representative of their institutions, but such disclaimers provide few if any legal protections for those who use them.

Some school districts and universities have policies in place with strict guidelines for what teachers can and cannot say both in the classroom and on social media. For example, in school districts across the country, in places as diverse as New York City and rural Georgia, teachers are prohibited from sharing their political views with students. Outside of school, teachers' free speech is protected only in situations wherein the speech addresses a matter of public concern and is not disruptive to the school environment. Of course, in many cases, speech that is protected by the former criterion is not protected by the latter. This means that, should a teacher post on social media a response to a political matter unrelated to the school, an action that seemingly is protected under the First Amendment, the subsequent backlash from others on social media can be cause for termination due to the publicity it heaps upon the school.

Behavioral guidelines for college-level educators tend to be more lax than those on the secondary level, if they exist at all, but the hiring structure of the academy may contribute to a culture of caution and concern for a majority of instructors. While there are departmental and university guidelines for the renewal or termination of contracts for university faculty members on the tenure track, there are far fewer requirements for terminating faculty members hired on a contractual basis, such as part-time adjunct and full-time non-tenure-track instructors. (Contingent faculty now make up more than 75 percent of college-level educators.[8]) At university systems with strong contingent faculty unions, such as the California State University or the City University of New York, there are guidelines in place for when and how adjunct faculty members may be released, but such university systems are few and far between.

Similarly, though there are protections for tenured schoolteachers, in many school districts, secondary teachers without tenure can be nonrenewed for any reason at all.

Cautious Classrooms

Inside the classroom, even when teachers do not share their personal political views, they may be apprehensive about sharing political material because of potential negative reactions from students, parents, and administrators. Though making connections between historical and contemporary events is among best practices in history and social studies education, many teachers became cautious about drawing too many comparisons to current events following Donald Trump's election. As one history teacher notes, "All of a sudden it seems to be taboo to talk about government, politics, civics."[9]

Contributing to that sense of taboo are situations like what happened to Frank Navarro in the days following the election in November 2016: Navarro, a Northern California high school history teacher and Holocaust scholar, was placed on leave after students and parents complained about a lesson he gave comparing Trump to Adolf Hitler.

Concerns about backlash from students may also cause instructors on the college level to limit the extent to which they discuss difficult topics in the classroom. Because negative student evaluations can contribute to a contingent faculty member not being hired the next semester, some instructors who lack the protections of the tenure track avoid addressing politically charged topics.[10] While it *may* be possible for an adjunct professor of earth sciences to talk climate change without getting into the politicized discourse around global warming, it's virtually impossible for an adjunct professor of political science to avoid talking politics or for an adjunct professor of sociology to avoid talking about society.

To those who advocate its usage, the trigger warning seems like a useful strategy for easing into conversations that may be contentious. The trigger warning, however, would not have prevented these situations from occurring. Race talk, and talk about other political and societal problems and hierarchies, are frequently referred to as *difficult discussions* or *controversial conversations*, but these euphemisms obscure the real issue. After all, it isn't the subject matter of talk that, for some, is seen as a problem; it is more so the critical nature of the talk, the viewpoints expressed, and the people who express them.

Who's at Risk?

In the current political climate, it sometimes seems remarkably difficult just to do one's job. For some educators, just doing one's job has always been difficult.

Given the overwhelming White majority of the teaching force in the United States, educators of color are often isolated in their departments or on their campuses. At the same time, they are expected to take on many different roles in addition to their teaching duties: POCI may be expected to mentor marginalized students, to advise student affinity groups, to serve as the voice of diversity on committees and task forces, and to "represent the views of a variety of ethnic groups in even the most informal conversations."[11]

Additionally, educators of color (and other marginalized groups, including members of the LGBTQIA+ community) are often assigned to teach what may be referred to as *diversity courses,* typically elective classes that highlight the experiences or work of marginalized individuals in a particular field. Whether teachers want to teach these classes is often left out of scheduling decisions; it is simply assumed that POCI will teach classes about POCI and mentor students who are POCI. This is even more troubling given that POCI, especially women, already wage an uphill battle talking about social and political issues in the classroom and are already subjected to discrimination in formal evaluation processes.

These expectations create situations in which those who are already marginalized are teaching complex material on campuses without the support structures to protect them from student resistance or parental complaints. As Patricia A. Matthew, an English professor and scholar of faculty diversity in higher education, so succinctly asked in the weeks following the 2016 presidential election: "If, generally speaking, classes that ask students to reexamine their assumptions about race and racism are challenging, what is in place to protect faculty who lead difficult class conversations in this particularly volatile moment?"[12]

There are indeed challenges to academic freedom in this country—but not necessarily for the people who are complaining about it the loudest. The victimization culture (see chapter 6) some sociologists blame for the rise of trigger warnings, safe spaces, and microaggressions is typically and reductively associated with youth, racial and ethnic diversity, and the political Left. According to conservative educators and political pundits, the academy is too liberal. Calls for *viewpoint diversity* might lead people to believe that voices from the political Right are silenced in school settings when, in fact, comprehensive research conducted *by conservative scholars* has concluded that right-wing activists are "overstating the extent to which conservatives are mistreated" on college campuses![13]

In nearly all of the cases identified in this chapter, faculty members were publicly attacked or officially disciplined (or both) for comments or actions that challenged, directly or implicitly, the white supremacy that undergirds U.S. institutions and policies and which is furthered by conservative political rhetoric.

Scholars who use their experience and expertise to point out racism are subject to attacks and threats then penalized by their institutions for being publicly victimized or for simply having the audacity to call out inequity. Women educators who violate puritanical norms of behavior by showing skin in a photograph or teaching pole dancing on the weekend to earn extra money must either self-censor or be subject to punitive measures. (That women in bikinis are plastered all over popular media and that pole dancing is an increasingly common fitness trend and competitive style of dance all over the U.S. only add to the hypocrisy of such measures.) As has always been the case, those most at risk in the current sociopolitical and educational climate are those whose identities or behaviors challenge the status quo.

The policies written to prevent teachers from crossing these lines (or to defend institutions for firing those who do) are both discriminatory, in that they disproportionately affect specific populations of educators, and out of touch with the realities of the contemporary United States. One such reality is the financial hardship faced by many of the nation's educators. A teacher shouldn't need to work a second job in the first place but, because of the cultural devaluing of the teaching profession and the inequities of American capitalism, such as the ever-growing costs of real estate and student loans, many teachers do.

In 2018, nearly 20 percent of all public school teachers in the United States held a second job, a percentage *five times* the national average for full-time working adults.[14] Many teachers take on teaching or tutoring assignments outside of their districts in addition to teaching summer classes or in after-school programs. In some areas, teachers work as drivers for ridesharing services like Uber or Lyft; in other areas, they work evening or weekend shifts at supermarkets, warehouses, and fast-food restaurants. Across the country, public school teachers moonlight as private tutors, athletic coaches, dance and fitness instructors, ushers at sporting events, animal trainers, and bus drivers.[15]

Three-quarters of college-level instructors are hired on a contingent basis, making it even more common to find postsecondary educators who hold more than one job. In some fields, teaching may be the second job for an adjunct faculty member, as in the case of medical practitioners who teach future nurses and doctors or business professionals who teach an evening course or two in their area of expertise each year. In other fields, it is common for graduate students to teach lower-division courses while they complete their master's or doctorate degrees.

Many other contingent faculty members, however, are experienced teachers with terminal degrees for whom teaching is their primary job. Earning a living as an adjunct, though, is exceedingly difficult: in the United States, the average compensation for teaching a college class is only $2,700 and a large majority of adjunct faculty are not eligible for medical or retirement benefits.[16] To eke out a living, many instructors are *freeway flyers* who teach numerous courses at different institutions, often commuting between campuses each day, and an increasing number also teach online. Despite being employed as part-timers at each individual school, these instructors very often teach the equivalent of a full-time course load for a third of the pay that full-time faculty members receive. Like public schoolteachers, many instructors also work second jobs outside of the education sector. Still, one-quarter of adjunct instructors receive public assistance.[17]

In this economic context, no teacher who works a second job to supplement her income should have to worry that the second job will cost her the first, especially when that second job is legal, necessary, and in no way hinders her ability to do what she was hired to do: teach.

Another example of the incongruity between policy and reality are social media policies, which disproportionately affect younger teachers and faculty members who have grown up with and are active on social media. While many policies have been written or amended in the years since the proliferation of social media, most have been created with the purpose of regulation as much as integration.

Schools may use social media to announce events and connect with the community, but they also regulate employee use, even when that use is unrelated to the school or its students. That Millennials are also the most racially and ethnically diverse generation in U.S. history means that younger educators of color may be at increased risk of being held accountable by their employers for what they do and say as educators and outside of school. This is especially problematic because, given that the teaching force in the United States is predominantly White, many young teachers of color who feel isolated on their campuses use social media to connect with educators in other schools who share their experiences.

GRIEF AND TRAUMA AMONG THE TEACHING FORCE

Teachers, of course, are immune to neither trauma nor marginalization, and they work in the same hegemonic educational institutions that their students attend. In educational research and scholarship, however, teachers' feelings and lived experiences are underacknowledged and understudied, often taking a backseat to seemingly more practical matters of professionalization, such as teacher preparation and pedagogical inquiry, or emphasis on students' well-being.

Professional and Personal Trauma

It would stand to reason that teachers are as likely as any other professional to experience trauma. The relationship between teaching and mental health, however, is complex: despite high turnover rates, teaching tends to be associated with high job satisfaction, largely because of the passion for the act of teaching itself. At the same time, considerable research demonstrates that teaching is more stressful than many other jobs.

Echoing the results of previous studies, a 2017 survey conducted by the American Federation of Teachers found that educators find work twice as stressful and report having poor mental health at twice the rate of other U.S. workers.[18] Some of this stress is due to the job itself: between teaching classes, planning lessons, conferencing with students during office hours, and participating in meetings and professional development, both secondary and college-level educators have very little downtime during the average workday. Educators experience additional stress as the result of administrative and bureaucratic pressures, and, since the 2016 presidential election, teachers feel increasingly unsupported and disrespected by elected officials and popular media.

Because full-time postsecondary positions, on or off the tenure track, are scarce, even accomplished, highly competitive teacher-scholars find themselves competing with possibly hundreds of other candidates for a single position. On-campus interviews, which may already require one to take time off from work, leave family, and travel to another state for a full day (or two) of interviews, research talks, and teaching demonstrations, are not always funded, which puts candidates with fewer financial resources at a disadvantage. These interviews, which often also require candidates to dine and socialize with search committee members, are physically, mentally, and emotionally exhausting.

Those who receive a job offer often are required to move, perhaps alone or perhaps with family, to another part of the country. For many faculty members, who may have already moved away from home for graduate school, this move will be one of many. Moving is already a difficult and potentially traumatic experience, compounded by the distance between the individual and their existing support systems. This is common practice in academia and, as such, but its normalization perpetuates and normalizes the emotional distress it causes.

Teachers, like anyone else, are susceptible to personal trauma and post-traumatic stress, and they may actually be at increased risk for secondary traumatization when compared with other professional populations. For example, though most research on the professional impact of another's suicide has been conducted on within the field of mental health care, the limited research that exists has shown that teachers experience considerable personal and professional deficits following a student's suicide.[19] Given that suicide is the second leading cause of death among adolescents and young adults in the United States,[20] it is not unlikely that a teacher will lose a student to suicide during her career.

Racial Trauma

Just as students who identify as POCI experience racial trauma in the school setting as a result of numerous factors including but not limited to the erasure of marginalized stories and voices from the curriculum (what some have called *epistemic genocide*), on-campus marginalization, teachers' biases, and the white supremacy of the curriculum, classroom pedagogies, and campus culture, teachers who identify as POCI experience the same.

Some research has shown that teachers are even more segregated in the United States than are students. POCI are far likelier to teach in schools that serve a diverse student population than in PWIs; those teachers of color and indigenous teachers who do teach on predominantly White campuses are often the only (or one of very few) POCI among the faculty. The incidence of workplace bullying is more than three times as high for teachers than for other U.S. workers,[21] and POCI, particularly in PWIs, are likely to be targeted by their colleagues. Black, Latinx, and Native American educators in particular report feeling that they must prove their worth as educators in order to be taken seriously by coworkers, administrators, students, and, on the K–12 levels, parents. Teachers who identify as POCI are questioned about their credentials, passed over for advancement over equally qualified or less qualified White colleagues, and may be ignored, insulted, or taunted by White coworkers. Black teachers, like their students, "feel pressured to police their own behavior so they could be seen as more professional" and avoid fulfilling others' stereotypes.[22]

While a majority of people in the United States would not encourage their children to become teachers,[23] people continue to be drawn to the profession. Because education so often is framed as liberatory and uplifting, particularly for members of underserved communities, those who do enter the field tend to feel hopeful and excited about the roles they intend to play in providing such an education. The pull toward college-level teaching can be even higher, not least because the title of *professor* has a certain allure to it (especially when it is not preceded by the modifiers that indicate the numerous rungs of the academic hierarchy).

Unfortunately, the realities of U.S. education provide an unwelcome wake-up call for new educators, particularly POCI. In addition to low salaries and limited job security, teachers see from a perspective unavailable to those outside of the system the inequities of schooling, from limited resources, prescriptive curricula, and standardized testing to discriminatory policies and draconian disciplinary measures. As Jerica Coffey and Stephanie Cariaga, former high school teachers who have each founded nonprofit organizations dedicated to educational justice, explain: "We each went into teaching because of the promise education represents in our communities' struggles for self-determination. What we didn't envision were the ways that poverty would manifest in our classrooms and, even worse, the ways our school would blatantly ignore our students' pressing needs."[24]

Those who recognize these inequities often feel powerless to do anything about them and, as a result, grapple with the role they play in the system that perpetuates them. Still, teachers like Coffey, Cariaga, and countless others across the country use their curricula to challenge the inequities their students experience and to subvert the neoliberalism and standardization that perpetuate those inequities—but such work in the classroom comes at a cost.

Curricular Labor

Every semester, Candace, a White, female writing professor in a PWI in the American South, assigns her first-year students an activity she calls In the News. For this assignment, students work in small groups to find and lead a discussion about a recent news article that stands out to them. "This is an exposure exercise," she says.

Though she has been using this assignment for many years, Candace introduced trigger warnings after three students with trauma histories confessed to experiencing discomfort when their classmates shared an article about sexual assault, which resulted in a hurtful discussion with "students questioning choices made by the victim." Now, she requires students to share their articles with her before bringing them in for the presentation so that she can determine whether a trigger warning will be necessary for that class session.

Still, for Candace, who describes herself as a "logical responder," attending to students' emotions can be difficult, even with the trigger warning: "With that assignment, I'm constantly feeling like I am not providing the support that's needed at that moment when it gets really intense."

One such intense moment arose when Candace, who always models the activity for her students before they complete the assignment, brought in a news story about racist threats on college campuses. The discussion that ensued exposed the racial illiteracy that prevails in predominantly White settings like Candace's university. Most of the White students in the class were confused by the mention of a noose in the article, as they were unaware of its violent racist implications. Candace was surprised by her White students' lack of awareness and what that signified about the gaps in their education. Mostly, though, she was worried about the three Black students in her classroom of twenty-two: "Having my [Black] students be subject to hearing that [White] students don't know what a noose is—and hearing the insensitivity that comes out of them because of that . . . as a teacher, you don't want that to happen."

Recalling the situation, Candace sighs. "Sometimes I find this assignment so exhausting," she says, "but every semester I get such positive feedback about it."

Like Candace, many educators who engage critical pedagogies, whether the focus of that pedagogy is trauma, racism, or another societal ill, are passionate about their work yet admit that it can be emotionally, physically, and mentally taxing. No matter how many resource guides are written, no matter how many professional development trainings are provided, designing equitable curricula is *not* easy: it requires the abilities to connect content and approach, establish rapport and trust with students, examine and check one's own positionality, and anticipate, recognize, and respond to the needs of the students in the classroom. Teachers often feel responsible for students' emotional well-being—whether or not they feel equipped to provide the support students may need.

Further, the types of teaching practices that have been proven to respond most equitably to a diverse student population do not blend easily with the standardization and white cultural hegemony of contemporary education. On the secondary level, teachers may feel torn between an emphasis on critical inquiry or culturally relevant pedagogy and the need to prepare students for statewide exams and to meet official curricular milestones. Many Latinx teachers who incorporate culturally relevant pedagogies have had to "think unconventionally" and "stretch school rules and/or policies to better serve their students," which "drew objections and criticism from other teachers and even school leaders."[25]

Some educational researchers have attributed the pressures placed on POCI educators to the systemic *double bind* of the education system, "reflected in conflicting approaches to improving educational outcomes for students from nondominant cultural and linguistic communities."[26] Though qualitative and quantitative research as well as anecdotal evidence demonstrate that exposure to culturally relevant pedagogies and opportunities to connect with teachers who are POCI are especially helpful in improving educational outcomes for marginalized students, the standardization of U.S. schooling, which has far worse implications for marginalized students, prevents easy implementation of those approaches that have proven effective. In other words, POCI are often expected "to be the racial conscience of their institutions while not ruffling too many of the wrong feathers."[27]

On the college level, as antiracist educator Irene A. Lietz points out, institutions often do not provide the "mechanisms of support"[28] integral to challenging inequity beyond the classroom, creating a troublesome disconnect between the work students do inside the classroom and the rest of their on-campus experiences. While this can be disappointing for students, it can also cause them to doubt the significance of the curricular work; if the rest of the campus is not on board, students unfamiliar with the inequities of educational structures might come to see the coursework as part of an individual teacher's so-called agenda. This dissonance can leave teachers feeling frustrated and defeated. As Lietz asks: "What are we to do when even our best students and teachers who are honestly struggling to create change are unable to sustain an anti-racist project longer than one sixteen-week course?"[29]

Extracurricular Labor

On some campuses, resources are available to extend the work of critical pedagogies outside the classroom. Teachers often are called upon to take on this work, but doing so comes with additional labor and emotional effects. Yet the emotional labor required of teachers outside of the classroom is an underacknowledged and understudied area of research and scholarship, often taking a backseat to pedagogical inquiry and emphasis on students' well-being.

Teachers like Larry, the adjunct professor with whose story this chapter began, may find that their seeming accessibility to students comes with additional work and challenges. For many educators, forming strong relationships with students is an important and even necessary part of the work; still, as Larry experienced, gaining students' trust can lead to longer work hours and new ethical conflicts. Though Larry knew not to provide legal advice to his student, he also struggled with how to convey that to her.

With a few exceptions, teachers aren't trained as psychologists and, as a result, may be unsure how to respond to their students' more personal shares. This work is *invisible labor*, not because it isn't seen (although sometimes it isn't) but because it is not typically counted among the contractual requirements for the job or the departmental requirements for reappointment, tenure, or promotion and, as such, comes with little formal acknowledgment or reward from the institution or one's colleagues.

There are, of course, more formal, better seen forms of extracurricular labor on high school and college campuses, typically referred to as *internal service*, unpaid work that contributes to the departmental and campus community. The labor of internal service is unevenly distributed, especially in postsecondary institutions: White women take on more of this labor than do White men, and women of color take on more of this labor than do men of color.[30] Because tenure and promotion guidelines typically give less weight to service than to research or teaching, women often find that their service works against rather than for them and can event postpone or prevent tenure. (Interestingly, women are not likelier to take on *external service*, a type of service that involves working within one's discipline or with the community, and which tends to carry more weight and add greater value to one's academic portfolio.)

On both the secondary and postsecondary levels, the types of labor requested or required of educators tend to differ, often according to normative societal expectations and stereotypes. For example, men are likelier to volunteer for projects related to their research agendas, while women are likely to do internal service related to regular departmental upkeep (the so-called housekeeping of the university), event planning, and extracurricular work with students. Female faculty members are also more frequently approached outside of class by students with requests both academic (such as individual conferences and letters of recommendation) and personal (such as help working through a romantic or family struggle or assistance with school matters unrelated to coursework) than their male colleagues. Younger faculty members are also likelier than are older faculty members to be approached by students, who may feel that younger teachers will understand them better due to the smaller generation gap.

Teachers who identify as POCI may find that, regardless of their research or teaching interests or experience, they are asked to participate in diversity initiatives, posts in which they may serve as resources from whom White faculty can learn about the experiences of POCI on the campus or in the community. Such service, while seemingly progressive and oriented toward equity, is actually highly problematic, for it often benefits White faculty members at a cost to faculty of color. The work may require that educators work outside their academic areas of expertise, which can add to existing workloads and lead to a decrease in their individual scholarly activity. Furthermore, for educators who are already minoritized in their institutions, this work can be emotionally painful; its ongoing nature can have deleterious effects on educators' mental health and lead to early career burnout.

In many cases, educators who are minoritized and overworked continue to do this extra work outside of the classroom and not always because it is required. As is often the case, teachers do what they do because they care about the students they serve. For many teachers, extracurricular emotional labor, even when it feeds inadvertently into a workforce dynamic that perpetuates educational inequity, is a labor of love—but teachers "can't pay their bills with love."[31]

SECONDARY STRATEGIES

There are more teachers in the United States than there were during the last two decades of the twentieth century, yet the average teacher of the twenty-first century is both younger and newer to the profession than was the case thirty years ago. Most troubling, teachers today are likelier to abandon the profession than they were some thirty years ago. In other words, teachers are entering the field—but they aren't staying in it. While some teachers leave their positions for personal reasons, such as health and familial obligations, nearly half of those who abandon teaching do so because of dissatisfaction with the job, citing poor working conditions, low salaries, limited classroom resources, and few growth opportunities.[32]

While there is clearly a need for broad structural change to improve working conditions in U.S. public schools, anecdotal and experiential research suggest that local support structures may help to lower rates of teacher attrition by improving teachers' experiences in their first few years in the profession. Mentorships, for example, in which new teachers are paired with more experienced teachers, can help new teachers become acquainted with the school setting, gain confidence as educators, broaden their teaching toolboxes, manage professional challenges, and cope with the feelings associated with the new position.

New teachers may struggle to meet both the requirements of the position and live up to the goals they have set for themselves as educators. Job security concerns, however, may prevent them from requesting the help they need. A mentor who has experience in the field or the particular school but who holds no supervisory power over the new teacher can be an important ally. Mentorships may be on-site, meaning the mentor teacher is a colleague in one's own school or department, or they may be arranged through professional networks. In addition to helping familiarize inexperienced teachers with the ins and outs of the school, on-site mentorships can be helpful for teachers who may not be new to the profession but who are new to the particular school or even grade level.

In this age of standardized testing and accountability measures, teachers may feel that they are under surveillance. Therefore, it is important that mentoring and evaluation are distinct, if related, practices. Though a department chair may be an invaluable resource, it is possible that a new teacher will be uncomfortable opening up to a supervisor responsible for conducting an in-class observation or writing an annual performance evaluation. A colleague serving as a mentor, however, may be able to contribute a letter of support for a teacher's file, should one be requested.

While most new teachers struggle to adapt to the school environment, the struggle to adapt to the school environment can be especially difficult for teachers who discover that the school is not adapting itself to them. Unfortunately, many teachers, particularly POCI, do not receive the support they need from their colleagues or supervisors. In such cases, mentoring initiatives organized by professional groups can provide support and guidance for new teachers. Many national professional groups for teachers, such as the National Council of Teachers of English, already have programs in place to support early career educators of color; when they don't, caucuses and affinity groups within larger professional organizations often serve as informal support networks.

Depending upon the professional organization through which teachers are paired, new teachers may be assigned mentors as close by as the other side of town or as far away as the other side of the country. Although mentors in different schools, cities, or states may not be able to offer their mentees the inside scoop on a particular school or department, they can help new teachers expand their content knowledge and increase their confidence as content area teachers. Depending upon their training, new teachers may enter the profession with more knowledge of pedagogical theory than the content area in which they are assigned to teach or they may have considerable experience in the subject matter but little experience in the classroom. For these reasons, professional organizations like the National Council of Teachers of Mathematics advocate for professional mentorships, which help to provide the much-needed "content knowledge, pedagogical knowledge, and knowledge of local, state, and national curricular expectations and their implications for high-quality" teaching.[33]

Anna J. Small Roseboro, an award-winning retired teacher, writer, and mentor, explains that new teachers "have questions and concerns that, if unanswered can lead to frustration, discouragement, and a sense of worthlessness that drive well-educated, highly motivated teachers to abandon the profession."[34] Veteran teachers, however, can provide support derived from experience and model for tentative or frustrated teachers "ways to balance personal and professional lives showing us when to push, when to pull, and when to step back and rest."[35] Importantly, these partnerships are mutually beneficial, and veteran teachers can benefit from exposure to new people, new practices, and new challenges.

Good teachers, after all, never stop learning.

COLLEGE CONSIDERATIONS

In most universities, faculty members fortunate enough to be tenured or on the tenure track are evaluated annually or biennially on their contributions to the school in three arenas: research, teaching, and service. There are various exceptions to this general rule, of course, such as the scientist who runs a laboratory at a major research university but who doesn't teach on a regular basis or the writing program coordinator who teaches one course each year and whose workload consists primarily of administrative service. In some schools, teaching is weighted more heavily than research; in others, new faculty are advised to avoid service obligations for the first few years while they build their research portfolios.

In light of considerable research describing the inequitable distribution of service work on college campuses, some departments have begun to use departmental workload boards that display each faculty member's teaching load, course releases, and service commitments during a given semester. These boards might include the following for each faculty member:

- the quantity and types of courses taught (because some courses, especially service learning courses and those that are writing intensive or have high enrollment caps, require more out-of-class mentoring or grading);
- course releases received for research or service, if applicable;

- service assignments, including requirements of the position, length of commitment, hourly commitment each week, and whether one is receiving a course release or compensation for the work;
- independent studies led, thesis projects overseen, and other student advisement duties, as well as whether they are compensated; and
- other work obligations suggested by faculty members.

Software programs already exist to manage individual workloads but, if technological or financial limitations are a concern, they can just as easily be created and shared as a digital file, displayed on a password-protected webpage, or even hung via poster board in a common office space. To ensure that no one is tasked unfairly with creating or maintaining this board—an assignment that might reproduce the labor inequities the board is designed to expose or rectify—it might be best for someone who is compensated for administrative work, such as the department chair or, if applicable, a staff associate, to take on the responsibility.

While some educators may be concerned that boards like these are an administrative tool for the oversight or micromanagement of faculty labor, if set to be visible only to those within the department, these boards can provide a useful visualization of the division of labor among colleagues. The workload board can be especially helpful for faculty members who, as the result of their own privileged positionalities, simply don't recognize the imbalances of labor within the department. For those who do take on greater service duties, such a board can contribute to a feeling of being seen. Just as importantly, it provides tangible data with which to demonstrate institutional inequities, should the need arise to lodge or even defend a formal complaint.

CONCLUDING THOUGHTS

Attending to teachers' well-being is a necessary part of the work toward equitable, trauma-informed classroom practices, but the work of taking care of teachers cannot be yet another addition to the already heavy workloads of equity-minded educators. Instead, it must be incorporated into the work teachers, administrators, and communities are *already* doing to improve their campuses and curricula, particularly in response to students' changing needs in the emotional and educational climate of the twenty-first century. "Teachers' psychological well-being and satisfaction with the school environment are crucial to their ability to assist students with mental health problems."[36]

When faced with the choice of supporting their students or tending to their own needs, many teachers, driven by their passion for the profession and their love for their students, support their students at the expense of their own time, resources, and emotional well-being. Rather than forcing educators to make a difficult choice, support structures should be put into place to ensure that teachers can both take care for their students and for themselves.

When the institutions and classrooms students and their teachers enter perpetuate societal inequities, it can be easy to claim that educational equity is impossible within a system created and maintained by white supremacist ideology. Yet while it may miseducate as often as it educates, this system, however inequitable, is the same one from which has emerged a great deal of scholarship on the necessity and challenges of working toward a more just system of education. Though educators' visions for better schools may be idealized and may differ in some ways from one to the next, there is some consensus among researchers and scholars of equitable education. The following are a few recommendations for creating more equitable classrooms and institutions of education in the United States:

BROAD RECOMMENDATIONS FOR CREATING EQUITABLE, TRAUMA-INFORMED CLASSROOMS AND SCHOOLS

- **Trauma must be reconceptualized to include perspectives beyond the white, masculine, and Western.** To that end, research into the effects of trauma should be conducted with diverse participant pools and in multiple geographic locations and cultural communities, including schools, to explore the contextual nature of experience, expression, and emotion.
- **Feelings must be understood as an integral part of learning, knowing, and experiencing in education.** Emotion and emotional expression should be interpreted and discussed as contextual, culturally situated, and intrinsically connected to logical reasoning, cognitive maturation, and student experience. Teachers and students should be encouraged to consider how their own positionalities contribute to their attitudes and expectations regarding emotional expression in the classroom.
- **Teacher candidates and future scholars should be trained in inclusive, trauma-informed pedagogy as part of their graduate education or certification process.** Teachers aren't counselors, but they are an important part of students' support systems. As such, new teachers should be adequately prepared to identify signs of emotional and psychological distress, respond responsibly, and refer appropriately.

- **Resources must be made available to support students with histories of trauma and trauma-based stress disorders.** These should include school-based counseling and psychological services as well as school-wide preventative mental health initiatives, classroom-based interventions, and professional development trainings for teachers. These services should be culturally responsive, asset based, and readily available, and should acknowledge the impact of emotional health on academic success.
- **Whiteness in content, pedagogy, and ideology should be interrogated, critiqued, and challenged.** Its influence on curriculum, classroom practice, and educational policy should be made explicit for teachers, administrators, and students. Teachers should engage in active personal and professional development to identify and implement practices that resist whiteness and inequity.
- **Voices, stories, and epistemologies of POCI should be incorporated into (rather than added to) all curricula.** It is not enough to include voices and stories of marginalized peoples; these stories must be woven into the curriculum critically and respectfully. Teachers who are white or white identified should pay particular attention to how content pertaining to marginalized peoples are represented in course materials.
- **Students should be allowed and/or encouraged—but never forced—to share their own stories of trauma, marginalization, recovery, and success.** Students should never be called upon to represent particular groups, even those with which they identify. Even when a student's experience illuminates a societal problem, no individual story should be used as evidence to be examined in the classroom, unless such inquiry is guided by the student. Institutional polices about mandated reporting should be made very clear to students to ensure that, should they share a traumatic experience, they know who their audience is and what might become of the information they share.
- **A trauma-informed approach to race talk must acknowledge that racial trauma is ordinary and ongoing and take steps to minimize the potential for classroom race talk to perpetuate that traumatization.** Practicing racial literacy requires examining and challenging the ways that intersecting systems of oppression (each which bolsters the others) maintain white cultural hegemony in the United States, even in classrooms. The focus of classroom race talk, then, must shift from highlighting and possibly exploiting the racialized experiences of POCI to exposing and critiquing the white supremacy that sustains racism and governs the discursive and emotive norms of classroom discourse.

- **Teachers who use the trigger warning should consider their goals for its implementation as well as the population of students likeliest to benefit from the warning.** Students should be invited into the discussion of the trigger warning's potential uses, misuses, benefits, and disadvantages. Teachers should examine what drives their interest in the trigger warning, whether it is student need, administrative oversight, individual hesitance or resistance, a combination of these factors, or something else entirely.
- **Difficult discussions must happen in the classroom.** Race talk, explorations of trauma and marginalization, and discussions about politics and the implications of policy and politic rhetoric are necessarily part of a comprehensive, socially just curriculum. Attempts to shut down conversation via displays of white fragility or misogyny should neither be heeded nor ignored but instead should be identified and examined. Safeguards should be put in place to ensure that students' experiences and feelings are honored during these discussions, and both students and teachers should have access to resources that help them understand and process their reactions, should they need them.
- **Classroom policies pertaining to behavior, language, and academic discourse should be cocreated with input from the students in the classroom.** Class policies should acknowledge the school context and the needs of the student population. Language policies should be informed by scholarship and guided as much by descriptive approaches to language and discourse as prescriptive. Prescriptive language pedagogies (those that teach a particular genre, dialect, or usage of oral or spoken communication) should be flexible, discourse community based, and critical and should consider the linguistic strengths students already bring to the classroom.
- **Schools and school districts should put into place formal policies and programmatic structures to support and uplift the teaching force.** Teacher mentorships should be established and encouraged by individual schools, colleges, local school districts, and university systems. Behavioral policies and tenure and promotion guidelines for schoolteachers and university faculty should be rewritten (and rewritten and rewritten) to continue to reflect the needs of instructors, students, the school community, and a changing society.
- **Instructor salaries, expenses, and resources should align with the economy and promote inclusivity and equity.** Schoolteachers must be paid salaries that align with the economy and local cost of living. Adjunct faculty on the college level should receive a per-course minimum based on the unit percentage of the institution's annual full-time teaching load and commensurate with experience

and level of education. On-campus interviews and all related travel for full-time faculty positions should be fully funded to ensure equal access for job candidates.
- **Efforts toward equitable, trauma-informed education must be outward facing, engaging the community as well as the classroom, and must influence and ultimately be reflected in policies pertaining to curriculum, assessment of students, evaluation of teachers, hiring practices, and distribution of resources.** Teachers and former teachers dedicated to educational equity should consider running for local office or applying for administrative positions in the education system to work toward creating and implementing policies that better represent the needs of teachers and students.

These recommendations may sound too general, fanciful, or even naïve, and they may not be easy to implement, but they are a start. Amend as you see fit. Add your own recommendations if you like. Then post them in the department office. Tape them to the refrigerator in the teachers' lounge. Hang a copy on the door to your office or classroom. Discuss them with colleagues. Share them with students and parents. Host a roundtable at a professional development workshop, a local conference, or a union meeting.

Most importantly, once you've got your list of strategies and steps toward educational equity, make sure to look at that list before you teach your students. Your students experience pain, trauma, and inequity, maybe on a daily basis. Teachers' actions, even with the best of intentions, have consequences—so do everything you can to ensure those consequences are positive ones.

NOTES

1. C. Schick, "By Virtue of Being White: Resistance in Anti-racist Pedagogy," *Race, Ethnicity and Education* 3, no. 1 (2000): 98.
2. Colleen Flaherty, "Last Minute Tenure Threat," *Inside Higher Ed* (May 17, 2019).
3. George Ciccariello-Maher, "Conservatives Are the Real Campus Thought Police Squashing Academic Freedom," *The Washington Post* (October 10, 2017).
4. Colleen Flaherty, "Trinity Suspends Targeted Professor," *Inside Higher Ed* (June 27, 2017).
5. American Association of University Professors, "Letter Issued in Trinity Prof Suspension Case," *AAUP Updates* (June 27, 2017), https://www.aaup.org/news/letter-issued-trinity-prof-suspension-case#.XPVS3MhKiUk.
6. Henry Reichmann, quoted in Flaherty, "Trinity Suspends Targeted Professor."
7. Kenneth Storey, quoted in Jeff Weiner, "Winter Park–Based Tampa Professor Fired after Harvey 'Karma' Tweet," *Orlando Sentinel* (August 29, 2017).
8. American Association of University Professors, *Trends in Instructional Staff Employment Status, 1975–2011* (Washington, DC: AAUP Research Office, 2013), https://www.aaup.org/sites/default/files/files/AAUP_Report_InstrStaff-75-11_apr2013.pdf.

9. Nathan McAlister, quoted in Josh Kenworthy, "Teachers' New Catch-22: Students Want to Talk Politics, but Their Parents Don't," *Christian Science Monitor* (March 13, 2017).

10. Robert Samuels, "Professional Insecurity in a Fraught Environment," *Inside Higher Ed* (April 24, 2017).

11. Patricia A. Matthew, "What Is Faculty Diversity Worth to a University?" *The Atlantic* (November 23, 2016).

12. Ibid.

13. Matthew Woessner, "Rethinking the Plight of Conservatives in Higher Education," *Academe* (2012), https://www.aaup.org/article/rethinking-plight-conservatives-higher-education#.XPa9qshKiUk.

14. Rick Hampson, "We Followed 15 of America's Teachers on a Day of Frustrations, Pressures, and Hard-Earned Victories," *USA Today* (October 17, 2018; updated April 2019).

15. Peter Rad and Erum Salam, "How I Survive: American Teachers and Their Second Jobs—A Photo Essay," *The Guardian* (September 5, 2018), https://www.theguardian.com/us-news/2018/sep/05/american-teachers-second-jobs-how-i-survive.

16. The Coalition on the Academic Workforce, *A Portrait of Part-Time Faculty Members: A Summary of Findings on Part-Time Faculty Respondents to the Coalition on the Academic Workforce Survey of Contingent Faculty Members and Instructors* (June 2012), http://www.academicworkforce.org/CAW_portrait_2012.pdf.

17. Ken Jacobs, Ian Perry, and Jenifer MacGillvary, *The High Public Cost of Low Wages: Poverty-Level Wages Cost U.S. Taxpayers $152.8 Billion Each Year in Public Support for Working Families*, UC Berkeley Center for Labor Research and Education (April 2015), 3.

18. American Federation of Teachers and the Badass Teachers Association (AFT/BTA), *2017 Educator Quality of Work Life Survey* (Washington, DC: AFL, 2017), i.

19. Kairi Kolves, Victoria Ross, Jacinta Hawgood, Susan H. Spence, and Diego De Leo, "The Impact of a Student's Suicide: Teachers' Perspectives," *Journal of Affective Disorders* 207 (2017).

20. Centers for Disease Control and Prevention (CDC) and the National Center for Health Statistics, "Adolescent Health," CDC/National Center for Health Statistics (March 3, 2017), https://www.cdc.gov/nchs/fastats/adolescent-health.htm.

21. AFT/BTA, *2017 Educator Quality of Work Life Survey*, i.

22. Ashley Griffin and Hilary Tackie, *Through Our Eyes: Perspectives and Reflections from Black Teachers* (Washington, DC: The Education Trust, 2016), 9.

23. Hampson, "We Followed 15 of America's Teachers."

24. Jerica Coffey and Stephanie Cariaga, "Collaborating to Capture Community Resilience," *Rethinking Schools* (Summer 2015): 20.

25. Ashley Griffin, *Our Stories, Our Struggles, Our Strengths: Perspectives and Reflections from Latino Teachers* (Washington, DC: The Education Trust, 2016), 9.

26. Betty Achinstein and Rodney T. Ogawa, "New Teachers of Color and Culturally Responsive Teaching in an Era of Educational Accountability: Caught in a Double Bind," *Journal of Educational Change* 13, no. 1 (2012): 27.

27. Matthew, "What Is Faculty Diversity Worth?"

28. Irene A. Lietz, "'When Do I Cross the Street?' Roberta's Guilty Reflection," *The Journal of the Assembly for Expanded Perspectives on Learning* 21 (2015–2016): 111.

29. Ibid.

30. Cassandra M. Guarino and Victor M. H. Borden, "Faculty Service Loads and Gender: Are Women Taking Care of the Academic Family?" *Research in Higher Education* 58, no. 6 (2017).

31. Karla Hernandez-Mats, quoted in Erin Richards and Matt Winn, "'Can't Pay Their Bills with Love': In Many Teaching Jobs, Teachers' Salaries Can't Cover Rent," *USA Today* (June 5, 2019).

32. Richard Ingersoll, Lisa Merrill, and Daniel Stuckey, *Seven Trends: The Transformation of the Teaching Force* (Philadelphia: Consortium for Policy Research in Education, April 2014), 25–26.

33. National Council of Teachers of Mathematics (NCTM), *Teacher Mentorship: A Position of the National Council of Teachers of Mathematics* (Reston: NCTM, October 2013), 2.

34. Anna J. Small-Roseboro, "Mentors Help New Teachers Manage," *Literacy & NCTE* (blog) (National Council of Teachers of English, January 24, 2017), http://www2.ncte.org/blog/2017/01/mentors-help-new-teachers-manage/.

35. Ibid.

36. Kolves et al., "The Impact of a Student's Suicide," 276. See also Meike Sisask, Peeter Varnik, Airi Varnik, et al., "Teacher Satisfaction with School and Psychological Well-Being Affects Their Readiness to Help Children with Mental Health Problems," *Health Education* 73 (2014).

Bibliography

Achinstein, Betty, and Rodney T. Ogawa. "New Teachers of Color and Culturally Responsive Teaching in an Era of Educational Accountability: Caught in a Double Bind." *Journal of Educational Change* 13, no. 1 (2012): 1–39.
Alim, H. Samy, and Geneva Smitherman. *Articulate while Black: Barack Obama, Language, and Race in the U.S.* Oxford: Oxford University Press, 2012.
Alvarez, Adam, H. Richard Milner IV, and Lori Delale-O'Connor. "Race, Trauma, and Education: What Educators Need to Know." In *But I Don't See Color: The Perils, Practices, and Possibilities of Antiracist Education*, edited by Terry Husband, 27–40. Rotterdam: Sense, 2016.
American Association of University Professors. "Letter Issued in Trinity Prof Suspension Case." *AAUP Updates* (June 27, 2017).https://www.aaup.org/news/letter-issued-trinity-prof-suspension-case#.XPVS3MhKiUk.
———. *Trends in Instructional Staff Employment Status, 1975–2011.* Washington, DC: AAUP Research Office, 2013.
American Federation of Teachers and the Badass Teachers Association (AFT/BTA). *2017 Educator Quality of Work Life Survey.* Washington, DC: AFL, 2017.
American Psychiatric Association (APA). *Diagnostic and Statistical Manual of Mental Disorders: DSM-5.* Arlington, VA: American Psychiatric Publishing, 2013.
Annual Report of the Board of Education of the City and County of New York, 1850. New York: William C. Bryant, 1850.
Arao, Brian, and Kristi Clemens. "From Safe Spaces to Brave Spaces: A New Way to Frame Dialogue around Diversity and Social Justice." In *The Art of Effective Facilitation: Reflections from Social Justice Educators*, edited by Lisa M. Landreman, 135–50. Sterling: Stylus, 2013.
Asia Society. "Asian Americans Then and Now: Linking Past to Present." Asiasociety.org. https://asiasociety.org/education/asian-americans-then-and-now.
Bass, Alison. "Report on Youth Violence Urges Prevention." *Boston Globe* (August 10, 1993).
Bauman, Dan. "After 2016 Election, Campus Hate Crimes Seemed to Jump. Here's What the Data Tell Us." *The Chronicle of Higher Education* (February 16, 2018).
Bellet, Benjamin W., Payton J. Jones, and Richard J. McNally. "Trigger Warning: Empirical Evidence Ahead." *Journal of Behavior Therapy and Experimental Psychiatry* 61 (2018): 134–41.
Belluck, Pam. "N.I.H. Head Calls for End to All-Male Panels of Scientists." *New York Times*, June 12, 2019.

Birdee, Gurjeet S., Anna T. Legedza, Robert B. Saper, Suzanne M. Bertisch, David M. Eisenberg, and Russell S. Phillips. "Characteristics of Yoga Users: Results of a National Survey." *Journal of General Internal Medicine* 23, no. 10 (2008): 1653–58.

Boler, Megan. *Feeling Power: Emotions and Education*. New York: Routledge, 1999.

Bonilla-Silva, Eduardo. *Racism without Racists: Color-Blind Racism and the Persistence of Racial Inequality in America*, 5th ed. Lanham: Rowman & Littlefield, 2017.

Bordo, Susan. *Unbearable Weight: Feminism, Western Culture, and the Body*. Berkeley: University of California Press, 1993.

Bourdieu, Pierre. *The Field of Cultural Production*. New York: Columbia University Press, 1994.

Boysen, Guy A. "Evidence-Based Answers to Questions about Trigger Warnings for Clinically-Based Distress: A Review for Teachers." *Scholarship of Teaching and Learning in Psychology* 3 (2017): 163–77.

Brumberg, Stephan F. *Going to America, Going to School: The Jewish Immigrant Public School Encounter in Turn-of-the-Century New York City*. New York: Praeger, 1986.

Campbell, Bradley, and Jason Manning. "Microaggression and Moral Cultures." *Comparative Sociology* 13 (2014): 692–726.

Centers for Disease Control and Prevention (CDC) and the National Center for Health Statistics. "Adolescent Health." CDC/National Center for Health Statistics, March 3, 2017. https://www.cdc.gov/nchs/fastats/adolescent-health.htm.

Chen, Michelle. "How Unequal School Funding Punishes Poor Kids." *Nation* (May 11, 2018).

Cherng, Hua-Yu Sebastian, and Peter F. Halpin. "The Importance of Minority Teachers: Student Perceptions of Minority versus White Teachers." *Educational Researcher* 45, no. 7 (2016): 407–20.

Cho, Sumi, Kimberle Williams Crenshaw, and Leslie McCall. "Toward a Field of Intersectionality Studies: Theory, Applications, and Praxis." *Signs: Journal of Women in Culture and Society* 38, no. 4 (2013): 785–810.

Cholewa, Blaire, Christina K. Burkhardt, and Michael F. Hull. "Are School Counselors Impacting Underrepresented Students' Thinking about Postsecondary Education? A Nationally Representative Study." *Professional School Counseling* 19, no. 1 (2015).

Ciccariello-Maher, George. "Conservatives Are the Real Campus Thought Police Squashing Academic Freedom." *Washington Post* (October 10, 2017).

Coalition on the Academic Workforce. *A Portrait of Part-Time Faculty Members: A Summary of Findings on Part-Time Faculty Respondents to the Coalition on the Academic Workforce Survey of Contingent Faculty Members and Instructors*. June 2012. http://www.academicworkforce.org/CAW_portrait_2012.pdf.

Coffey, Jerica, and Stephanie Cariaga. "Collaborating to Capture Community Resilience." *Rethinking Schools* (Summer 2015): 20–33.

Coleman, Taiyon J., Renee DeLong, Kathleen Sheerin DeVore, Shannon Gibney, and Michael C. Kuhne. "The Risky Business of Engaging Racial Equity in Writing Instruction: A Tragedy in Five Acts." *Teaching English in the Two-Year College* 43, no. 4 (2016): 347–70.

Collins, Cory. "Hate at School: January 2018," *Teaching Tolerance* (February 7, 2018).

Comas-Diaz, Lillian, Gordon Nagayama Hall, and Helen A. Neville. "Racial Trauma: Theory, Research, and Healing: Introduction to the Special Issue." *American Psychologist* 74, no. 1 (2019): 1–5.

Condon, Frankie. *I Hope I Join the Band: Narrative, Affiliation, and Antiracist Rhetoric*. Logan: Utah State University Press, 2012.

Cooper, Janice L., Rachel Masi, Sarah Dababnah, Yumiko Aratani, and Jane Knitzer. *Unclaimed Children Revisited: Working Paper No. 2: Strengthening Policies to Support Children, Youth, and Families Who Experience Trauma*. National Center for Children in Poverty, 2007. http://nccp.org/publications/pdf/download_204.pdf.

Cottom, Tessie McMillan. "Should There Be Trigger Warnings on Syllabi?" *Society Pages* (March 13, 2014). https://thesocietypages.org/socimages/2014/03/13/should-there-be-trigger-warnings-on-syllabi/.

Crane-Newman, Molly, Graham Rayman, and Rocco Parascandola. "Manhattan's Pace University Evacuated after Studs on Student's Belt Get Mistaken for Ammo." *New York Daily News* (September 14, 2017).
Crowley, Sharon. *Composition in the University: Historical and Polemical Essays.* Pittsburgh: University of Pittsburgh Press, 1998.
DiAngelo, Robin. "White Fragility." *International Journal of Critical Pedagogy* 3, no. 3 (2011): 54–70.
D'Mello, Sidney, Blair Lehman, Reinhard Pekrun, and Art Graesser. "Confusion Can Be Beneficial for Learning." *Learning and Instruction* 29 (2014): 153–70.
Domonoske, Camila. "Segregated from Its History, How 'Ghetto' Lost Its Meaning." NPR.com (April 27, 2014).
Downey, Sharon. "The Evolution of the Rhetorical Genre of Apologia." *Western Journal of Communication* 57, no. 1 (1993): 42–64.
Dutro, Elizabeth. "Writing Wounded: Trauma, Testimony, and Critical Witness in Literacy Classrooms." *English Education* 43, no. 2 (2011): 193–211.
Ellison, John (Jay). "Dear Class of 2020 Students." The University of Chicago, accessed February 10, 2019, https://news.uchicago.edu/sites/default/files/attachments/Dear_Class_of_2020_Students.pdf.
Fairbanks, Eve. "The 'Reasonable' Rebels." *The Washington Post* (August 29, 2019).
Filipovic, Jill. "We've Gone Too Far with 'Trigger Warnings.'" *The Guardian* (March 5, 2014).
Finkelstein, Martin J., Valerie Martin Conley, and Jack H. Schuster. "Taking the Measure of Faculty Diversity." *Advancing Education* (2016).
Flaherty, Colleen. "Last Minute Tenure Threat." *Inside Higher Ed* (May 17, 2019).
———. "Trigger Unhappy." *Inside Higher Ed* (April 14, 2014).
———. "Trinity Suspends Targeted Professor." *Inside Higher Ed* (June 27, 2017).
Fonow, Mary Margaret, Judith A. Cook, Richard S. Goldsand, and Jane K. Burke-Miller. "Using the Feldenkrais Method of Somatic Education to Enhance Mindfulness, Body Awareness, and Empathetic Leadership Perceptions among College Students." *Journal of Leadership Education* 15, no. 3 (2016): 116–30.
Foucault, Michel. *The Archaeology of Knowledge.* New York: Harper, 1972.
Frankenberg, Ruth. *The Social Construction of Whiteness: White Women, Race Matters.* Minneapolis: University of Minnesota Press, 1993.
Freire, Paulo. *Pedagogy of the Oppressed*, translated by Myra Bergman Ramos. New York: Continuum, 2005.
Gee, James Paul. *An Introduction to Discourse Analysis: Theory and Method*, 4th ed. London: Routledge, 2014.
———. "Literacy, Discourse, and Linguistics: Introduction." *Journal of Education* 171, no. 1 (1989): 5–17.
Glover-Graf, Noreen M., Eva Miller, and Samuel Freeman. "Accommodating Veterans with Posttraumatic Stress Disorder Symptoms in the Academic Setting." *Rehabilitation Education* 24, no. 1–2 (2010): 43–56.
Godfrey, Erin B., Carlos E. Santos, and Esther Burson. "For Better or Worse? System-Justifying Beliefs in Sixth-Grade Predict Trajectories of Self-Esteem and Behavior across Early Adolescence." *Child Development* 90, no. 1 (2019): 180–95.
Goodman, Rachael D., and Cirecie A. West-Olatunji. "Educational Hegemony, Traumatic Stress, and African American and Latino American Students." *Journal of Multicultural Counseling and Development* 38 (2010): 176–86.
Grayson, Mara Lee. "Race Talk in the Composition Classroom: Narrative Song Lyrics as Texts for Racial Literacy." *Teaching English in the Two-Year College* 45, no. 2 (2017): 143–67.
———. "The Surreal World: Racism, Capitalism, and Complacency, Millennial-Style: Review of *Sorry to Bother You*." *The St. John's Humanities Review* 16, no. 1 (2019): 26–28.
———. *Teaching Racial Literacy: Reflective Practices for Critical Writing.* Lanham: Rowman & Littlefield, 2018.
———. "Want to Connect with Your Students? Be a Person." *Education Week: Classroom Q& A with Larry Ferlazzo.* October 20, 2018. http://blogs.edweek.org/teachers/class-

room_qa_with_larry_ferlazzo/2018/10/response_dont_just_teach_the_curriculum_teach_the_students.html.

Grayson, Mara Lee, and Adam Wolfsdorf. "Courageous Conversations in the Age of the Trigger Warning." In *From Disagreement to Discourse: A Chronicle of Controversies in Schooling and Education*, edited by Beth Duroyode and Rhonda Bryant. Charlotte: Information Age Publishing, 2019.

Green, Erica L. "Why Are Black Students Punished So Often? Minnesota Confronts a National Quandary." *The New York Times* (March 18, 2018).

Greenfield, Laura. "The 'Standard English' Fairy Tale: A Rhetorical Analysis of Racist Pedagogies and Commonplace Assumptions about Language Diversity." In *Writing Centers and the New Racism: A Call for Sustainable Dialogue and Change*, edited by Laura Greenfield and Karen Rowan, 33–60. Logan: Utah State University Press, 2011.

Griffin, Ashley. *Our Stories, Our Struggles, Our Strengths: Perspectives and Reflections from Latino Teachers.* Washington, DC: The Education Trust, 2016.

Griffin, Ashley, and Hilary Tackie. *Through Our Eyes: Perspectives and Reflections from Black Teachers.* Washington, DC: The Education Trust, 2016.

Grinage, Justin. "Reterritorializing Locations of Home: Examining the Psychopolitical Dimensions of Race Talk in the Classroom." *Journal of Curriculum Theorizing* 30, no. 2 (2014): 88–102.

Guarino, Cassandra M., and Victor M. H. Borden. "Faculty Service Loads and Gender: Are Women Taking Care of the Academic Family?" *Research in Higher Education* 58, no. 6 (2017): 672–94.

Guinier, Lani. "From Racial Liberalism to Racial Literacy: Brown v. Board of Education and the Interest-Divergence Dilemma." *The Journal of American History* 91, no. 1 (2004): 92–118.

Halberstam, Jack. "Trigger Happy: From Content Warning to Censorship." *Signs* 42, no. 2 (2017): 535–42.

Hamblin, James. "What Are Active-Shooter Drills Doing to Kids?" *The Atlantic* (February 28, 2018).

Hampson, Rick. "We Followed 15 of America's Teachers on a Day of Frustrations, Pressures, and Hard-Earned Victories." *USA Today* (October 17, 2018; updated April 2019).

Harmon-Jones, Eddie. "Cognitive Dissonance." In *Encyclopedia of the Mind*, edited by Harold E. Pashler. Los Angeles: Sage, 2013.

Helms, Janet. "Toward a Model of White Racial Identity Development." In *Black and White Racial Identity: Theory, Research, and Practice*, edited by Janet Helms. Westport: Praeger, 1990.

Hoffman, Diane M. "Reflecting on Social Emotional Learning: A Critical Perspective on Trends in the United States," *Review of Educational Research* 79, no. 2 (2009): 533–56.

Holling, Michelle A., Dreama G. Moon, and Alexandra Jackson Nevis. "Racist Violations and Racializing Apologia in a Post-racism Era." *Journal of International and Intercultural Communication* 7, no. 4 (2014): 260–86.

hooks, bell. *Teaching to Transgress: Education as the Practice of Freedom.* New York: Routledge, 1994.

Ingersoll, Richard, Lisa Merrill, and Daniel Stuckey. *Seven Trends: The Transformation of the Teaching Force.* Philadelphia: Consortium for Policy Research in Education, April 2014.

Inoue, Asao B. *Labor-Based Grading Contracts: Building Equity and Inclusion in the Compassionate Writing Classroom.* Fort Collins: WAC Clearinghouse, 2019.

Jacobs, Ken, Ian Perry, and Jenifer MacGillvary. *The High Public Cost of Low Wages: Poverty-Level Wages Cost U.S. Taxpayers $152.8 Billion Each Year in Public Support for Working Families.* UC Berkeley Center for Labor Research and Education, April 2015.

Jones, Sarah. "Fed Up with Liberal Academia, Conservatives Call for Their Own Safe Space." *New York* (January 5, 2019).

Kaestle, Carl F. *The Evolution of an Urban School System: New York City, 1750–1850.* Cambridge: Harvard University Press, 1973.

Kareem, Jamila. "A Critical Race Analysis of Transition-Level Writing Curriculum to Support the Racially Diverse Two-Year College." *Teaching English in the Two-Year College* 46, no. 4 (2019): 271–96.

Kashdan, Todd B., and J. Q. Kane. "Posttraumatic Distress and the Presence of Posttraumatic Growth and Meaning in Life: Experiential Avoidance as a Moderator." *Personality and Individual Differences* 50, no. 1 (2011): 84–89.

Kataoka, Sheryl, Audra Langley, Marleen Wong, Shilpa Baweja, and Bradley Stein. "Responding to Students with PTSD in Schools." *Child and Adolescent Psychiatric Clinics of North America* 21, no. 2 (2012): 119–33.

Keisch, Deborah M., and Tim Scott. "U.S. Education Reform and the Maintenance of White Supremacy through Structural Violence." *Landscapes of Violence* 3, no. 3 (2015): 1–44.

Kenworthy, Josh. "Teachers' New Catch-22: Students Want to Talk Politics, but their Parents Don't." *Christian Science Monitor* (March 13, 2017).

Kim, Dae-Joong, and Bobbi Olson. "Deconstructing Whiteliness in the Globalized Classroom." In *Performing Antiracist Pedagogy in Rhetoric, Writing, and Communication*, edited by Frankie Condon and Vershawn Ashanti Young, 123–58. Fort Collins: WAC Clearinghouse, 2017.

King, LaGarrett. "Black History as Anti-racist and Non-racist: An Examination of Two High School Black History Textbooks." In *But I Don't See Color: The Perils, Practices, and Possibilities of Antiracist Education*, edited by Terry Husband, 63–79. Rotterdam: Sense, 2016.

Knox, Emily J. M., ed. *Trigger Warnings: History, Theory, Context*. Lanham: Rowman & Littlefield, 2017.

Kolves, Kairi, Victoria Ross, Jacinta Hawgood, Susan H. Spence, and Diego De Leo. "The Impact of a Student's Suicide: Teachers' Perspectives." *Journal of Affective Disorders* 207 (2017): 276–81.

Kretzschmar, Jr., William A., and Charles F. Meyer. "The Idea of Standard American English." In *Standards of English: Codified Varieties around the World*, edited by Raymond Hickey, 139–58. Cambridge: Cambridge University Press, 2013.

Ladson-Billings, Gloria. "Just What Is Critical Race Theory and What's It Doing in a *Nice* Field Like Education?" In *Foundations of Critical Race Theory in Education*, 2nd ed., edited by Edward Taylor, David Gillborn, and Gloria Ladson-Billings. New York: Routledge, 2016, 25.

Lea, Mary, and Brian Street. "Student Writing in Higher Education: An Academic Literacies Approach." *Studies in Higher Education* 23, no. 2 (1998): 157–73.

Leyva, Yolanda Chavez. "The Mexican Schools: An Invisible History." *Fierce Fronteriza* (May 23, 2017).

Lietz, Irene A. "'When Do I Cross the Street?' Roberta's Guilty Reflection." *The Journal of the Assembly for Expanded Perspectives on Learning* 21 (2015–2016): 100–113.

Lippi-Green, Rosina. *English with an Accent: Language, Ideology, and Discrimination in the United States*. London: Routledge, 1997.

Looft, Ruxandra. "How Do Trigger Warnings Fit into the Classroom Lesson Plan?" *Shakesville* (blog) (February 12, 2013). http://www.shakesville.com/2013/02/how-do-trigger-warnings-fit-into.html.

Lopez, Omar S., Stephen B. Springer, and Jeffrey B. Nelson. "Veterans in the College Classroom: Guidelines for Instructional Practices." *Adult Learning* 27, no. 4 (2015): 143–51.

Lukianoff, Greg, and Jonathan Haidt. "The Coddling of the American Mind." *The Atlantic* (September 2015).

———. *The Coddling of the American Mind: How Good Intentions and Bad Ideas Are Setting Up a Generation for Failure*. New York: Penguin, 2018.

Marcotte, Amanda. "The Year of the Trigger Warning." *Slate* (December 30, 2013). https://slate.com/human-interest/2013/12/trigger-warnings-from-the-feminist-blogosphere-to-shonda-rhimes-in-2013.html.

Matthew, Patricia A. "What Is Faculty Diversity Worth to a University?" *The Atlantic* (November 23, 2016).

Mayor, Christine. "Whitewashing Trauma: Applying Neoliberalism, Governmentality, and Whiteness Theory to Trauma Training for Teachers." *Whiteness and Education* (2019): 198–216.

Melin, Julia. "Desperate Choices: Why Black Women Join the U.S. Military at Higher Rates than Men and All Other Racial and Ethnic Groups." *New England Journal of Public Policy* 28, no. 2 (2016): 1–14.

Miron, Lynsey R., Holly K. Orcutt, and Mandy J. Kumpula. "Differential Predictors of Transient Stress versus Posttraumatic Stress Disorder: Evaluating Risk Following Targeted Mass Violence." *Behavior Therapy* 45, no. 6 (2014): 791–805.

Morrison, Toni. *Playing in the Dark: Whiteness and the Literary Imagination*. Cambridge: Harvard University Press, 1992.

Moss, Hilary J. *Schooling Citizens: The Struggle for African American Education in Antebellum America*. Chicago: University of Chicago Press, 2009.

Murphy, Rosalie. "Why Your Yoga Class is So White." *The Atlantic* (July 8, 2014).

National Center for Education Statistics. "Fast Facts: Race/Ethnicity of College Faculty." https://nces.ed.gov/fastfacts/display.asp?id=61.

National Council of Teachers of Mathematics (NCTM), *Teacher Mentorship: A Position of the National Council of Teachers of Mathematics.* Reston: NCTM, October 2013.

National Institutes of Health. "PTSD: A Growing Epidemic." *NIH MedlinePlus: The Magazine* 4, no. 1 (2009).

Nielsen, Kathryn. "On Class, Race, and Dynamics of Privilege: Supporting Generation 1.5 Writers across the Curriculum." In *WAC and Second Language Writers: Research toward Linguistically and Culturally Inclusive Programs and Practices*, edited by T. M. Zawacki and M. Cox, 129–50. Fort Collins: WAC Clearinghouse, 2014.

Obama, Barack. *Audacity of Hope: Thoughts on Reclaiming the American Dream*. New York: Crown Publishers, 2006.

Omi, Michael, and Howard Winant. *Racial Formation in the United States: From the 1960s to the 1990s*, 2nd ed. New York: Routledge, 1994.

Orem, Sarah, and Neil Simpkins. "Weepy Rhetoric, Trigger Warnings, and the Work of Making Mental Illness Visible in the Writing Classroom." *Enculturation: A Journal of Rhetoric, Writing, and Culture* (2015). http://enculturation.net/weepy-rhetoric.

Paul, Annie Murphy. "Your Brain on Fiction." *New York Times* (March 18, 2012).

Payne, Michelle. *Bodily Discourses: When Students Write about Abuse and Eating Disorders*. Portsmouth: Boynton/Cook, 2000.

Pena, Richard Perez. "Fight against Sexual Assault Holds Colleges to Account." *New York Times* (February 3, 2015).

Pierce, Chester. *Television and Education*. Beverly Hills: Sage, 1978.

Price, Margaret. *Mad at School: Rhetorics of Mental Disability and Academic Life*. Ann Arbor: University of Michigan Press, 2011.

Pritchett, Wendell. *Brownsville, Brooklyn: Blacks, Jews, and the Changing Face of the Ghetto*. Chicago: University of Chicago Press, 2002.

Rad, Peter, and Erum Salam. "How I Survive: American Teachers and Their Second Jobs—A Photo Essay." *The Guardian* (September 5, 2018). https://www.theguardian.com/us-news/2018/sep/05/american-teachers-second-jobs-how-i-survive.

Richards, Erin, and Matt Winn. "'Can't Pay Their Bills with Love': In Many Teaching Jobs, Teachers' Salaries Can't Cover Rent." *USA Today* (June 5, 2019).

Rosenblatt, Louise M. *Literature as Exploration*, 5th ed. New York: The Modern Language Association of America, 1995.

Roy, Nance. "The Rise of Mental Health on College Campuses: Protecting the Emotional Health of Our Nation's College Students." *Higher Education Today* (December 17, 2018). https://www.higheredtoday.org/2018/12/17/rise-mental-health-college-campuses-protecting-emotional-health-nations-college-students/.

Ruiz, Iris D., and Raúl Sánchez. *Decolonizing Rhetoric and Composition Studies: New Latinx Keywords for Theory and Pedagogy*. New York: Palgrave Macmillan, 2016.

Rush, Benjamin. "A Plan for the Establishment of Public Schools and the Diffusion of Knowledge in Pennsylvania; to Which are Added, Thoughts upon the Mode of Education, Proper

in a Republic." In *Essays on Education in the Early Republic*, edited by Frederick Rudolph. Cambridge: Harvard University Press, 1965.
Said, Edward. "Michel Foucault 1926–1984." In *After Foucault: Humanistic Knowledge, Postmodern Challenges*, edited by Jonathan Arac. New Brunswick: Rutgers University Press, 1988.
Samuels, Robert. "Professional Insecurity in a Fraught Environment." *Inside Higher Ed* (April 24, 2017).
Sanchez, Claudio. "Tougher Times for Latino Students? History Says They've Never Had It Easy," NPR.org (November 15, 2016).
Sauter, Michael B. "Faces of Poverty: What Racial, Social Groups Are More Likely to Experience It?" *USA Today* (October 10, 2018). https://www.usatoday.com/story/money/economy/2018/10/10/faces-poverty-social-racial-factors/37977173/.
Schick, C. "By Virtue of Being White: Resistance in Anti-racist Pedagogy." *Race, Ethnicity and Education* 3, no. 1 (2000): 83–101.
Schmidt, Lauren M. "Trauma in English Learners: Examining the Influence of Previous Trauma and PTSD on English Learners and within the Classroom." *Current Issues in TESOL* (2018): 1–10.
Sibrava, Nicholas J., Andri S. Bjornsson, A. Carlos I. Perez Benitez, Ethan Moitra, Risa B. Weisberg, and Martin B. Keller. "Posttraumatic Stress Disorder in African American and Latinx Adults: Clinical Course and the Role of Racial and Ethnic Discrimination." *American Psychologist* 74, no. 1 (2019): 101–16.
Singleton, Glenn E., and Curtis Linton. *Courageous Conversations about Race: A Field Guide for Achieving Equity in Schools*. Thousand Oaks: Corwin, 2006.
Sisask, Meike, Peeter Varnik, Airi Vaarnik, et al. "Teacher Satisfaction with School and Psychological Well-Being Affects Their Readiness to Help Children with Mental Health Problems." *Health Education* 73 (2014): 382–93.
Skiba, Russell J. "When Is Disproportionality Discrimination? The Overrepresentation of Black Students in School Suspension." In *Zero Tolerance: Resisting the Drive for Punishment in Our Schools; A Handbook for Parents, Students, Educators, and Citizens*, edited by William Ayers, Bernadine Dohrn, and Rick Ayers. New York: New Press, 2001.
Smagorinsky, Peter. "Huck and Kim: Would Teachers Feel the Same If the Language Were Misogynist?" *English Journal* 106, no. 2 (2016): 75–80.
Small-Roseboro, Anna J. "Mentors Help New Teachers Manage." *Literacy & NCTE* (blog). National Council of Teachers of English, January 24, 2017. http://www2.ncte.org/blog/2017/01/mentors-help-new-teachers-manage/.
Smith, Cheryl Hogue. "'Diving in Deeper': Bringing Basic Writers' Thinking to the Surface." *Journal of Adolescent & Adult Literacy* 53, no. 8 (2010): 668–76.
Smith, James E. "Race, Emotions, and Socialization." *Race, Gender, and Class* 9, no. 4 (2002): 94–110.
Song, Ah-Young. "Voice and Experience: Forming Counter-narratives through Personal Poetry." *English Journal* 108, no. 3 (2019): 74–80.
Spear, Rachel N. "'Let Me Tell You a Story': On Teaching Trauma Narratives, Writing, and Healing." *Pedagogy: Critical Approaches to Teaching Literature, Language, Composition, and Culture* 14, no. 1 (2013): 53–79.
Strauss, Valerie. "The Myth of Common Core Equity." *The Washington Post* (March 10, 2014).
Sue, Derald Wing. *Microaggressions in Everyday Life: Race, Gender, and Sexual Orientation*. Hoboken: Wiley, 2010.
———. "Race Talk: The Psychology of Racial Dialogues." *American Psychologist* (2013): 663.
Sue, Derald Wing, Christina M. Capodilupo, Gina C. Torino, Jennifer M. Bucceri, Aisha M. B. Holder, Kevin L. Nadal, and Marta Esquilin. "Racial Microaggressions in Everyday Life: Implications for Clinical Practice." *American Psychologist* 62, no. 4 (2007): 271–86.
Swartz, Ellen. "Emancipatory Narratives: Rewriting the Master Script in the School Curriculum." *Journal of Negro Education* 61, no. 3 (1992): 341–55.

Tatum, Beverly Daniel. "Talking about Race, Learning about Racism: The Application of Racial Identity Development Theory in the Classroom." *Harvard Educational Review* 62, no. 1 (1992): 1–24.

Trainor, Jennifer Siebel. "From Identity to Emotion: Frameworks for Understanding, and Teaching Against, Anticritical Sentiments in the Classroom." *JAC* 26, no. 3–4 (2006): 643–55.

Tsai, Jeanne L., Diana I. Simeonova, and Jamie T. Watanabe. "Somatic and Social: Chinese Americans Talk about Emotion." *Personality and Social Psychology Bulletin* 30, no. 9 (2004): 1226–38.

Turner, Cory, Reema Khrais, Tim Lloyd, Alexandra Olgin, Laura Isensee, Becky Vevea, and Dan Carsen. "Why America's Schools Have A Money Problem." NPR.org (April 18, 2016).

Twine, France Winddance. "A White Side of Black Britain: The Concept of Racial Literacy." *Ethnic and Racial Studies* 27, no. 6 (2004): 881.

Tyng, Chai M., Hafeez U. Amin, Mohamad N. M. Saad, and Aamir S. Malik, "The Influences of Emotion on Learning and Memory." *Frontiers in Psychology* 8 (2017).

UNC Charlotte Writing Project Collaborative. "The Five-Paragraph Essay and the Deficit Model of Education." *English Journal* 98, no. 2 (2008): 16–21.

U.S. Department of Justice, Federal Bureau of Investigation. *2016 Hate Crimes Statistics* (2017). https://ucr.fbi.gov/hate-crime/2017/tables/table-10.xls.

Vieira, Paul, and Kim Makrael. "Trudeau Apologizes Again as Another Old Image in Blackface Emerges." *The Wall Street Journal* (September 19, 2019).

Villanueva, Victor. "Whose Voice Is It Anyway? Rodriguez's Speech in Retrospect." *English Journal* 76, no. 8 (1987): 17–21.

Ware, B. L., and Wil A. Linkugel. "They Spoke in Defense of Themselves: On the Generic Criticism of Apologia." *Quarterly Journal of Speech* 59, no. 3 (1973): 274.

Weiner, Jeff. "Winter Park–Based Tampa Professor Fired after Harvey 'Karma' Tweet." *Orlando Sentinel* (August 29, 2017).

Weir, Kristen. "School Psychologists Feel the Squeeze." *Monitor on Psychology* 43, no. 8 (2012): 34.

Wenger, Christy. *Yoga Minds, Writing Bodies: Contemplative Writing Pedagogy*. Fort Collins: WAC Clearinghouse/Parlor Press, 2015.

White, Edward M. "My Five-Paragraph-Theme Theme." In *What Is College-Level Writing? Volume 2*, edited by Patrick Sullivan, Howard Tinberg, and Sheridan Blau. Urbana: NCTE, 2010.

Williams, Raymond. *Problems in Materialism and Culture: Selected Essays*. London: Verso, 1980.

Winans, Amy. "Cultivating Racial Literacy in White, Segregated Settings: Emotions as Site of Ethical Engagement and Inquiry." *Curriculum Inquiry* 40, no. 3 (2010): 475–91.

Woessner, Matthew. "Rethinking the Plight of Conservatives in Higher Education." *Academe* (2012). https://www.aaup.org/article/rethinking-plight-conservatives-higher-education#.XPa9qshKiUk.

Wolfsdorf, Adam. "Reflecting on Functioning in Trigger Happy America." *Changing English* 24, no. 3 (2017): 299–317.

———. "When It Comes to High School English, Let's Put Away the Triggers." *English Journal* 108, no. 1 (2018): 39–44.

Young, Richard L., Alton L. Becker, and Kenneth L. Pike. *Rhetoric: Discovery and Change*. New York: Harcourt Brace Jovanovich, 1970.

Zahn-Waxler, Carolyn. "Socialization of Emotion: Who Influences Whom and How?" In *The Role of Gender in the Socialization of Emotion: Key Concepts and Critical Issues*, edited by A. Kennedy Root and S. Denham. San Francisco: Jossey-Bass, 2010.

Zurbriggen, Eileen L. "Preventing Secondary Traumatization in the Undergraduate Classroom: Lessons from Theory and Clinical Practice." *Psychological Times: Theory, Research, Practice, and Policy* 3, no. 3 (2011): 223–28.

Index

1990 Americans with Disabilities Act, 30. *See also* accommodations

academic freedom, 28, 32, 144, 145, 148
academic protocol, xiv, xix, xxiii, 36, 66, 67, 72, 73, 76, 83, 84. *See also* discourse, classroom norms
accommodations, 2, 30; trigger warning as fair accommodation, 30–31
adjunct faculty, xxiv, 143, 146, 147, 149, 162
administrative policy on trigger warnings, 27, 28, 32–33
African Americans. *See* Black people
The American Dream, 6, 7. *See also* myth of meritocracy
antiracism: definition of, 15–16; examples of, 14–15; vs. nonracism, 15
anti-Semitism. *See* hate crimes; Jewish people
anxiety, 31, 55, 74, 94–95, 103, 104. *See also* eating disorders; mindfulness techniques; symptoms of trauma-related stress disorders; yoga
apologia, xix–xx; trigger warning as, xx. *See also* hedging
Asian Americans. *See* Asian people
Asian people, 2, 6, 9, 53, 119
assessment, 6, 14, 98, 108, 131–133, 134–135, 136, 163
avoidance coping, 95–96

banking model of education, 83, 98
blackface, xx
Black English, 115–117, 119, 131, 134. *See also* multiple academic Englishes; standardized English
Black history in schools, 11, 12
Black Panther Party, 11
Black people, 51, 53, 90
Black students, 1–2, 5, 9, 10, 11, 56, 97, 143, 153
Black teachers, 13, 152
Black Lives Matter, 145

capitalization of race terms, xxv–xxvi
catharsis, 126. *See also* critical witnessing
censorship, 144, 146–147. *See also* academic freedom; job security
charter schools, 9
The Chicago Letter, 27–28. *See also* administrative policy on trigger warnings
Chinese Exclusion Act, 6
Civilization Fund Act. *See* Indian Civilization Act
classroom protocol. *See* academic protocol; discourse, classroom norms
The Clery Act, 57
cognitive dissonance, 74–75, 103; and racial identity development, 75–76, 78. *See also* disintegration
colonization, 2, 52, 59

175

colorblind racism, 121. *See also* hedging
Common Core State Standards, 10, 135
communication styles, 67–68, 80, 81–82; of collectivist societies, 68, 80; of individualist societies, 67, 68, 80. *See also* culturally situated practices; discourse; emotion, cultural situatedness of
content note, 25–26; on syllabus, xiv, 21, 36–38, 63, 83
contingent faculty. *See* adjunct faculty
contract grading, 132. *See also* assessment
counternarrative, 124, 125, 138. *See also* master script
critical race theory, xx
critical witnessing, 125, 126, 126–127, 129
culturally relevant pedagogy, 4, 14, 16, 97, 99
culturally situated practices, xx, 13, 14, 23, 38, 66, 70, 80, 93, 102, 107, 119, 122, 125, 127, 128, 130, 160. *See also* communication styles; discourse; emotion, cultural situatedness of
curriculum, standardization of, 3, 10–11
curriculum, potential for traumatization, 59
cross-cultural communication, xvi, 64, 66, 83, 105, 128. *See also* communication styles; race talk

depression, 31, 50, 55, 110. *See also* symptoms of trauma-related stress disorders
Diagnostic and Statistical Manual of Mental Disorders, 44, 45, 46, 51
dialect. *See* multiple academic Englishes; standardized English
discourse, 85, 121, 131; classroom norms, 69, 71, 74, 80, 83, 85, 90, 91, 97, 99, 125, 132, 161, 162; definitions of, 68, 69, 70–71. *See also* classroom protocol; communication styles; race talk
discourse analysis, xxi, 71
disintegration, 75. *See also* cognitive dissonance; white fragility
double bind, 154. *See also* POCI teachers

eating disorders, 22–24; and trigger warnings, 24

elective classes, xv, 8, 12, 34, 148. *See also* curriculum
emotional labor: definition of, 79; of POCI, 79; of teachers, 143, 153, 155, 156. *See also* race talk, dangers of
emotion: and classroom norms, 73, 80, 84, 92; cultural situatedness of, 89, 90, 91, 93, 105, 130; role in learning, 89, 94–96, 112; role in racial literacy development, 78, 79. *See also* communication styles; cultural practices; emotional labor; emotion socialization; Social Emotional Learning; white fragility
emotion socialization, 89–90, 93. *See also* Social Emotional Learning
empathy, 31, 64, 79, 129. *See also* race talk, benefits of
exceptionalism, 119, 129
expressive individualism, 67

faculty professional development. *See* professional development
firing of teachers, 145, 146. *See also* academic freedom; social media policies
first-generation college students, 56, 83

grading. *See* assessment
graduation rates of POCI, 1, 9, 48, 54, 136

feminism, 23; and social media, 24; and theories of emotion, xviii, 84, 92; and the trigger warning, 24, 25, 33
First Year Composition (FYC), 71, 83

gentrification, 110

hate crimes, 1, 52, 53; examples of, 1, 123, 153. *See also* racial trauma; racism
hedging, xvii, xix. *See also* apologia; colorblind racism
hidden curriculum, 92–93
Hispanic people. *See* Latinx people

The Immigration Act of 1917, 6
immigration as trauma, 47
Indian Civilization Act, 5

internalization of white supremacy, 7, 52, 93–94, 116, 124, 133
intersectionality, xviii
invisible labor, 155. *See also* emotional labor

Jewish people, xiv, 4, 14, 116, 122
job security, xxiv, 20, 32, 58, 65, 152, 157. *See also* academic freedom; adjunct faculty
job stress, 150–151

King, Martin Luther, 11

Latinx people, 14, 51; Latinx students, 1, 9, 10, 53, 97; Latinx teachers, 152, 154
literature, 31, 109, 125–126
Lukianoff, Greg, and Jonathan Haidt, 28–29, 33, 120, 122, 124

mandated reporting, 54, 56–58, 161
manifestoes of white supremacists, 123
master script, 11, 130, 138; definition of, 11. *See also* counternarrative
media: trigger warnings in, 19, 27; representation of POCI, 52, 124, 130; representation of teachers, 65, 142–143; violence in, 21, 49; as trauma, 45, 46, 59
mentoring of teachers, 157–158
Mexican schools, 5–6
microaggressions, xxv, 2, 13, 52, 84, 93, 120, 121, 123, 124, 148; comparison to trigger warnings, 111, 120; definition of, 2, 13
military veterans, 20, 24, 44, 46, 48, 96, 110, 124
Millennials, xiv, 29, 150
mindfulness, 102–103; definition of, 102; techniques, 104, 105, 110
multiple academic Englishes, 133–134. *See also* standardized English
myth of meritocracy, 6, 77, 93. *See also* The American Dream

National Council of Teachers of English (NCTE), 35, 157. *See also* professional organizations

Native American people, 5, 51–71; students, 1, 5, 97; teachers, 13, 152
natural disasters, 44, 47, 49, 54
neoliberalism, xxiv, 32, 58, 60, 153
new teachers, 69, 156–157, 160. *See also* mentoring of teachers
New York City Board of Education, 3

Obama, Barack, 26, 115, 122, 134
Oberlin College, 27
objectivity, 12, 32, 72, 90, 93, 94
Observe, Describe, Participate, 103–105. *See also* mindfulness

Pace University, 50
Parks, Rosa, 11
People of Color and Indigenous Peoples. *See* POCI; POCI, use of term
personal narratives, 13, 38, 100, 129, 130, 135
POCI: in the curriculum, 11, 59, 64, 78, 79, 151, 161; students, 12, 15, 53, 56, 58, 73, 79, 92, 112, 129, 130, 133, 135, 136, 161; teachers, 147–148, 151–152, 152, 154, 156, 157; use of term, xxvi. *See also* Asian people; Black people; Latinx people; Native Americans; racial trauma
poetry, 135
politeness protocol. *See* discourse, classroom norms of
political correctness, 32
political rhetoric, 52, 129, 142, 148; conservative, 33, 123, 144–145, 148
Post-Traumatic Stress Disorder, xiii, 20–21, 24, 26, 29, 30, 46, 47, 49, 51, 55, 95, 96; in adolescents, 47, 51; definition of, 44, 45, 51, 59; incidence of, 46, 47, 48, 49, 50, 51; research into, 52, 53. *See also* secondary traumatic stress; symptoms of trauma-related stress disorders; triggers; vicarious traumatization
poverty, 51, 129, 138, 152
predominantly white institutions, xvi, 13, 56, 152, 153
professional development, xvi, xxii, 109, 151, 154, 161, 163

professional organizations as resources for teachers, 109, 157–158
Protestant influences on education, 4, 10
psychological services, school-based, 54–56, 161. *See also* mandated reporting
PTSD. *See* Post-Traumatic Stress Disorder
public school funding, 8–9
public schools, history of, 3–5
PWI. *See* predominantly white institutions

race-based stress. *See* racial trauma
race talk: benefits of, xv, 64, 79, 162; dangers of, 64, 67, 73, 79; definition of, xxv, 147; and the trigger warning, xvi, 83, 84. *See also* classroom discourse, norms of; emotional labor; white fragility
racial identity, xvii, 56. *See also* disintegration
racial literacy, critical framework of, xvii
racial microaggressions. *See* microaggressions
racial trauma, 51–53, 59, 76, 80, 130, 151–152, 161
racist violence. *See* hate crimes
rape. *See* sexual assault
rape trauma syndrome, 24. *See also* Post-Traumatic Stress Disorder; sexual assault
ratings systems, media, 22
reading about trauma, 126–127
research on trigger warnings, xxi–xxii, 19, 31, 32, 95, 96, 120
rhetorical violence, 53, 124

Sacagawea, 11
safe spaces, 27–28, 111, 148
school-based discipline, 2, 48, 92
school psychologists. *See* psychological services, school-based
school shootings, 29, 47, 49–50
secondary traumatic stress, xiii, 46, 59, 60, 126, 151. *See also* vicarious traumatization
SEL. *See* Social Emotional Learning
sexual assault, 24, 26, 46, 57, 58, 59, 75, 103, 108, 141; of LGBT individuals, 49; on college campuses, 26, 27, 48, 49; reporting of, 49, 54
Social Emotional Learning, 82, 91, 105, 109
social media, 22, 29; and the trigger warning, 24, 25; in the curriculum, 108, 137; policies, 146, 150; teachers' use of, 144–145, 146, 150
somatic awareness. *See* mindfulness
somatization, 105
special education, 2, 54
Standard English. *See* Standardized English
Standardized English, 72, 98, 117–119, 131, 133–134, 135, 138; as part of assessment, 137; origins of, 118
standardized testing, 11, 98, 134, 152, 157
structures of feeling, 92
suicide, 54, 151
Sulkowicz, Emma, 26
syllabus note. *See* content note
symptoms of trauma-related stress disorders, 44, 45, 46, 47, 50, 54, 55
System Justification Theory, 94

teachers, stereotypes of. *See* media, representation of teachers
Telecommunications Act of 1996, 22
television content warnings. *See* viewer discretion advisory
terrorism, 50
Title IX, 26
trauma, definition of, 44, 46, 51, 56, 59. *See also* Post-Traumatic Stress Disorder
trauma among POCI. *See* racial trauma
treatment of PTSD, 29, 52, 55, 59
treatment seeking among trauma survivors, 44, 49, 51, 56
triggers, xiii, 20–21
trigger warning, definition of, xiv, 20–21
Trump, Donald J., 9, 145, 147
Twitter, 25, 146. *See also* social media

University of California, Santa Barbara (UCSB), 26, 33

viewer discretion advisory, 21–22, 36
vicarious traumatization, 46, 59, 60, 126. *See also* secondary traumatic stress

victimhood culture, 120, 121, 123–124
vindictive protectiveness, 28

white fragility, 67, 76, 77. *See also* cognitive dissonance; disintegration
whiteliness, xv, 65–66, 78
White people, xxv, 72, 75, 78, 119; in the curriculum, 11, 12; students, xvi, 2, 78, 79, 97, 107, 128, 153; teachers, xxiv, 66, 138, 143, 153, 161. *See also* white fragility; whiteliness

white supremacist manifestoes. *See* manifestoes of white supremacists
workload boards, 158–159
writing about trauma, 127–130
Writing Program Administration listserv (WPA-L), 15

X, Malcolm, 11

yoga, 54, 110–111. *See also* mindfulness techniques

About the Author

Mara Lee Grayson is assistant professor of English at California State University, Dominguez Hills. Her first book, *Teaching Racial Literacy: Reflective Practices for Critical Writing*, was published by Rowman & Littlefield in 2018. Her research and scholarship have also appeared in *English Education*, *Teaching English in the Two-Year College*, *The Journal of the Assembly for Expanded Perspectives on Learning*, *The St. John's University Humanities Review*, and numerous edited collections. Her creative work can be found in *Columbia Journal*, *English Journal*, *Fiction*, *Construction*, and *Mr. Beller's Neighborhood*, among other publications.

Mara Lee earned a PhD in English education from Columbia University and an MFA in creative writing from the City College of New York. She chairs the Jewish Caucus of the National Council of Teachers of English and serves on multiple committees of the Conference on College Composition and Communication. Her awards and honors include the 2018 Mark Reynolds *TETYC* Best Article Award and a CCCC Emergent Researcher Grant.

A native New Yorker, Mara Lee now lives in Southern California with her spouse and their two cats. Learn more at maragrayson.com or follow her on Twitter: @maraleegrayson. She welcomes your correspondence at maraleegrayson@gmail.com.

www.ingramcontent.com/pod-product-compliance
Lightning Source LLC
Chambersburg PA
CBHW021849300426
44115CB00005B/79